AS YOU LIKE IT

SHAKESPEARE AT STRATFORD

Published by The Arden Shakespeare in association with
The Shakespeare Birthplace Trust

General Editor: Robert Smallwood, (formerly of) The
Shakespeare Centre

Associate Editors: Susan Brock, The Shakespeare Centre Library
Russell Jackson, The Shakespeare Institute

SHAKESPEARE AT STRATFORD

AS YOU LIKE IT

ROBERT SMALLWOOD

The Arden website is at
http://www.ardenshakespeare.com

Shakespeare at Stratford: *As You Like It*
first published 2003 by The Arden Shakespeare
in association with The Shakespeare Birthplace Trust

© 2003 Robert Smallwood

The Arden Shakespeare is an imprint of Thomson Learning

Thomson Learning
High Holborn House
50/51 Bedford Row
London WC1R 4LR

Typeset by LaserScript, Mitcham, Surrey

Printed by Zrinski in Croatia

British Library Cataloguing in Publication Data
A catalogue record for this book is available from the British Library

Library of Congress Cataloguing in Publication Data
A catalogue record has been applied for

ISBN 1-903436-15-X (pbk)
NPN 9 8 7 6 5 4 3 2 1

THE AUTHOR

obert Smallwood is an Honorary Fellow of the Shakespeare Institute and the General Editor of this *Shakespeare at Stratford* series. He recently retired as Head of Education at the Shakespeare Centre, Stratford-upon-Avon, where the courses he directed for twenty-five years on plays in the repertoire of the Royal Shakespeare Company for university students from many countries brought him into regular contact with actors, directors and other members of the RSC. The series *Players of Shakespeare*, of which he is editor, developed from this work, as well as the idea for this series of volumes on Shakespeare's plays in performance at Stratford. Since retiring he has been Visiting Professor at the University of Bourgogne and has also taught in the United States.

FOR

THE LIBRARY STAFF OF THE SHAKESPEARE CENTRE,
PRESENT AND PAST, GUARDIANS AND ADMINISTRATORS
FOR NEARLY FORTY YEARS OF THE ARCHIVE OF
STRATFORD THEATRE, WHOSE EFFICIENCY,
KNOWLEDGE AND HELPFULNESS ARE SO GENEROUSLY
GIVEN TO ALL WHO USE THE LIBRARY AND HAVE
MADE POSSIBLE THIS BOOK, AND THIS SERIES

CONTENTS

LIST OF ILLUSTRATIONS

Cover photograph
Rosalind and Orlando, 1961
Photograph: Thomas Holte

SOURCES

Joe Cocks Studio: The Joe Cocks Studio Collection, The Shakespeare Centre Library, Stratford-upon-Avon
Copyright: The Shakespeare Birthplace Trust

Malcolm Davies: The Shakespeare Centre Library, Stratford-upon-Avon
Copyright: The Shakespeare Birthplace Trust

Thomas Holte: The Tom Holte Theatre Photographic Collection, The Shakespeare Centre Library, Stratford-upon-Avon
Copyright: The Shakespeare Birthplace Trust

Angus McBean: The Shakespeare Centre Library, Stratford-upon-Avon
Copyright: The Royal Shakespeare Company

Central Press Photos Ltd/Hulton Picture Company
Zoë Dominic
John Haynes
Alastair Muir

Every effort has been made to contact copyright holders and the publishers will be happy to include further acknowledgements.

GENERAL EDITOR'S PREFACE

The theatre archive housed in the Shakespeare Centre Library here in Stratford-upon-Avon is among the most important in the world; for the study of the performance history of Shakespeare's plays in the twentieth century it is unsurpassed. It covers the entire period from the opening of Stratford's first Shakespeare Memorial Theatre in 1879, through its replacement, following the fire of 1926, by the present 1932 building (renamed the Royal Shakespeare Theatre in 1961) and the addition of the studio theatre (The Other Place) in 1974 (closed, lamentably, in 2001), and of the Swan Theatre in 1986, and it becomes fuller as the years go by. The archive's collection of promptbooks, press reviews, photographs in their hundreds of thousands, and, over the last couple of decades, archival video recordings, as well as theatre programmes, costume designs, stage-managers' performance reports and a whole range of related material, provides the Shakespeare theatre historian with a remarkably rich and concentrated body of material. The wealth and accessibility of this collection have sometimes tended to give general performance histories of Shakespeare's plays an unintentional Stratford bias; the aim of this series is to exploit, and indeed revel in, the archive's riches.

Each volume in the series covers the Stratford performance history of a Shakespeare play since World War II. The record of performances at Stratford's various theatres through this period unquestionably offers a wider, fuller, and more various range of productions than is provided by any other single theatre company. It may fairly be said, therefore, that a study of the Stratford productions since 1945 of any Shakespeare play provides a representative cross-section of the main trends in its theatrical interpretation in the second half of the twentieth century. Each volume in the series will, however, begin with an introduction that sets this Stratford half-century in the wider context of the main trends of its play's performance history before this period and of significant productions elsewhere during it.

The organization of individual volumes is, of course, the responsibility of their authors, though within the general aim of the series to avoid mere chronicling. No volume in the series will therefore offer a chronological account of the Stratford productions of its play: some will group together for consideration and analysis productions of similar or comparable style or approach; others will examine individual aspects or sections of their plays across the whole range of the half-century of Stratford productions' treatment of them. Illustrations are chosen for what they demonstrate about a particular production choice, a decision that, on some occasions, may be more important than photographic quality. Given the frequency with which individual plays return, in entirely new productions, to the Stratford repertoire, most volumes in the series will have some ten or even a dozen productions' approaches and choices to consider and contrast, a range that will provide a vivid sense of the extraordinary theatrical diversity and adaptability of Shakespeare's plays.

The conception and planning of this series would not have been possible without the support and enthusiasm of Sylvia Morris and Marian Pringle of the Shakespeare Centre Library, Kathy Elgin, Head of Publications at the Royal Shakespeare Company, Jessica Hodge and her colleagues at the Arden Shakespeare, and above all, my two Associate Editors, Susan Brock of the Shakespeare Centre Library and Russell Jackson of the Shakespeare Institute. To all of them I am deeply grateful.

ROBERT SMALLWOOD
The Shakespeare Centre, Stratford-upon-Avon

ACKNOWLEDGEMENTS

The dedication to this book records my most significant debt of gratitude: the staff of the Shakespeare Centre Library makes enterprises of this kind possible. I am grateful also to Roger Pringle, Director of the Shakespeare Birthplace Trust, who could not have been more encouraging in the early stages of this 'Shakespeare at Stratford' project, and to Kathy Elgin, who, in her capacity as Head of Publications at the RSC, was an enthusiastic and constructive supporter. Elaine Bradley very kindly gave me a batch of *As You Like It* programmes and press cuttings from her RSC collection and Roger Howells (former RSC Production Manager) generously shared his memories of productions when other sources of information failed.

I am grateful also to the team at the Arden Shakespeare: Jessica Hodge and Andrew McAleer have been both encouraging and immensely patient, and no one could have wished for a more thorough, meticulous, helpful and understanding editor than Hannah Hyam. I owe a great debt also to my fellow authors in the series: reading their work as their books grew and developed has been a great stimulus to getting on with my own. My Associate Editors, Susan Brock and Russell Jackson, have been a constant source of support and good humour. I began the early stages of writing this book in the beautiful city of Dijon in Burgundy and am immensely grateful to my friend Professor Terence McCarthy of the Université de Bourgogne for the invitation to be Visiting Professor there after my retirement from the Shakespeare Centre. For his hospitality in Dijon I thank also my good friend Gilles Monsarrat. For briefer teaching visits to Furman University, South Carolina, and to Hanover College, Indiana, where the writing progressed a little further, I thank Professors Willard Pate and Jonathan Smith.

It is a pleasure to record also my gratitude for the opportunity of working over the second half of the period covered by this book with many of the actors whose performances it attempts to record: to share their insights into this play in classroom sessions with student groups, and in personal conversation (and in some cases in essays for the *Players of Shakespeare* series), was a privilege and a joy. For arranging nearly all those sessions and, more importantly, for all the years of friendship and of good talk about the work of the Stratford company, and about theatre more generally, I am grateful to Sonja Dosanjh, RSC Company Manager in Stratford for nearly half the productions dealt with in this book. Finally I thank Liz, partner and mainstay, who put up with me through the tensions of finishing the book against a looming deadline and helped in so many ways to get me there.

ROBERT SMALLWOOD

Eastham, Worcestershire, June 2002

INTRODUCTION

I t is a curious fact that one of the most notorious episodes in the performance history of *As You Like It* at Stratford (or anywhere else for that matter) was caused by a stuffed stag. On the evening of 22 April 1919 there opened at Stratford's old Memorial Theatre a production of *As You Like It* that shocked the town. Its guest director was Nigel Playfair, invited down from London by Sir Frank Benson, who had been responsible for most of Stratford's annual theatre festivals since they began in 1879. Playfair had acted with Benson companies on several occasions before, but he had also worked with Harley Granville-Barker and his production showed Barker's influence. With an uncut text, a set designed by Claude Lovat Fraser that placed the action on the edge of the forest, with formalized trees based on fifteenth-century manuscripts, and a background of open country, and with vividly coloured costumes, the production swept away a forty-year Stratford tradition at a stroke. For audiences used to Benson's fern-and-ivy-covered canvas flats (that wobbled when Orlando fixed his poems to them), to costumes in autumnal hues, and to a stage ankle-deep in leaves, this sudden inrush of the new was seriously destabilizing. Even more shocking, however, in a symbolic way at least, was the absence of a stuffed stag, on loan (since it had been borrowed for Barry Sullivan's production of *As You Like It* in the very first Stratford festival of 1879) from neighbouring Charlecote, where, so the legend has it, the young Shakespeare had poached its ancestors.

1

This venerable beast, by now a little moth-eaten, had made its ritual appearance in every Stratford production of *As You Like It* since Sullivan's, and the play had been in two dozen of the festival seasons before 1919. To leave it out, Playfair wrote later, was 'a piece of iconoclasm ... never heard of in Stratford before'. He found himself cut by his fellow hotel guests after the performance and his designer was accosted in the street and told 'not to meddle with our Shakespeare' (Beauman, 64–7; see also Trewin, 86–7).

The story tells us two things: first, that *As You Like It* has always been a popular play at Stratford – it had, indeed, been performed there in the town's first attempt to get a theatre started, in the garden of New Place in 1827, and it was in the small repertoire of plays performed in the temporary pavilion as part of the tercentenary celebrations in 1864 (Kemp and Trewin, 4–5); and, second, that, from its inception and for many decades beyond that, there was a traditionalism and provincialism about Stratford theatre that was to take a great deal of shifting. Both these characteristics effortlessly survived the onslaught of Playfair's production. There were productions of *As You Like It* in thirteen of Stratford's festival seasons between its stageless manifestation in 1919 and the first of the post-war productions with which this book is concerned, that of Herbert Prentice in 1946. These were mostly produced by the resident artistic directors of the company, William Bridges-Adams from 1919 to 1934 and Ben Iden Payne from 1934 to 1942, though a production by the actor–director Balliol Holloway in 1939 was twice revived, and Robert Atkins directed the play in the first of his two seasons as festival director in 1944. *As You Like It*, altogether unsurprisingly, was among the seven plays presented in Elisabeth Scott's new Shakespeare Memorial Theatre in its inaugural 1932 season, with Fabia Drake as Rosalind, whose speaking of the role 'glinted like a stream in sunlight' (Trewin, 137). But the way the Stratford seasons were organized in those years, with half a dozen or so productions opening within a few days of each other, made fresh thought about the plays virtually impossible. Sally Beauman provides evidence of both Bridges-Adams and Iden Payne being forced, by the very nature of the theatre's schedules and their own workloads, to direct from old promptbooks, and she quotes the critic of the *Era*, reviewing the very first performance in the new Memorial Theatre, declaring that at Stratford 'there is hardly a single play in the repertory which does not require a new production' (Beauman, 121).

The message was long in being heard, but when the war ended Stratford theatre at last began to develop the major international artistic reputation that it was soon to enjoy (and that justifies this series of books). Its new chairman of governors, Sir Fordham Flower, and its new artistic director, Sir Barry Jackson, the latter with innumerable theatrical successes (including the first important modern-dress Shakespeare productions) behind him at his Birmingham Repertory Theatre, were to oversee this new phase in its evolution. And along immediately came a production of *As You Like It*, in that first post-war season of 1946, the work of a guest director from Sheffield, Herbert Prentice, a friend and associate of Jackson's. Unlike so many pre-war Stratford versions, it was an entirely new production of the play – as have been its twelve successors, down to the end of the century, that form the subject of this book. Two or three of the most successful of them would be revived in the succeeding season in Stratford, and from 1961 onwards all (except the 1973 production) would go to London, to the Aldwych Theatre or (from 1985) to the Barbican. But the days of reviving and revamping existing productions were not to return to Stratford: each of the productions with which we are here concerned is essentially a new artistic creation and only once in the sequence, in 1957, after the success of his 1952 production, does a director (in this case Glen Byam Shaw, with his original design team Motley) return to the play.

Thirteen productions, twelve directors and designers, thirteen different actors in each of the major roles of Rosalind, Orlando, Jaques, Touchstone: there has been little of the repetitive about the treatment of *As You Like It* at Stratford in the past half century.

The cast lists in Appendix 1 allow some amusing tracing of career moves here and there: Michael Siberry takes a dozen years to graduate from Jaques de Boys to Jaques (senior); Tony Church moves from wickedness to goodness on the ducal moral register; two Silviuses (Ian Bannen and Peter McEnery) become Orlandos; a Celia (Janet Suzman) becomes a Rosalind and, more surprisingly, a Rosalind (Samantha Bond) becomes a Celia; an Audrey (Susan Fleetwood) becomes a Rosalind; a youthful Donald Sinden and a youthful Ian Richardson each give us a youthful Monsieur Le Beau. In the bigger roles, though, post-war Stratford has allowed actors only a single chance, and one has occasionally felt a great sense of lost opportunity, especially about a potentially splendid Rosalind, that there should be something about the circumstances, or the conception, of a production that did not really permit them to do themselves justice, to achieve the effect that ought to have been possible.

One notable fact about these thirteen productions of *As You Like It* is that they have all been on Stratford's main stage, the stage of the Royal Shakespeare Theatre (or, as it was known before 1961, the Shakespeare Memorial Theatre). Since the opening of the studio theatre (The Other Place) in 1974, and of the medium-sized, vaguely Elizabethan, Swan Theatre in 1986, the RSC has mounted productions of all but six of Shakespeare's plays in one or other of these smaller spaces. That *As You Like It* (along with just four other comedies and *Henry V*) has remained resolutely a 'main house' play is due partly, perhaps, to its amplitude of form – two dozen speaking parts is high, though not exceptionally so – but much more to the very popularity that has given it a place in over fifty seasons in the 120-year history of Stratford theatre. A popular play will sell tickets throughout a season for a house with fifteen hundred seats; to perform it in a smaller space is to fail to take advantage of its financial potential. No Stratford director in the last fifty years, it seems, has had so strong an artistic reason to want to try it in a smaller auditorium for this financial imperative to be gainsaid.

Another curious characteristic that these thirteen productions have almost in common is the point at which they broke for the interval: all but two of them took their interval at the same point. The 1961 production broke after the interrogation of Oliver (3.1), and in 1967 David Jones's production drove right through to the end of the first wooing scene (3.2) before breaking. All the rest took the interval after the scene of Duke Senior's forest meal (2.7). (Glen Byam Shaw's two productions (1952 and 1957) added another short interval after 4.1.) Such directorial unanimity about where to break play is unusual.

The constancy of *As You Like It* in Stratford's repertoires is a reflection of its more general theatrical reputation. It was presumably played at the Globe by Shakespeare's company, though in fact no documentary evidence of a performance of it exists for Shakespeare's lifetime (this is not, of course, unusual among his plays) and it was not printed until the Folio collection of 1623. The first firmly recorded performance was in 1740 when it was played on 20 December at Drury Lane. A hybrid piece by Charles Johnson entitled *Love in a Forest*, adapting it and adding bits from several other Shakespeare plays (and marrying Celia to Jaques), had had a few performances in 1723. The beginning of the play's performance history in the mid-eighteenth century derived, as Alan Brissenden makes clear in his introduction to the Oxford edition (Brissenden, 54ff.), from an increasing interest at that period in 'breeches parts' (women dressed as men) and in cross-dressing more generally. But that, in a sense, is just another way of saying that the play's theatrical fortunes depended on its Rosalind, a situation that has never changed and is never likely to. Most of the major actresses of the eighteenth and nineteenth centuries played Rosalind at some time in their careers – even the great tragedienne Sarah Siddons attempted it, though with less than dazzling success – and some played the role over many years; and from that first performance in 1740, few years went by without a production of *As You Like It* at one of the London theatres. William Charles Macready's Drury Lane production of 1842, in his usual style of archaeological exactness – fifteenth-century France was his chosen period – was among the more notable of the nineteenth century. Its Rosalind was Louisa Nesbitt, but the mid-century's most famous Rosalind was certainly Helena Faucit, whose performances in the part over more than twenty years shifted it in a decisively romantic direction, following the more boisterous, 'tomboyish' interpretation of earlier fashion. A paragraph in Helena Faucit's essay on the role describes this shift and provides a benchmark for the future theatrical interpretation of the part:

> It was surely a strange perversion which, we read, assigned Rosalind … to actresses whose strength lay in comedy. Even the joyous, buoyant side of her nature could hardly have justice done to it in their hands; for that is so inextricably mixed with deep womanly tenderness, with an active intellect disciplined by fine culture, as well as tempered by a certain native distinction, that a mere comedian could not give the true tone and colouring even to her playfulness and her wit. These forest scenes between Orlando and herself are not, as a comedy actress would be apt to make them, merely pleasant fooling. At the core of all that Rosalind says and does, lies a passionate love as pure and all-absorbing as ever swayed a woman's heart. (Faucit, 236)

The nineteenth century's commitment to archaeological and pictorial realism in the theatrical presentation of *As You Like It*, which kept the play for the most part in late medieval costume throughout the century, seems to have reached its zenith at the Queen's Theatre, Manchester, in 1908 when a small herd of deer added to the verisimilitude of the grass and moss and ferns which filled a stage crossed by one of those 'running brooks' (2.1.16) to which Duke Senior refers.[1] Frank Benson's ivy and scattered leaves at Stratford (not to mention just one dead deer instead of several living ones) at about this time must have seemed rather unadventurous in comparison.

The Stratford production that swept away the old approach to the play, Nigel Playfair's in 1919, had as its Rosalind Athene Seyler. Accounts of her performance emphasize its humour and gaiety, as well as the tenderness upon which Helen Faucit had insisted. This combination of qualities is what the two most notable Rosalinds of the inter-war years brought to the role, Peggy Ashcroft (directed by Harcourt Williams) in 1932 and Edith Evans (directed by Esmé Church) in 1936, when she was forty-eight and playing opposite the Orlando of the youthful Michael Redgrave. Many reviewers of the earlier post-war Stratford productions of *As You Like It* look back to Edith Evans's Rosalind as the standard by which to judge those who came after. (The fact that Evans almost always comes off better in such comparisons should not surprise us: those productions that we see in our formative theatre-going years seem always to retain their allure.) An undated gramophone record of some of Edith Evans's Rosalind scenes was issued some time in the late 1950s and the vivacity, wit and energy with which the language is handled are a joy to hear. The exasperated disbelief with which she ticks off the 'foolish shepherd' Silvius, 'puffing' – and she gives the word sharp emphasis and a very plosive initial consonant – 'with wind and rain' in his pursuit of Phebe, and the little gurgle of amusement with which she thinks of the idea that it is 'such fools' as he 'that makes the world full of ill-favour'd children' (3.5.50, 52–3) are particularly engaging.

After these two Old Vic productions in the pre-war years the most significant events in the performance history of *As You Like It* in this country have really occurred on Stratford's stage and are the subject of this book. Two all-male productions elsewhere during the period it covers were also, however, important. The first, in 1967, for the National Theatre (at London's Old Vic) was directed, in modern dress on an abstract set, by Clifford Williams, with Ronald Pickup as Rosalind. The director's programme note expressed his wish to evoke 'an atmosphere of spiritual purity which transcends sensuality in the search for poetic sexuality'. Dennis Kennedy suggests that Williams avoided 'making the all-male casting a mere gimmick ... chiefly because of Ralph Koltai's set, which transformed Arden into a man-made forest, a dream-space of modern art' (Kennedy, 258). Then, in 1991, came Declan

Donnellan's all-male production, with Adrian Lester as Rosalind, for his Cheek by Jowl company, like Williams's on an abstract set (the appearance of green strips of hanging silk signified the move to Arden) and in more or less modern costume. The production was, thought Peter Holland, 'a revelation ... like watching a much-loved picture restored'; it defined love and desire 'as lying beyond gender, simply coming into being, irresistibly and unaccountably' (Holland, 1997, 91–2). The National Theatre offered the play again in 1979, with Sarah Kestelman as Rosalind, in a production by John Dexter; Fiona Shaw, Stratford's Celia in 1985, was Rosalind at the Old Vic in Tim Albery's production in 1989; Anastasia Hille was Rosalind at the replica Globe Theatre in 1998 in a production that pandered, as so much of the Globe's work has so far done, to the lowest common denominator of audience taste; and Victoria Hamilton, Phebe in Steven Pimlott's 1996 production at Stratford, gave a 'vulnerable, febrile, dark-haired, small, even birdlike' Rosalind in 2000 in Michael Grand-age's Sheffield production later seen in London (Dobson, 268).

Within this larger context, then, belong the post-war Stratford productions of *As You Like It*. I have divided my discussion of them into seven chapters – not over-influenced, I hope, by Jaques's division of the stages of human life – which seem to me to reflect the main areas which a production of the play must take into account. The first two chapters deal with the environments that successive directors have created for the play, in their presentations of court and forest. The next two chapters deal respectively with Rosalind and Celia and Rosalind and Orlando, her movement from one relationship to the other being the fundamental 'journey' (to use the term so often found useful by actors) depicted in the play. The fifth chapter considers the roles of Touchstone and Jaques, the two anti-romantic characters that Shakespeare added to those he inherited from his principal source, Thomas Lodge's pastoral romance *Rosalynde*, published in 1590. The penultimate chapter considers the treatment of the not inconsiderable population of Arden-dwellers, beyond the principal characters, and the final chapter covers the thirteen versions of the play's final movement, with the very particular challenge of bringing Hymen, the god of marriage, to the boards of the Royal Shakespeare Theatre.

The source material for the analyses that follow, as for all the volumes in this series, is the remarkable theatre archive in the Shakespeare Centre at Stratford. The promptbooks and photographic collections, and press cuttings of reviews for all thirteen productions, have been consulted; so too have the more retrospective reviews in such journals as *Shakespeare Quarterly* and *Shakespeare Survey*. There are valuable essays on their roles by the 1980 Orlando, the 1985 Rosalind and Celia and the 1985 Jaques, the 1989 Rosalind, and the 1996 Touchstone. The highly praised Michael Elliott production of 1961, with Vanessa Redgrave as Rosalind, was redirected for television by Ronald Eyre and broadcast in 1963. In it Patrick Allen replaces Ian Bannen as Orlando and there are textual cuts (including Touchstone's long speech on the stages of the lie – no need to cover a costume change in a film – and Rosalind's epilogue); it is an adapted version of the stage production, therefore, and not a precise record of it – but hugely valuable (not to say enjoyable) nevertheless.

To these sources must be added personal memory – that disconcertingly selective faculty: I saw all but the first four productions myself. Where the source of information is unassigned, therefore, it is usually my own memory (inevitably, and regrettably, less full for the earlier productions than for the more recent ones, some of which I was guilty of reviewing for one or other of the Shakespeare journals mentioned above). Memory has been a little replenished by a study also of the archival video recordings of the five productions since 1985 (the first Stratford *As You Like It* to come within the policy of making such a recording of each production). These are an extremely valuable extra resource, but the extent to which these filmings of one performance from a single fixed camera (which frequently shows very little when the stage lighting is low) should not be overestimated.

Given the nature of the source material, therefore, I inevitably have more to say on the more recent productions than on the earlier ones, and it will be obvious that my reliance on the press reviews is much greater for the early productions. In the 1940s and 1950s a vigorous policy of reviewing Stratford productions in the local as well as the national press (and not just the local press of the Stratford region) means that there are often several dozen accounts of a production in the archive, and one often finds oneself grateful to a reviewer from a small local newspaper for catching some aspect of, or moment in, a production that would otherwise be lost. The aim of newspaper reviewers, however, is to provide their immediate readers with opinions of a production rather than posterity with descriptive information about it, and as my aim here is much more to allow readers to form their own opinions than to inflict on them my own or those of critics from the past, I have frequently found myself trying to sift the informative from the merely opinionated. Inevitably, though, and in the end perhaps rightly, enthusiasm, and sometimes disappointment, will frequently make themselves apparent.

To try to deal with thirteen productions of the same play sliced into seven segments is indisputably to risk bewildering the reader about which production is under discussion at any one time. For this reason I have, for the most part anyway, followed a basically chronological structure within each chapter. With the same intention of mitigating confusion, I want now to say something in general terms about each of the productions in the hope of giving some sense of the individual character and flavour which each most certainly possessed.

The local press was full of post-war optimism about the new Stratford season when Sir Barry Jackson's former associate Herbert Prentice came down to Stratford from Sheffield to direct *As You Like It* in 1946. Phrases such as 'quality before profit' were being used about the ideals of the Memorial Theatre under its new chairman and artistic director, and there was much discussion about whether Stratford could manage to keep pace with the West

End in the matter of actors' salaries – *plus ça change, plus c'est la même chose*! In choosing a late medieval setting for the play ('Plantagenet' is the word reviewers frequently come up with for the court) Prentice was clearly following an older tradition, but his choice of Ruth Lodge as his Rosalind brought to Stratford an actress who had had a considerable success as Cressida in Michael MacOwan's famous modern-dress *Troilus and Cressida*, produced at the Westminster Theatre on the eve of the war (Trewin, 177), and his production's extensive use of the apron stage and the simplicity of its musical arrangements, eliminating the orchestra and integrating the songs more closely into the fabric of the play, were innovative choices that were widely welcomed. It is phrases such as 'lightness of touch', 'gaiety of tone' (*Leam. Spa Cour.*), 'subtle simplicity' (*Evesham J.*) that chime through the reviews, and the *Times*, in all its authoritative anonymity of the period, welcomed its 'freshness of impact'.

Stratford's next two productions of *As You Like It* were directed by Glen Byam Shaw, the first in 1952, as a guest director, the second in 1957 when he was in charge of the Stratford company. Both were designed by the Motley team, which had been responsible for many celebrated Shakespeare productions before and after the war. Neither design was altogether specific about period, but the first, heavier and more realistic in style, clearly alluded to seventeenth-century France, and the second, lighter and more abstract in tone, drew strongly on early sixteenth-century images for the court scenes. Margaret Leighton was Rosalind in the first production, returning to a role in which she had had a great success a few years earlier at Birmingham Repertory Theatre; Dame Peggy Ashcroft, the Rosalind of 1957, was also returning to the role but in her case the gap was longer: she was now almost fifty and her last Rosalind had been twenty-five years earlier at the Old Vic. On the whole, and in spite of the respect and affection for Ashcroft evident throughout the reviews, the earlier production seems to have been the more warmly received: the *Birmingham Gazette*'s reviewer is representative of many in praising its swift scenes, 'lightsome' music, and 'infectiously simple approach'; that enthusiasm for the freshness of the music ('one of the gayest things in the production', *Stage*) runs through much of the critical comment, above all for the penny-whistle-accompanied singing of the two boys who performed 'It was a lover and his lass'. The same composer, Clifton Parker, was responsible for the music in 1957 – the repetition of play, director, designer and composer would be inconceivable today – but failed to elicit the same enthusiastic response from reviewers, and though Philip Hope-Wallace admired the 'lovely unforced nimbleness' of the production (*Time & T.*), little murmurings about chilliness, and a failure to offer much by way of variation of tempo, are to be heard occasionally in the critical commentary.

In every sense the production of 1961 was a landmark. This was Peter Hall's second season in charge at Stratford, the predominantly young company had just received its new 'Royal Shakespeare' appellation, and Michael Elliott, a guest director from the Old Vic with big success in Ibsen behind him, came to work for the first (and, as it transpired, the only) time in Stratford. His *As You Like It*, with Vanessa Redgrave as Rosalind and Max Adrian as Jaques, received the most ecstatic set of reviews of any post-war Stratford production of the play and was the only one to be remade for television. Robert Speaight, former actor and hugely experienced reviewer, called it 'by far and away the best production of *As You Like It* I have ever seen and one of the most richly satisfying Shakespearean performances in all my fairly long experience' (*SQ*, 432). Its music, by George Hall, was in Elizabethan style, the early songs decidedly melancholy in tone, and its single set for court and forest, a green, tree-crowned knoll, used 'cross fades' for scene changes and kept the action moving fast. It is the first production for which reviewers make more than passing mention of the contribution of lighting design to mood creation. Above all, there was the extraordinary response to the joy and energy of Vanessa Redgrave's Rosalind. A few of the older critics felt their younger colleagues were going overboard because they hadn't had the good fortune to see Edith Evans a quarter of a century earlier; a quarter of a century later reviewers of Stratford Rosalinds would be using Vanessa Redgrave as the standard of comparison. This was undoubtedly a darker production than many of its predecessors – the bleakness of Arden, the ferocity of the deer-killing, the chilling brutality of the court, are often mentioned – but what J.W. Lambert called 'the pure delight' of Redgrave's Rosalind (*S. Times*) seems to have shone the more brightly in contrast with them. It was a little Birmingham Sunday newspaper that stuck its neck out and predicted that it would 'go down in history as a classic production' (*S. Mercury*).

David Jones, then, had a hard act to follow when he came to direct the play in 1967 with Dorothy Tutin as his Rosalind. It was to be her last appearance at Stratford after much-praised performances in such roles as Juliet and Viola. There was much advance publicity for this production because the well-known television comedian Roy Kinnear had been cast as Touchstone – and very funny he was, particularly in the ruefulness of his realization that 'when I was at home I was in a better place' (2.4.13–14), a reference, one sometimes allowed oneself to think, to his own misjudgement in accepting such a script as Touchstone's, rather than to Touchstone's having been so foolish as to accept an invitation to Arden. Where Elliott's Arden had been a single tree, Jones's was two huge cantilevered tree trunks, swinging ominously into different positions from time to time, like outsized stick insects. The music, by William Mathias, was again rather sombre – 'taut' the *Morning Star* called it – like the production itself. This was, thought J.C. Trewin, a 'low-key' production, by a director who didn't want to 'nudge' us and had no interest in 'point-making' (*Birm. Post*); in Ronald Bryden's view it therefore allowed its actors to demonstrate that 'this is one of the most theatrical things Shakespeare ever achieved' (*Observer*).

There was nothing 'low key' about the *As You Like It* of 1973. Directed by Buzz Goodbody, the first woman to direct on Stratford's main stage since Dorothy Green in 1946, the production had a rock-and-roll score by Guy Woolfenden, an Edwardian court, and 1970s denim jeans for Rosalind and Orlando in the forest scenes. Eileen Atkins played Rosalind and Richard Pasco a Chekhovian Jaques that attracted great critical acclaim. The abstract set used steel tubes in straight lines to suggest court pillars or random arrangements to suggest forest trees. Many reviewers thought the setting destroyed the play's stylistic contrasts – 'nothing much stirs in Arden', thought Michael Billington, except Jaques (*Guardian*), and Eileen Atkins herself later said that she thought that 'modern dress is a nightmare for Rosalind' (Hemming). But critical response was far from wholly negative: the *Oxford Mail* thought that Goodbody had, 'in her kinky way, captured the spirit of Arden', and Jack Tinker was moved by the scenes of the exiled court which he thought caught 'something of the true anguish of the displaced person' (*D. Mail*).

The next two productions of *As You Like It*, in 1977 and 1980, were by the then incumbent artistic directors of the RSC, Trevor Nunn and Terry Hands. After his success the previous year with a musical version of *The Comedy of Errors*, Nunn's 1977 production of *As You Like It* turned the play in the direction of baroque opera. Staged in consciously artificial mid-seventeenth-century style, it had a design by John Napier of two-dimensional 'screens' that were raised and lowered behind the players. The score was by Stephen Oliver, and songs were danced as well as sung to choreography by Gillian Lynne. There was a full-scale (if tongue-in-cheek) cloud-borne, theophanic descent for Hymen at the end, in seventeenth-century masque mode. Kate Nelligan played Rosalind. A side-stage orchestra of a dozen was kept busy through the evening, and a frame for the play was created by bringing Hymen on at the beginning in a prologue trio woven from passages in Jonson and Spenser in which he arbitrated between Fortune and Nature. Reception of the production ranged from the outraged – 'Shakespeare as librettist for Stephen Oliver' (*Guardian*), a 'team of good Shakespearean actors ... exposed as amateur vocalists' (*Times*) – to the delighted: 'gorgeous mock-baroque music transcends pastiche' (*S. Telegraph*), 'the sugar-plum of the season' (*D. Telegraph*). The magnitude of directorial intrusion on the text provoked a good deal of serious discussion: Shakespeare had applied 'all his skill and sophistication to turning the rigid pastoral form into warm human drama and here comes Trevor Nunn and turns it back into elaborate artifice', wrote John Peter (*S. Times*). At a more basic level, the sheer length of the evening that resulted from Nunn's treatment was the source of much rueful comment.

Artifice gave way to boisterous energy in Terry Hands's 1980 *As You Like It*, a production of 'fearlessly extrovert animation' that suggested to Irving Wardle 'the work of a ring master more than a director' (*Times*). Susan Fleetwood's Rosalind was a creature of total commitment, and the production aimed at presenting a play about the sheer force of love and sexuality, with actors 'freezing' to emphasize the episodes of love at first sight. Guy Woolfenden, returning to the play after his rock version seven years earlier, provided a score (much admired by Michael Coveney, *FT*, reviewing the Aldwych transfer), that supported Hands's timeless, somewhat folkloric approach, particularly in a frenetic final dance with corn dollies and other fertility symbols. The court scenes vaguely suggested the eighteenth century, the forest carefully suggested timelessness. 'Explosive fertility' was John Peter's phrase for it, 'mystical and somewhat primitive' (*S. Times*).

Adrian Noble's 1985 production, music in modern style by Howard Blake, was tagged by Michael Billington 'Jung ones in Arden' (*Guardian*), and the phrase offers a helpful mnemonic to its chief identifying characteristic. There were several quotations from Jung in the programme and a double-page spread entitled 'In search of herself'. Noble doubled the two Dukes, and offered a way to Arden through a looking glass, or a large round hole in the back of the set that might have been a rabbit hole but might also have been the moon. Juliet Stevenson played a Rosalind whose Ganymede (in white suit and bowler hat) had a somewhat Chaplinesque quality. Michael Ratcliffe thought it 'as near to abstract Shakespeare as you are likely to find in any theatre this side of Bochum' (*Observer*). An abstract, treeless, modern-dress Arden became a sort of playground in which role-playing was the pastime. The production received as divided a set of reviews as any post-war Stratford version of *As You Like It* (though there was competition for that distinction from the next two): for the *Spectator* it destroyed the 'fundamentally celebratory power of Arden', yet for the *Daily Telegraph* (and I deliberately choose two publications so often on the same side), it was 'an *As You Like It* for our generation', giving us the play 'as fresh as if we were seeing it for the first time'.

The 1989 production, with Sophie Thompson as Rosalind, offered a directly metatheatrical approach to *As You Like It*, presenting its opening scenes on the apron stage in a replica of the Royal Shakespeare Theatre's foyer areas and showing its characters reaching the playing space of Arden by physically breaking through behind the proscenium arch to the original stage of the theatre. In keeping with this approach one actor again played both Dukes. Music was by Ilona Sekacz 'alternately haunting and jolly' (*Birm. Post*). From the false elegance, and simmering violence, of the court, the production moved to an abstract Arden, again a sort of playground, which Peter Kemp tartly described as 'a place where actors go to camp' (*Independent*) and Hugo Williams regarded as providing the environment for 'a brilliant experiment in interpretative director's theatre' (*S. Corresp.*).

After two highly conceptualized versions of the play, David Thacker's 1992 production, with Samantha Bond as Rosalind (Kate Buffery took over the role in September of the Stratford season), returned to a much more traditional interpretation. Gary Yershon's rather fulsomely romantic score ('of almost cinematic dimensions', *Birm. Post*) featured a number of big set-piece songs with orchestral backing and there was a full-scale transformation scene from a black court in Velasquez style to a realistic forest with mossy banks, a rustic bridge and a murmuring stream. And yet again the critics were divided, many responding to its 'fresh, spirited, straightforward' qualities (*S. Telegraph*), others finding it an affair of 'routine dullness' (*Observer*). Terry Grimley, in the *Birmingham Post*, asked the obvious question: was it, he wondered, just a little 'too traditional'.

There was nothing traditional about the juxtaposition, in Steven Pimlott's production in 1996, of an abstract box set in shining metal (with shining metal poles flown in for the forest scenes) and costumes of rigorous Elizabethan exactness, even to the faintly absurd puffy behinds of the men's breeches. Niamh Cusack's Rosalind was the first for many a long Stratford year to carry a boar spear with her to Arden and to be able to ask, quite literally, what she should do with her 'doublet and hose' (3.2.215–16). After the fullness of the musical score in 1992, this production was almost musicless, except for modern, and rather difficult, settings of the songs by Jason Carr. It was marked by some very deliberate directorial choices – the death of Adam at the interval, for example, or a much older Jaques than usual, or Hymen's manifestation as a figure from among the audience – all of them intellectually defensible and all of them dividing reviewers and audiences, as their treatment in the following pages reveals.

Gregory Doran's *As You Like It* in 2000 will be remembered for taking us, in Michael Billington's wicked phrase, 'to Liberty's and not to banishment' (*Guardian*), for its needlework and tapestry set, designed by Kaffe Fassett, did indeed leave Arden (with its embroidered cushions and magnificent pullovers) looking like a fashion shop rather than a forest. The jazz score, by Django Bates, with the singers miked and a large stage-side orchestra, took the songs in a Broadway direction, while the set was taking the play in quite another: 'the lighting glares and the music blares', as Susannah Clapp put it (*Observer*). And yet, as John Gross remarked, the evening still had the Rosalind of Alexandra Gilbreath, and she makes any evening in the theatre worthwhile (*S. Telegraph*). And for all one's sense that the production was doing nothing to help her, there was about her Rosalind a directness, an emotional charge and vulnerability, and at times a sheer joy, that reminded one of why one had come to see this play. In the much simpler restaging of the production at the Barbican's Pit studio theatre, these qualities were allowed the freedom they deserved.

Thirteen productions of *As You Like It* in fifty-four years gives, on average, a Stratford production approximately every four years. I hope that this summary of the broad characteristics of each of them will have established the play's hospitality to such regular theatrical re-exploration. I turn now to the seven different aspects of the play I have isolated to examine the variety of directorial approaches in more detail. Before doing so, however, it may perhaps be useful to admit that the sort of account that one can offer of past performances in a book of this scope is necessarily highly selective. Even though theatrical performance, as has been often said, is an essentially evanescent art, enough information survives in the Stratford archive for a volume of encyclopaedic proportions to be compiled if one attempted to give a moment-by-moment account of what happened on stage in the twenty-two scenes of *As You Like It* in these thirteen post-war Stratford productions. I have had to allow the difficult process of selection to be steered by what seemed significant, characteristic, innovative, perhaps even eccentric about each production; the focus therefore varies somewhat from production to production, with episodes, even characters, coming into prominence in one version that hardly merit a mention in another. If this seems inconsistent and frustrating to the reader, the remedy probably lies in a personal exploration of the Stratford theatre archive – and there are few more enjoyable ways of spending time. The only criterion of selectivity amongst the mass of available material that I can proffer is what interested me personally. The book makes no claim to be an exhaustive treatment of its topic; it is, as Touchstone says (5.4.58) of his chosen partner – apologetically but perhaps, after all, unrepentantly – 'mine own'.

NOTE

1 My quotations and references throughout are to Agnes Latham's Arden edition of the play.

1

THE ENVIOUS COURT

> Now my co-mates and brothers in exile,
> Hath not old custom made this life more sweet
> Than that of painted pomp? Are not these woods
> More free from peril than the envious court?
>
> (2.1.1–4)

As You Like It, like many another play of the late sixteenth and early seventeenth centuries, takes its characters on a journey to a 'green world' where, the dramatic convention proposed, life could be lived, and its assumptions examined, tested and reassessed, with a freedom and candour impossible in the restricted world of urban, or courtly, existence. It is a structural pattern to which Shakespeare frequently has recourse, most obviously (in addition to *As You Like It*) in *A Midsummer Night's Dream* and *The Winter's Tale*, but it is latent in a long list of comedies from *The Two Gentlemen of Verona* to *The Tempest* and controls also, of course, the form of *King Lear*. Its principal effect on performance in any kind of naturalistic theatre is to create the need for two basic sets, one for the 'court' and one for the 'country', with the opportunity, irresistible to some directors, of a spectacular transformation scene to mark the move from one to the other.

Shakespeare has complicated things in *As You Like It*, however, by providing a text that fails to make that move in one clean break. We begin at court – or rather near it, since Oliver's 'orchard'

(1.1.41) is apparently easily visited by Charles the court wrestler –
and we pass three scenes there before the move out to Arden and
to the exiled Duke insisting on the contrast with the world we
have just left:

> Are not these woods
> More free from peril than the envious court?
>
> (2.1.3–4)

But, greatly to the inconvenience of the set designer and the scene
builder, we do not stay in Arden after this initial excursion, but
return to court, not once but twice, first for Duke Frederick's
discovery of his daughter's and Rosalind's escape (2.2), second –
and after no fewer than five more scenes, four in the forest and
one of Orlando's flight, with Adam, from his brother's dwelling –
for Frederick's interrogation of Oliver, the first scene of the third
act in the Folio's division. How are directors to cope with this
bewildering locative toing and froing?

The answer, interestingly as far as post-war Stratford productions are concerned, is mostly with patient acquiescence. Only the
1992 production, with a major transformation scene for the move
from court to country, put all of the court scenes together at the
beginning of the play; its playing order was thus as follows: 1.1,
1.2, 1.3, 2.2, 2.3, 3.1, 2.1, 2.4, 2.5, 2.6, 2.7, 3.2 and then in Folio
order through to the end of the play. Apart from this there were
changes to the Folio order only in the following productions: 1946,
which put the arrival in Arden of Orlando and Adam (2.6) immediately before the scene of Jaques's first appearance (2.5) and so played
Jaques's first scene and the exiled Duke's feast (2.7) as one long
sequence; 1952 and 1957, which played the escape of Orlando and
Adam (2.3) before Duke Frederick's discovery of the flight of his
daughter and Rosalind (2.2); and 2000. This last created a five-
scene pre-Arden group by playing the sequence 1.1, 1.2, 1.3, 2.2,
2.3, followed by a major resetting of the stage (though not quite
on the scale of 1992) and a sequence 2.1, 2.4, after which the
scenes were played through to the end in Folio order, with 3.1 (the

interrogation of Oliver) enacted downstage as the first scene after the interval with the upstage Arden set unlit. Oliver's interrogation has been an immediately post-interval scene in all productions except 1992 (when the scene was moved) and 1961 and 1967 (when the interval was taken later). Most productions have used the sort of downstage playing, with lighting effect, employed in 2000 to make clear the return to court here and for the discovery of the escape of Rosalind and Celia (2.2); alternatives have been to play 'in front of tabs' (1946 promptbook), before a 'curtain' or 'cloth' (1952 and 1957 promptbooks), or with a different backdrop (1961, 1977). It is surprising, perhaps, that more directors have not been tempted to tidy and compartmentalize the playing order of scenes.

Whether the 'painted pomp' and 'peril' of the envious court is an experience we 'take all at once, and have it over' (in Scrooge's phrase about his ghostly visitors), or whether (as has been the norm at post-war Stratford) we pay return visits to encounter further facets of its nastiness, any production of *As You Like It* needs to establish the fact that the court is an environment from which escape is to be wished – devoutly so in the case of some recent productions, for the dangerous and threatening atmosphere of Frederick's court, and the unpredictable violence and cruelty of Frederick himself, have certainly increased during the sequence of thirteen versions of the play with which this book is concerned.

When the sequence began, in 1946, it was the 'painted pomp' and the 'dignity' of a court with a 'striking Plantagenet air' (*Birm. W. Post*) that reviewers noticed. Any sense of villainy was 'rather muted' (*Evesham J.*). Frederick, indeed, seemed 'subdued' (*SA Herald*), though the 'close' atmosphere of his court, its 'simmering' sense of 'man's inhumanity to man' were also noticed (*Birm. Post*). The wrestling attracted only adverse comment – 'something wants doing about it' – though the young Donald Sinden, playing Le Beau, apparently cheered things up somewhat by providing 'jolly fun' (*Birm. E. Desp.*). The threat in this Plantagenet world, however, clearly came from Paul Scofield's Oliver, occupying a larger proportion of reviewers' space than any Stratford Oliver since and a performance several times referred to as a triumph. This 'sharply twisted' (*SA Herald*), 'calculating' villain (*Evesham J.*), with his sinister 'darkling' quality (*Birm. Post*), contrasted strikingly with Douglas Seale's 'quite exceptionally sympathetic' Adam (*Birm. E. Desp.*), which showed 'all the courage and humour of old age' (*SA Herald*) and enjoyed a warmth of companionship with Myles Eason's Orlando that was much noticed.

From the painted Plantagenet pomp of Joyce Hammond's sets to the ostentation of seventeenth-century France was the move Duke Frederick's court made between 1946 and 1952, when the first of Glen Byam Shaw's two Stratford productions of *As You Like It* (both designed by Motley) was staged. The court costumes were 'nearer to Molière than to Shakespeare' (*Bolton E. News*), though Philip Hope-Wallace was reminded of Van Dyke cavaliers (*Man. Guardian W.*). The promptbook indicates an elaborate court procession before the second scene (off to see the wrestling between Charles and the old man's three sons (1.2.109ff.), no doubt) which returned for the bout with Orlando. The comments of reviewers offer little evidence of any particularly striking threat posed by Duke Frederick or his régime. The *Stage* thought he had 'the right toughness and incisiveness', but on this occasion it was the wrestling that drew nearly everyone's attention: it was 'the real thing' (*Birm. W. Post*); it had 'brilliant reality' (*West. D. Press*); it made people in the front row apprehensive and Orlando's virility was evinced in the energy of his 'youthful attack rather than his technical accomplishment' (*Nott. Guardian*). The undulating green sward of the forest in Motley's designs spilled over the edge of the stage and was therefore visible in the court scenes, which for some reviewers anxious for a more complete court/forest distinction 'spoiled the illusion' (*Nott. Guardian*). It clearly had no such effect, however, on the opening confrontation in Oliver's orchard, in which Ivor Brown (in the *Observer*) found James Wellman's 'codger' of an Adam unusually appealing. This 'quite enchanting' scene (*Nott. Guardian*) was played before a drop curtain, 'a cross between a Christmas card and a bookplate from Grimm's Fairy Tales' (*West. D. Press*) that to one reviewer 'seemed to offer a distant prospect of Moscow' (*Bolton E. News*). But for all its apparent internationality, neither the envious court itself, nor its neighbouring orchards, struck anyone in 1952 as particularly frightening places.

Five years later, however, when Glen Byam Shaw returned to *As You Like It*, again with the Motley design team, Mark Dignam gave 'a forceful, malignant touch to Duke Frederick' (*Birm. E. Desp.*), so that he seemed to come, as J.C. Trewin suggested, 'straight out of a Holbein canvas in a tearing temper' (*Birm. Post*). The promptbook again calls for a grand processional entry crossing the stage before the second scene and returning for the wrestling. Reviewer after reviewer comments on the unusual (and apparently at the time surprising) power of Dignam's Frederick – 'perpetually on the boil' as *Punch* observed – which brought unexpected 'life and purpose' to the early scenes (*Stage*). Dignam's turning on Oliver to roar 'more villain thou' (3.1.15) was particularly remarked. The early sixteenth-century appearance of the court is clearly seen in Angus McBean's photograph (posed, but certainly capturing a moment from the performance) of the wrestling scene (Figure 1), with Richard Johnson's Orlando swinging a defeated Charles on his shoulder and Dignam's broad-shouldered, threatening Frederick looking on dourly from the framed dominance of his raised pavilion – 'a Tudor portrait with a particularly nasty scowl' (*West. Indep.*). The references to the Tudors, and to Holbein, of which the reviews were full, did not convince Muriel St Clare Byrne, who felt that director and designer had been true to the play's French setting and that Dignam's Duke was exactly modelled on the Clouet portrait of François I in the Louvre (*SQ*, 481). Inevitably, however, it was Henry VIII who provided the point of reference for most commentators: no wonder, thought Cecil Wilson (*D. Mail*), that in this threatening environment Peggy Ashcroft's profoundly melancholy Rosalind seemed to be in constant fear of beheading.

With the court so powerfully evincing fear and threat, Oliver's orchard passed more or less unnoticed, though St Clare Byrne did observe, very sharply, that, in keeping with the wintry chill over the early stages of the play, the weather-vane indicated that the wind was in the north-east (*SQ*, 480). Orlando and Adam were discovered, statuesque, rather than entering in conversation as they had done in Shaw's earlier production (not a well-received change), and Adam (James Wellman again) seemed to Rosemary Anne Sisson 'too mincing and namby pamby' (*SA Herald*). But it was surprise at the way Dignam had made Frederick's anger and wickedness 'a much more vital thing than usual' (*Times*) that dominated reaction to these early scenes.

If some little spillage of forest greensward into the edges of the Holbeinesque court had been bothersome in 1957, Michael Elliott's decision to offer the whole play in 1961 on Richard Negri's single set – a tree-crowned knoll whose lower slopes extended into the auditorium (see Figure 42) – was unlikely to escape without comment. A backcloth of a many-windowed palace wall (visible in Figure 2) looked 'like a comprehensive school' (*Liv. Post*) or 'a totally unacceptable block of modern flats gone astray from some architectural exhibition' (*Guardian*). The *Morning Advertiser*, too, wondered about all the court scenes 'being placed on the lawn in front of the palace', even though a threatening effect might be achieved by projecting the shadow of a grilled iron gate across its greenery. For the most part, however, the single set for court, orchard and forest was accepted and comment concentrated on the acting. A fresh point of reference for the wrestling match had entered the national consciousness since the last production and reactions were full of comparison

FIGURE 1 (*opposite*) Watched by the assembled court in Motley's early sixteenth-century designs and with Mark Dignam's Duke Frederick in his pavilion to the rear, Orlando (Richard Johnson) lifts the defeated Charles (Ron Haddrick) onto his shoulder. Rosalind (Peggy Ashcroft, second from right) and Celia (Jane Wenham, to Rosalind's right) are in the foreground. (1.2, 1957) (all favourable) with all-in wrestling on commercial television, reviewer after reviewer making clear how they spent their Saturday afternoons; some even observed that the stage version was more 'realistic' than its television counterpart. The 'obscene ferocity' with which the ladies of the court followed the wrestling caused Bamber Gascoigne a 'shudder' (*Spectator*). Court costumes were more or less straightforwardly Elizabethan, making this the first post-war Stratford production to leave the play in its period of composition. Tony Church followed the lead set by Mark Dignam in offering a Duke Frederick of disturbing malevolence, who gave to the early scenes what one reviewer (presumably absent in 1957) thought 'moments of unexpected force' (*Leam. Spa Cour.*). But where Dignam had been overt and powerful in his anger, Church was, thought Bernard Levin, 'tormented' (*D. Express*), a man of 'sinister ferocity' (*Stage*), 'vicious and brooding' (*Warwick Adv.*) and with 'an incisive touch of neurosis' (*FT*). For Robert Speaight that neurosis helped explain the sudden conversion at the end; he was also impressed by the placing of the interval following the interrogation of Oliver, so that our image of Frederick in fury against the tree was displaced (after the gin and tonic) by Orlando hanging his sweet and silly love poems on it (*SQ*, 432). Other reviewers were struck by that pre-interval moment of Frederick's 'glowering, white-faced look over his shoulder at the departing Oliver in a slow fade while in the distance a dog howls' (*Leam. Spa Cour.*), and of his hunching 'grey and hollow-eyed across the stage in a dream of guilt' (J.W. Lambert, reviewing the Aldwych transfer, *S. Times*). Unrepresentative of the general admiration for Church's performance, but worth recording, for he clearly flirted with the danger, is that it 'smacked of melodrama' (*Coventry E. Tel.*). To watch it now, on the film made for BBC television, is to feel that the majority got it right and to concur with Irving Wardle that the court scenes in this production reached 'an astonishing pitch of intensity' (*Observer*, reviewing the Aldwych transfer).

Alongside Church's court, where Ian Richardson, near the beginning of his Stratford career, offered a 'deliciously effete Le

FIGURE 2 Beneath the large tree that dominated Richard Negri's set throughout, and in front of a backcloth representing a wall of the palace, Ian Richardson's elegantly effete Le Beau announces the wrestling to a smiling Rosalind (Vanessa Redgrave, right) and a more sombre Celia (Rosalind Knight). A reclining and amused Touchstone (Colin Blakely) looks on. (1.2, 1961)

Beau' (*D. Express*; see Figure 2), the orchard scene, too, presented a surprising level of psychological intensity. Ian Bannen's Orlando impressed reviewers as 'an angry man ... writhing under injustice', 'manly', and 'tender with Adam' (*Yorks. Post*), winning against Charles only through 'one last mighty effort' (*Morn. Adv.*). Once again the court scenes had provided an unexpectedly exciting prelude to what had apparently always been regarded in the past as the play's only real business in the Forest of Arden.

The extraordinary critical success of Elliott's 1961 *As You Like It* produced a larger than average gap before Stratford's next presentation of the play, David Jones's production in 1967, which pushed the potentially melodramatic element of the court scenes further. In Timothy O'Brien's designs, Duke Frederick's court now had black walls, and his courtiers' costumes were of stiff watered silk that swished sinisterly – except for Charles the wrestler in his black leather, 'pretending to be an Italian poisoner' (*Times*). There was a processional entry, with trumpets, for the wrestling. This was 'a darkly devious Renaissance court', thought Ronald Bryden in the *Observer*; a 'stuffy, somewhat vulgar Tudor palace' suggested Hilary Spurling in the *Spectator*, offering 'a fit setting for Duke Frederick and his uneasy court' while to the *Stage* (reviewing the 1968 revival) it all seemed 'more suggestive of the headquarters of an inquisition than a palace'. Even the orchard had become gloomier the second time round: surely it hadn't been such 'an austere mausoleum in black slate' the previous year, mused B.A. Young in the *Financial Times*, while the *Stratford-upon-Avon Herald* described the court in its second manifestation as a place of 'great plain black walls, duskily lit, which ... have rather the ascetic air of a monk's cell or an interrogation room' – the former possibility suggesting, perhaps, a Duke Frederick subconsciously anticipating his later conversion. Michael Billington, briefly writing for the *Times* when the production returned to Stratford in 1968, thought Clifford Rose presented a Duke more 'humorous' than 'full-scale neurotic' – as, by implication, Morgan Sheppard had been the year before, and when, indeed, 'violent neurotic', was the epithet W.A. Darlington had chosen (*D. Telegraph*).

Knowing eyes were again on the wrestling, and verdicts were uniformly favourable – magnificent, superbly rehearsed, spectacular in its precision, very realistic, the praises ring out with the *Morning Star* pronouncing it (on undisclosed authority) 'the most vigorous and effective wrestling match ever staged at Stratford'. Those Saturday afternoons on the television had clearly put pressure on director and performers alike to come up with the goods. On this occasion, interestingly, Orlando's bout with Charles was his second wrestling match of the evening: the play had begun with a more than usually fierce confrontation of the de Boys brothers watched, ditheringly, by a 'rheumy, toothless Adam, chumbling improbably as stage ancients will' (*Spectator*); Darlington found it all 'very exciting' (*D. Telegraph*).

FIGURE 3 Clement McCallin's Duke Frederick, complete with theatrical villain's black eye patch, invades the bedroom privacy of Rosalind (Eileen Atkins, right) and Celia (Maureen Lipman), already in their night attire, to announce the banishment of Rosalind (and, adding insult to injury, to light his cigar). Several productions have used this contrast between the young women in nightdresses and the intrusive male to emphasize Frederick's tyranny. (1.3, 1973)

The drift towards stylization and melodramatic effect in the court scenes took a step further in Buzz Goodbody's more or less modern-dress production in 1973. The forest wooing scenes were presented in wholly contemporary denim, but Christopher Morley's designs for the court looked vaguely Edwardian, the women in long dresses, the courtiers in high collars. Elegant Edwardian gilt chairs and a folding bedroom screen for the scene of Rosalind's banishment (see Figure 3) contrasted with the variable arrangements of vertical tubes that formed the abstract background for court and forest alike, the direction and design here reacting, consciously or unconsciously, against the realism of its immediate Stratford predecessors. Clement McCallin's Duke Frederick, with 'nervous facial twitches' and with a cigar described, rather alarmingly, by one reviewer as 'cynical' (*Malvern Gaz.*), 'prowled his court in a black eye patch, bolstering his authority with arbitrary banishments like some seedy Greek Colonel' (*Jewish Chron.*). The black eye patch contrasted with his banished brother's monocle, a bit of simple symbolism mocked by B.A. Young (*FT*), but hinting, perhaps, at future productions that would double the roles. The performances of Frederick and Oliver reminded J.C. Trewin of the villains' roles in a 'turn-of-the-century Drury Lane melodrama' (*Birm. Post*); for John Elsom (in the *Listener*) the court resembled a casino, for Benedict Nightingale (in the *New Statesman*) it was more of 'a jaded cocktail party', with Frederick 'raffish in velvet-lapelled black' and his courtiers bored and depressed. Michael Billington, now with the *Guardian*, felt that the modern dress had led to the neglect of 'real issues of text', with something of the court/country opposition lost and the courtiers seeming 'like well-heeled Kensington smoothies' who would, if they found themselves in Arden, soon build 'a bijou little cottage'.

The opening confrontation of the brothers retained its power, however, Orlando evincing a 'passionate hatred' (*Stage*) for an Oliver whose tight-fitting jodhpurs acted (as stage jodhpurs have an odd tendency to do) as a strong focus for audience dislike; and the wrestling once more cast its spell with the Charles of Brian Glover (himself a former professional wrestler) demonstrating 'swaggering cruelty' (*D. Mail*) and showing off outrageously in a fight which featured 'artificial half-nelsons, arm locks, and eye-gougings' much admired by Milton Shulman in the *Evening Standard*. 'To me the wrestling is always the main attraction of an *As You Like It* performance' wrote Bernard Shaw (only half ironically, one suspects), in 1896 (Shaw, 28): one might suppose from the energy and expertise with which the scene has been staged, and observed, in so many of Stratford's post-war productions that there is still much sympathy with this view.

It was not so, however – and one contemplates the fact with a sort of perverse relief that directorial energies seem to have gone elsewhere – in Trevor Nunn's 1977 production, when the wrestling provoked much complaint. There was a silver cup ready for the victor, into which the assembled lords put jewels and which the Duke ostentatiously filled with money and then (as the prompt-book records), snatched it from Celia, who was about to present it, on the news of Orlando's paternity. Roger Warren enjoyed the fact that, most unusually in his experience, Duke Frederick was passionately interested in the fighting and dragged his court around after him observing it (*SS*, 147). To Gareth Lloyd Evans, however, the wrestling seemed 'the worst staged I've ever seen at Stratford' (*SA Herald*). It featured an Orlando (Peter McEnery), whose victory no one found credible, and a Charles made into 'a believable and sympathetic character' by Jack Klaff (*SA Herald*), whose heart was clearly not in the service of Duke Frederick. He had earlier spoken with yearning about the 'golden world' of Arden (1.1.119), and would be warmly greeted by the forest lords when, at that telling moment just before the interval, he turned up there (as the promptbook indicates), during the singing of 'Blow, blow thou winter wind' (2.7.174ff.). This was, indeed, a court that leached away to Arden as the play progressed, several attendant lords being recognizable as they joined the exiled Duke's retinue. Last of them to arrive, just before the final weddings, was Graham Crowden's 'huge, laughingly ready-to-oblige Le Beau' (*SA Herald*), speaking 'volumes of courtly distress' – in John Peter's phrase (*S. Times*) – as he warned Orlando to make his escape.

Nunn placed the play in the later seventeenth century, with John Napier's settings presented in the theatrical style of the period, a drop cloth of a country chateau for Oliver's orchard, something more akin to Versailles for the Duke's establishment. In this satin and lace world of 'peacockishly caparisoned males' (*Oxf. Times*) who 'dandymince onto the stage in a stately dance' (*Guardian*), and whose appearance was in the sharpest contrast to the plain linen of the foresters, it was not the 'temperamentally incontinent' (*SA Herald*) Duke Frederick of John Rhys-Davies, reminiscent for one reviewer of a 'Caucasian Idi Amin' (*Coventry E.*

Tel.), who caught the eye, but the handsome figure cut by Charles Dance as Oliver, whom Irving Wardle (who had obviously not seen Scofield thirty years earlier) thought 'the best performance I have ever seen of this unappetizing part' (*Times*). Peter McEnery, who made Orlando 'deeply moving in his protestations about his brother's treatment of him' (*Jewish Chron.*), was first seen practising wrestling moves, which John Peter thought 'a nice touch', even if the wrestling itself failed to live up to this anticipatory promise (*S. Times*).

Duke Frederick's court returned in Terry Hands's 1980 production to the path of energetic and perhaps slightly overstated symbolism along which productions before Nunn's had been heading. Farrah's designs also moved it towards, if not quite clearly into (except in the men's tricorn hats), the eighteenth century. Characters in black and silver costumes occupied a strange world of sheepskin-clad walls seen through a row of vertical posts that crossed the stage near the front. Whether it was all taking place inside 'a sheepskin coat' (*SA Herald*) or 'a very large bedroom slipper' (*Punch*), the court décor was certainly enough to explain, as Jeremy Treglown observed (*TLS*), Duke Senior's preference for exile. My own assumption, I recall, based on the behaviour of the occupants and on that confining line of posts, was that director and designer had it in mind to allude to the idea of a padded cell. For this was a court populated by some seriously tense people. Robert Cushman noted that Jonathan Hyde 'gave the full melodramatic works to Oliver' and that even his inconspicuous servant Dennis 'shot off his two functional lines in a sinister ecstasy of bad temper' (*Observer*). 'The baddies', remarked Alan Drury in the *Listener*, 'stamp about and rant a lot', and 'Oliver and Frederick actually shriek at moments of high stress' – which for Oliver included his little soliloquy describing his brother as 'enchantingly beloved' (1.1.165–6). On hearing the name de Boys after the wrestling Frederick recoiled in Victorian melodramatic mode, taking 'four steps back and gibbering with horror at the very name' (*Guardian*). (See Figure 4.) He pulled Celia

FIGURE 4 On Farrah's sheepskin-covered court set, with its restrictive line of posts, an angry Duke Frederick (Bruce Purchase) learns that Orlando (John Bowe), who has just won the wrestling match, is the son of his former enemy. Touchstone (Joe Melia, left, in tricorn hat), Celia (Sinead Cusack) and Rosalind (Susan Fleetwood, right) look on in disgust. (1.2, 1980)

violently from Rosalind's arms in the banishment scene and quivered all over as he pronounced the sentence. Charles Spencer and Michael Billington, reviewing the Aldwych transfer, described Frederick (respectively) as 'a tyrant to be feared, twitchy, irrational, hovering on the brink of madness yet capable of snuffing out the lives of the play's innocents at a word' (*New Stand.*); and as 'juddering and starting as if he had seen a whole regiment of ghosts' (*Guardian*).

These early scenes were played with great energy and speed; Robert Cushman had 'never known the opening scene go at such a lick, with John Bowe as Orlando trying to make you feel you've never heard it before' (*Observer*). Orlando's fight with Oliver, which thrashed about all over the downstage area, turned out to be only a prelude to the wrestling with Charles, when every audience was invited to believe that it was only at their performance that Orlando had leapt back onto the stage to continue the fight after a fall into the front row of the stalls (business that led, late in the Stratford run, to a series of appearances by the understudy as this spectacular bit of showmanship resulted in a shoulder injury (Bowe, 70–1)). Such playing of the wrestling to encourage more laughter than earlier productions had sought was also manifested in Charles's fighting so ostentatiously dirtily that the hissing and pummelling, and hair-pulling and hand-stamping, of Sinead Cusack's self-assertive Celia seemed legitimate interventions.

If the highly demonstrative performances elicited by Terry Hands's direction pushed Duke Frederick's court a little too far for some tastes towards the unreality of melodrama, Adrian Noble's 1985 production was founded in a concept that was dedicated to taking the entire play, Duke Frederick's court and the Forest of Arden alike, out of any theatrical zone in which the word 'realism' had any relevance at all. The production was widely hailed as presenting a directorial breakthrough, but its basic proposition, that Arden is a state of mind rather than a place, was hardly new to critical discourse. It did, however, find a way of staging the notion that court and country are merely two ways of looking at the same world, and that a route between the two can be found by a little manipulative metatheatre. The trick upon which it was based was to have Joseph O'Conor play both Duke Frederick and his banished brother, the same group of actors doubling as the two Dukes' followers. They 'changed roles' simply by throwing dust sheets over their dress suits, Duke Frederick leading the way to Arden by stepping through a tall upstage mirror. The sheets were simply thrown off again (without the journey through the mirror), for the two scenes (2.2 and 3.1) when the action returns to court. Inevitably, therefore, this was the production, of the thirteen with which this book is concerned, in which court and forest were least differentiated, for the object of the exercise was to propose their interchangeability. Bob Crowley's single set (with a change of lighting) served for both, with the strong suggestion that it was neither ducal palace nor forest, but the stage of a theatre.

The play began before a billowing curtain, Orlando discovered in silhouette with his arms hitched over a staff which lay across his shoulders, a striking initial image of crucifixion that couldn't really lead very far. Dress was more or less modern: Orlando wore a donkey jacket, Oliver a trilby hat; a storm, with a howling wind, raged during their quarrel. Michael Ratcliffe, in the *Observer*, described Hilton McRae's Orlando as 'tousled ... scruffy, humorous, brave, and enormously likeable, if in need of a bath' and felt that he provided 'the only reference to any humanity warming the cerebral chill of the first half' of the play. A specific example of that warmth came as Orlando got the upper hand in the fight with Oliver: with his brother helpless beneath him he suddenly looked at him pityingly and hugged him, before allowing him to free himself – a curious and touching gesture looking forward to their later reconciliation.

The fight over, the curtain flew out and we were removed to a surreal world, a room with its furniture covered in white dust sheets. Rosalind entered alone, ahead of Celia, removed a sheet from the tall mirror that would soon provide the route to Arden, and gazed at herself for a long moment in a way that demanded that the audience register it as significant. Touchstone, complete with umbrella, emerged from under another dust sheet. The contemporary look of the first scene was now somewhat qualified: the long dresses worn by the young women and the formal evening dress of the men (see Figure 18) seemed to belong to the first third of the twentieth century, perhaps, rather than to the last. During the wrestling scene the men smoked cigars and half a dozen flaming hemispherical containers marked out the fighting space like so many miniature Olympic flames (when the play moved to the forest they doubled as braziers for the exiled lords to huddle round). Charles the wrestler wore a diamond-studded pink silk dressing-gown and Orlando found a moment during their bout to tweak his nipples. Joseph O'Conor's natural qualities as an actor were so obviously more akin to one's perception of the benignity of the exiled Duke than to the irascibility of his younger brother that his reaction to the news of the identity of Orlando's father, and his banishment of Rosalind, were as unthreatening as they had been for many Stratford productions. The court, indeed, had rarely seemed less 'envious'.

The tendency for one Stratford production of a play to react strongly against its predecessor (never deliberately, of course – or so it is always said) was notably conspicuous in John Caird's production of *As You Like It* four years later. Where Noble had gone out of his way to homogenize the physical presentation of court and forest, Caird and his designer Ultz made the move from one to the other so extreme and so violent that it actually involved the physical dismantling of the floor of the stage. We were still, however, in a broadly metatheatrical frame of reference. Few productions in Stratford's history can have been designed so specifically for the Royal Shakespeare Theatre. As the audience entered the theatre a little onstage band was playing tangos and sambas with couples in evening dress dancing on a stage that looked at first glance like a 1930s art deco ballroom but that one quickly realized precisely imitated the marquetry, panelling, chaises-longues and elegant lamps of the dress-circle bar. The silver-figured clock on the panelled wall, showing the real time, was a replica of the clock in the theatre foyer (see Figure 5). Actors in the uniforms of front-of-house staff moved between stage and auditorium, joining in the dancing when on stage, pretending to help with the ushering when at the front of the stalls. The house lights were up and there was no discernible boundary between playing area and auditorium: the audience was being invited to see the theatre building itself as the 'set' for the play – 'all the world's a stage', as it were. It is a curious fact, therefore, that among more than three dozen reviewers of the production whose notices are preserved in the archive at the Shakespeare Centre, only a handful saw the point. One reviewer thought the sets looked like 'the lobby of a seedy provincial hotel' (*Birm. Post*)

FIGURE 5 Beneath a clock replicating the one in the theatre foyer and showing the real time, Rosalind (Sophie Thompson, right) and Celia (Gillian Bevan) dance with court/theatre ushers (Eric Francis and George Malpas) who will later become, respectively, Adam and Corin. On the occasion of the photocall the performance was clearly running a few minutes behind schedule: the dance normally ended with Orlando's 'Prologue' at the normal performance starting-time of 7.30 p.m. (Prelude to 1.1, 1989)

while another even managed to refer to 'Duke Frederick's oppressively fascist décor' (*TLS*), a remark that must surely rank as one of the harsher judgements on Elisabeth Scott's Memorial Theatre building.

In this 'old Café de Paris' world (as Michael Billington called it in the *New York Herald Tribune*) of dinner jackets and ball gowns, one identified Clifford Rose's Duke Frederick by the red silk sash he wore across his jacket and by the gum-chewing 'minders', in their sunglasses, who kept him constantly in sight. Their presence was the one thing that prevented a number of reviewers from feeling that the whole event was rather jolly, though several still found it a puzzling way of presenting the court of the usurper Duke. The underlying mood, however, was profoundly tense, and the dancing had about it a joyless slickness that was rather menacing. As the hands of the clock reached 7.30 a young man in simple fawn breeches moved downstage with a frail old figure who looked as if he might be a court butler: 'As I remember Adam . . .'. The speech was delivered out to the audience rather than to Adam, so that it formed a kind of prologue from 'the lord' to balance the epilogue from 'the lady' (5.4.198–9) at the other end of the evening. The dancers (who had included Rosalind and Celia) sat at the sides of the stage watching the fraternal quarrel, but drifted away during it to leave the young women alone for the second scene. The wrestling was preceded by a processional entry for Duke Frederick down the stalls aisle to the ducal box (in the dress circle slips) to a vulgar national anthem for which the bodyguards demanded that the audience stood. Reviewing the production at the time for *Shakespeare Quarterly* I wrote:

> On most of the occasions I saw the production the majority of the audience was remarkably obedient to this demand, whether through pleasure in the performance or fear of the bodyguard; failure to obey, of course, did not necessarily mean failure to respond to the production: it might also signal an involvement so deep that one could not allow oneself to stand for the usurper. (492)

Orlando's victory in the wrestling (Charles wore a leopard-skin leotard and Frederick's minders were all over the auditorium, forcing us to support their man) was followed by his presentation, as cameras flashed and autographs were signed, with an ostentatious silver cup (a bit of business recalling the 1977 production). At the revelation of his parentage the cup was snatched from him and the revolvers of bodyguards flashed out, pointing at his head. Later, on Duke Frederick's order to search for the missing princesses (2.2), powerful searchlights raked the auditorium, and ducal henchmen prowled the stalls and circle.

Duke Frederick's court in this production was all forward of the proscenium arch, forward of what would have been regarded as the playing area when the theatre was built, the period that was being reproduced in the staging. There was no way on or off the stage other than by the auditorium; the audience, as well as the play's characters, were trapped in Duke Frederick's brutal little dictatorship. To force a way to Arden Duke Senior and his men (and again forest duke and followers were doubled with court duke and followers) had to come up from below ground, like Harry Lime from the sewers of Vienna in *The Third Man*, forcing a way through the stage floor. Only by means of what Paul Lapworth called 'the ultimate theatrical metaphor of demolishing the set' (*SA Herald*) would Rosalind and Celia ever escape from court and find their way to Arden. The way through to the theatre's originally intended playing space thus became the route to the magic of Arden, a bit of metatheatre that paid tribute, perhaps, to the half century and more of productions of *As You Like It* that the building had witnessed and that this book is attempting to chronicle.

Three years later, in David Thacker's 1992 production, the play returned to a more traditional mode, with quite separate, fully representational sets for court and forest, all the court scenes grouped together at the beginning, and an old-fashioned transformation scene for the move to Arden. Johan Engels's designs for the court made it a claustrophobic, ominous place, a windowless room in black marble with a vaulted ceiling, very reminiscent of the sort of set on which the RSC might, during the 1970s, have presented one of the Italianate tragedies of John Webster or Thomas Middleton. Before we entered it, however, we had been in Oliver's orchard 'where even the orchard trees stand to attention in sculptured duty' (*D. Mail*). Peter de Jersey's Orlando seemed to Nicholas de Jongh 'almost at the end of his emotional tether' (*E. Standard*); Benedict Nightingale had 'seldom

... seen an Orlando more distraught by his treatment by his elder brother' and thought that Oliver radiated 'Iago-like hate waves' (*Times*); they certainly had Alfred Burke's Adam growling in resentment. De Jongh described the brothers' confrontation:

> In a midnight garden, where tall, sinister trees rear up into the shadows, a half-hysterical Orlando, dressed in twentieth-century black leather, wrestles his wicked and even more leather-bound brother to the ground, while incidentally trying to choke the life out of him.

It was, he thought, 'a good flourish of ominous dramatics to start'.

Velasquez was the painter many reviewers thought of when describing the court scenes – 'all white ruffs beneath sour yellow faces', as Benedict Nightingale put it in the *Times*. In the black-lacquered walls of this mausoleum-like world, automaton courtiers in dark costumes, the men in heavy greatcoats and boots, the women in swishing silks, with ruffs and bustles, paraded and postured, 'looking as if they only need an *auto da fe* to make their day' (*Times*). The combination of the Victorian and the Jacobean was taken further with the huge black grand piano at which Rosalind and Celia were discovered (see Figure 19). The sense grew as one watched these scenes that one was in some sort of horrible nightmare, with Andrew Jarvis's Duke Frederick its central figure. His entrance for the wrestling had a deliberately absurd magnificence, coming after a succession of courtiers had each swept through the great studded black doors upstage, each one falsely anticipated as the Duke, until, to an even more pompous fanfare than his predecessors, and then ominous silence, and with his smoothly shaven head shimmering in the infernal red of the light, the man himself strode in, spurred and booted, pointed black beard jutting in front of him. Here was a melodramatically nasty man, 'fetishistically fondling the hair of Orlando, of Oliver, of Hisperia (Celia's gentlewoman, making a rare appearance) as he cross-examined them, then grabbing them by the chin to fling them aside in contempt' (*SQ*, 347). Figure 6 captures one such

FIGURE 6 Andrew Jarvis's Duke Frederick, booted and spurred, demonstrates his fetishistic tendency to fondle his victims' hair at moments of anger or disturbance. Here he is reacting to the news that Orlando (Peter de Jersey) is the son of Sir Rowland de Boys. (1.2, 1992)

moment, as Frederick learns of Orlando's parentage. This was a man 'to whom a little light torture comes naturally' (*E. Standard*), 'bald, mean, and paranoid to the point of psychosis' (*Times*). The sense of relief at Rosalind's (and our) escape from this flamboyantly melodramatic world of menace and violence was like awakening from a nightmare: Arden, in 1992, was no dream world – in comparison with Duke Frederick's court it seemed normality itself.

Where Andrew Jarvis's villainous Duke had been ostentatiously larger than life, Colum Convey's Frederick, tetchy and goggle-eyed in Steven Pimlott's 1996 production, was altogether smaller and meaner – 'a weak, shrill hysteric' (*D. Telegraph*), 'tiny, pink and nasty, like a rabid prawn' (*Times*). Robert Hanks noticed his 'swelling paranoia' (*Independent*) and others wrote of him in terms of the unhinged violence of the psychopath, or as 'chilling, sadistic ... a man who enjoys cruelly tormenting servants and watching his wrestling champion tear people's arms off' (*S. Mercury*). The court costumes here were Elizabethan, but Ashley Martin-Davies's set, a rectangular box of ribbed aluminium, was abstractly modern in a sternly uncompromising way – as if the play were happening inside a container lorry, as I heard someone remark over interval drinks. The 'orchard scene' was played downstage in front of what looked like the fourth wall of this box, Orlando and Adam stepping through a central slot that rose to give them egress. Liam Cunningham's Orlando was later to impress Benedict Nightingale as 'an unusually tough and dangerous wrestler' (*Times*), but here at the beginning John Peter thought him 'surly, difficult, unattractive, and well past his first youth' and objected to the whole presentation of these early scenes as 'designer visuals at the expense of reality, physical and spiritual' (*S. Times*). Charles Spencer, on the other hand, thought that the 'clinical' set suited 'the harsh, cold world of the court' (*D. Telegraph*), a world in which Sebastian Harcombe's Oliver evinced a genuinely creepy nastiness. Comparisons by a number of reviewers of Oliver to Richard III – which for some made his final conversion very suspect – relate curiously to comparisons of his immediate predecessor to Iago. Stratford Olivers were apparently going through a phase of particular villainy in the 1990s.

Since the rectangular metal set remained the same for Arden – with the addition of varying numbers of metal poles that one might (or might not) imagine as tree trunks – there was no question of following the preceding production's decision to group all the court scenes together at the beginning of the play. Indeed Steven Pimlott voiced an objection to this method of staging in an interview with me for the production's programme; movement between court and forest, he felt, was an important part of the play's design in its early stages. The last return to court came, therefore, immediately after the interval and showed Duke Frederick interrogating a half-drowning Oliver as Charles the wrestler, between the questions, forced his head into a tin bath full of water. Reviewing the production for *Shakespeare Survey*, I thought that Frederick's arrival at 'the last stages of psychopathic dementia ... made the final news of his entering a monastery oddly plausible' (204–5). The 'envious court' of *As You Like It* had, in the last production of the century, achieved what was, perhaps, its gloomiest manifestation.

Not that the first production of the new century offered anything very much lighter. In Gregory Doran's 2000 version we were once again in a more or less Elizabethan world, giving, for the only time in the period covered by this book, an unbroken sequence of three Stratford productions that all offered the play in Elizabethan or Jacobean costume. The designs, by Kaffe Fassett and Niki Turner, the former better known for his work in the fashionable world of knitwear and tapestry than as a theatre designer, presented the court scenes in monochrome, Rosalind in a black and white dress, Celia in a white and black one; even Touchstone's motley was black and silver. Ian Hogg, who doubled the two Dukes, wore a dark, heavy costume as Frederick, with a somewhat helmet-like headpiece that looked as if it might have been inspired by something in Gengis Khan's battle wardrobe. The bullet-headed look added to the impression of a 'chunky tyrant with a fondness for violence' (*Times*), a violence that evinced itself in a fierce blow to Touchstone's face in response to a jokey bit of mimed wrestling (with himself) just before Orlando's bout with Charles – a 'slightly excessive reaction', thought Michael Billington, to Touchstone's 'terrible jokes' (*Guardian*).

The court scenes, including an energetic version of the wrestling match in which Orlando's victory 'owed more to dirty tricks than honest valour' (*Guardian*) – he jumped on an unprepared Charles from the rear during a lull in the fighting and nearly throttled him – were played in a somewhat shadowy light on a stage dominated by an enormous monochrome tapestry in Elizabethan style (see Figure 7). Below this mural Rosalind was discovered, at the beginning of the banishment scene, working at a sewing frame with a vividly coloured piece of needlework emerging from her labours, the brightness that her imagination, and her weaving skills, were creating contrasting absolutely with the gloom of the court and with the monochrome stylized leaves and fabulous beasts of the mural. Was this, the production asked, our first glimpse of Arden, and was Arden, then, Rosalind's dream of escape? The doubling of the roles of the Dukes seemed to be part of this idea, as did the cousins' exit ('To liberty, and not to banishment', 1.3.134) through a hitherto unnoticed door in the middle of the big tapestry, while the proposition that Arden was an artistic construct, specifically of the art of the needleworker, was to be made manifest when the play moved out to the forest.

Stratford's thirteen post-war productions of *As You Like It* have moved Duke Frederick's court through a wide range of period settings, from the Plantagenet world of the 1946 production to various parts of the twentieth century – Edwardian, 1930s, contemporary. In between these extremes, it has been placed in the later seventeenth century (in both France and England), in the earlier sixteenth century, and (vaguely, at any rate) in the eighteenth century. Only five of the thirteen productions (including, interestingly, the three most recent) have costumed it, more or less, in the period of its composition. It has been

FIGURE 7 In front of the enormous monochrome tapestry in Elizabethan style, with its trees and mythical beasts, Touchstone (Adrian Schiller) tells the story of the knight and the mustard and the pancakes to Rosalind (Alexandra Gilbreath, left) and Celia (Nancy Carroll). The young women's later departure 'to liberty, and not to banishment' (1.3.134) will be through a previously unnoticed and unsuspected door in the tapestry. (1.2, 2000)

sternly realistic and deliberately whimsical; intentionally (and perhaps unintentionally) melodramatic, and genuinely nasty; it has striven to be as different from Arden as possible and it has been indistinguishable from it; it has been experienced all in one sequence at the start of the play but more often (and as the text proposes) as a place to revisit at intervals after an initial introduction to its allurements. But however it has been presented, it has always demanded attention on the one hand as an environment to be compared (for difference or for similarity) with the play's 'other world' of the forest, and on the other as the setting for what is certainly Shakespeare's most significant portrayal of friendship between women. To these two aspects of the play I turn in the next two chapters.

2

NOW AM I IN
ARDEN

Ay, now am I in Arden, the more fool I; when I was at home I was in
a better place, but travellers must be content.   (2.4.13–15)

A former house manager at the Royal Shakespeare Theatre
once told me of a rather unnerving experience he had
had during the interval of one of those RSC productions
of *As You Like It* that did not offer a particularly naturalistic vision
of Arden. He was on duty in the foyer, elegant as always in the
regulation black tie and dinner-jacket, when a very large patron
indeed, his face ablaze with rage, bore down on him and grabbed
him by the lapels. 'Listen to me, son', he shouted, pushing his
face down close to my friend's, 'I've travelled thousands of miles
from ...' – and he named somewhere on the other side of the
planet – 'and when I get to the Royal Shakespeare Theatre in
Stratford-on-Avon to watch *As You Like It* I expect to see some real
trees in the Forest of Arden!' The end of the story need not
concern us – house managers defuse such incidents, with aplomb,
on a nightly basis, and my friend continued unscathed in his job
for several years – but the incident is a valuable reminder of the
expectations of playgoers, built up over many decades of pictorial
theatre, about the wonderful escape to the greenwood that going
to watch *As You Like It* will offer them. No use explaining that the
word 'forest' did not necessarily imply trees in the sixteenth
century, and could simply mean 'a wild uncultivated waste, a

wilderness' (*OED sb.* 3), and that Orlando refers to Arden as a 'desert' (2.7.110): the play is simply too full of references to the trees of Arden (which include a 'palm' (3.2.173) and a 'tuft of olives' (3.5.75)), to their barks (in which Orlando carves his love's name (3.2.6, etc.)), and to their branches (on which he hangs the manuscript versions of his poetic efforts (3.2.1, etc.)) for this excuse to divert the tree-hungry punter. Indeed, in the very line after calling Arden a 'desert', Orlando refers to the exiled Duke and his companions spending their time 'under the shade of melancholy boughs' (2.7.111) and the first line of the play's first song is 'Under the greenwood tree' (2.5.1). Director and designer have somehow to respond to the sylvan and arboreal aspects of Arden.

'Ay, now am I in Arden, the more fool I' – and the look of despair and disbelief that he could ever have let himself in for this deplorable idea, written large over the face of Roy Kinnear's Touchstone in 1967, is indelibly inscribed on my memory – and quite well captured in Figure 28. That particular Touchstone's was rather a gloomy Arden – though he did a lot to cheer it up as the evening wore on. How has the location in which four-fifths of the action of *As You Like It* takes place varied its appearance and mood over half a century on Stratford's stage?

It seems clear from the reviews of Glen Byam Shaw's first production in 1952 that Stratford playgoers were not used to quite so wintry an Arden as he at first introduced them to – in spite of Duke Senior's references to the 'icy fang / And churlish chiding of the winter's wind' (2.1.6–7) and the invitation (in the song that accompanies his meal) to that same 'winter wind' to 'blow' (2.7.174). Commenting disbelievingly that the Duke in 1952 had his 'al fresco meal in the snow' – the first of several Stratford dukes to do so – and that only in the second half of the play did summer come to Arden, the *Times* remarked, surprisingly, that 'the bleakness of the opening scenes is a high price to pay for the novelty'. A few productions later, and an Arden that did not progress from winter to summer would be very hard to find. The play's songs propose a most odd progression of seasons, of course, beginning with the summer of 'greenwood' and birdsong, following with the blowing of the 'winter wind', and then progressing by way of a deer hunt (a basically autumnal activity) to the spring in which 'a lover and his lass' wander through the countryside (5.3.14ff.), but it would be a literal-minded director who tried to follow such a progression.

The only seasonal adjective in reviews of the 1946 production refers to the 'autumnal trees' against which the 'lively colours of the fifteenth-century costumes looked well' (*Stage*). Surviving monochrome photographs of Joyce Hammond's set of painted flats depicting a forest clearing, with a sloped bank down to the playing area, don't help us to be specific about summer or autumn, but there is certainly nothing of wintry leaflessness about them; the photograph (Figure 8) of the arrival in Arden of Rosalind, Celia and Touchstone, so wintry an event in later productions, shows it happening in what is clearly a fairly benign season. It was certainly the colourfulness of costumes against trees that most caught the attention of reviewers in 1946 – and not always with pleasure. The disapproving reviewer for the *Malvern Gazette* quoted the explanation offered by the theatre's artistic director, but remained unconvinced:

> I am told that Sir Barry Jackson has decided that the customary sombreness of the exiled court's dress has in his opinion been overdone and that there is nothing unlikely in the court being able to dress in the usual manner despite the exile.

The reviewer from neighbouring Worcester – how assiduous the not-so-local press was in covering Stratford productions in the first decade or two after the war – was, on the other hand, delighted to be 'dazzled' by colour 'to which we are no doubt particularly susceptible after the drab war years' (*Berrow's Worcs. J.*). One aspect of the first forest scene in 1946 that was to return later was the reception of the Duke's speech to his 'co-mates and brothers in exile' (2.1.1). It was greeted with 'only murmurs of polite approval' which 'suggested that they had heard those words ...

FIGURE 8 Against the background of Joyce Hammond's set design of trees and rolling hills, Ruth Lodge's Rosalind – a boar-spear in her hand as the text requires (1.3.114) – comforts the weaker vessel, Celia (Joy Parker). Hugh Griffith's Touchstone, in a jester's costume described by one reviewer as magpie-like, reflects that home was a better place. (2.4, 1946)

a good many times before' (*Leam. Spa Cour.*). That suggestion would recur, though not always with the same politeness.

Glen Byam Shaw's two productions, both designed by Motley, offered a rather literal presentation of the forest in 1952 and a more abstract and delicate one five years later. Figures 20 and 40 show the 1952 forest (complete with central palm tree) in its summer guise, after 'the leafless trees which stretch disconsolately to the skies' of the early forest scenes had become a 'tropical exuberance' in which 'palms and cacti flourish' (*Nott. Guardian*). The 'enchanting superficiality' reminded this reviewer of a seventeenth-century French tapestry, a curious premonition of the needlework inspiration for the production of 2000. Such pleasure was certainly not shared by W.A. Darlington, who found it all 'too whimsical' (*D. Telegraph*) or by the reviewer for the *Birmingham Gazette*, who admitted that it might be picturesque but complained that it was 'hardly an English forest, more a tropical garden'. That assumption that Arden is English, and must be seen to be so (in spite of its olives, and palm, and lioness), runs through many of the reviews. So subtropical did it all seem to a visitor from Lancashire that he found himself waiting 'to hear the distant chugging of the "African Queen"' (*Bolton E. News*), while T.C. Worsley grumbled that the palm tree, 'transplanted apparently from the front at Torquay', was 'an absurd piece of textual literalism' (*New States.*). In the middle of his long and distinguished career as a writer on Shakespearean performance, J.C. Trewin was clearly seeing his first Arden winter (of many), and joined the chorus of surprise and disapproval:

> The trees are bare – like a rank of scaffold poles – and we know that the cast lie in the bleak air … Pass the fruit at the December picnic and try to forget that pneumonia lies just around the corner.
>
> (*Jack O'L.*)

When winter turned to summer and the exotic leaves came out, he was equally unimpressed: there was about it all, he thought, 'less of Arden than the Ardennes' – anticipating by over three decades the textual decision of the Oxford editors of the *Complete Works* (Wells *et al.*).

An aspect of the 1952 production that will strike a chord with many actors who have found themselves as forest exiles on the Stratford stage (including the cast of a production exactly forty years later) was the arena that it provided for struggle between players and environment. The green undulations spread beyond the front of the stage (and were visible, unacceptably for some, in the court scenes), there was a rocky pool (the first of many in Stratford Ardens, some more genuinely watery than others), the cuckoo called, trees sprouted in abundance, and 'saplings, palm trees and Arcadian castles' left actors 'a bumpy postage stamp to play on' (*Leam. Spa Cour.*). There was even a cave-like structure for the Duke to 'abandon' later (5.4.195), and in front of it Jack Gwillim's Duke, 'all dignity' (*Coventry E. Tel.*), held court, his 'serenity' apparently overwhelming any tendency to irreverence on the part of his followers, for he made 'the attractions of his forest hideout magnetic' (*Solihull N.*).

Motley's second design for a Stratford *As You Like It* five years later took audiences to a much less literal location. The 'stencil' effect of the trees referred to by many reviewers is visible in its winter and its summer guises in Figures 9 and 41, the hoar-frosted twigs reaching beyond the proscenium arch in the scene of the Duke's feast. Again there were hankerings for a more Warwickshire Arden, the set suggesting 'less an English greenwood ... than an elysian idyll amid a silver-birch type of elfin elegance' (*Liv. Post*). The thinness of this forest, the sketchy, aspen-like prettiness of it, delighted some with its artificiality – 'like the massed pressings of leaves from the folios of a thousand botanists' (*Oxf. Times*) – and seemed to others a 'spidery', 'arty-crafty forest of spindly trees' (*Birm. W. Post*, *D. Mail*). Again the wintry start drew hostile comment, though not on the scale of five years earlier, and several reviewers also commented disparagingly on 'autumnal' colours: 'surely this is a spring play' grumbled the *Yorkshire Post*, apparently unheeding of the range of seasonal reference in the text. But Byam

Shaw was apparently beginning to make his point about the play's seasonality: Derek Granger enjoyed the moment when the Arden snows melted 'to reveal a quivering fabric of young greenery' (*FT*) and Rosemary Anne Sisson provides an early comment on the work of the lighting designer in the creation of Arden, admiring 'moments of great beauty ... as when the cold morning light slowly gives way to gold and green as the sun strikes upon the shivering tender trees' (*SA Herald*). The *Warwick Advertiser*, too, drew attention to the effects produced by lighting: 'pale sunlight glinted through the trees of a grove through which meandered a stream crossed by a rustic bridge'.

In this idyllic (or arty-crafty) world Cyril Luckham's exiled Duke seems to have earned the confidence of most audiences. The 'genuine goodness' about him made his forest repast 'a moment of deep, almost religious emotion' (*SA Herald*) – a curiously eucharistic note there – and phrases suggesting humanity, gentleness and calm are frequent in the critical response. Nor is there any indication (in the promptbook or the reviews) that his followers greeted his reflections on the forest life with anything other than rapt attention, though one reviewer, 'despite the ruddy face and cheerful smile', remained unconvinced: 'Surely, one felt, having made the necessary gesture of encouragement to his shivering band, he would now go sensibly back to a blazing fire' (*Coventry E. Tel.*). Such *fin de siècle* cynicism is a little surprising so early in our half century.

No such irreverence intrudes into accounts of the scene in 1961; and in the version of the production redirected for

FIGURE 9 (*opposite*) With the frosted trees of Motley's wintry set reaching beyond the proscenium arch, Orlando (Richard Johnson) brings Adam (James Wellman) to the forest meal. Robert Harris's Jaques is seated in the centre, with Duke Senior (Antony Brown, understudying Cyril Luckham) seated at the table to his left. One of the pageboys who featured prominently in this and the same director's 1952 production is visible in the foreground. The Duke's 'cave' (5.4.195) seems a geologically unlikely phenomenon on the right of the picture. (2.7, 1957) television the followers of Paul Hardwick's banished Duke (he had replaced Redmond Phillips for the Aldwych transfer) listen with affectionate attention to his eagerly persuasive homily (delivered in that wonderfully rich baritone) and quietly murmur their approval of Amiens's respectful response. The sense of 'closeness in friendship and loyalty' (*Yorks. Post*) of the exiled court, huddled in their fur-edged, faintly Russian-looking clothes, is certainly very palpable in the television remake.

The Forest of Arden consisted, in Richard Negri's design, of one large tree (rather, it would seem from Figure 42, of the cedar genus, though many reviewers refer to it as an oak) behind which different backdrops could be flown in (including the architectural forms used for the outdoor court scenes described in the preceding chapter). The tree stood on the top of a green mound or knoll that looked 'like the cap of a huge green mushroom' (*D. Herald*). This simple set was almost universally admired by reviewers – and survived, for certain scenes at least, into the television film. Gerard Fay described its merits: 'It makes changes of time and place smooth and presents a foreground for backgrounds of woods and rolling valleys' (*Guardian*). Bernard Levin thought it 'superb': 'a huge greenwood tree backed by a succession of perfectly judged flats' (*D. Express*). Only one reviewer (among the five dozen and more whose opinions are preserved in the Stratford theatre records) was now to be found objecting to the season chosen for the initial episodes in Arden: 'altogether too wintry', he thought, 'so that some of the early scenes seem to be taking place in Tibet' (*D. Mail*). The rest express constant admiration for the way lighting, and a soundtrack, were used to mark the play's progress through the seasons, and the days. The word 'dappled' runs like a leitmotif through accounts of 1961's Arden, with its transitions 'from winter to summer and from dawn, to high noon, to dusk' (*Warwick Adv.*) and its imagined pond (somewhere backstage) 'over which the summer insects hum' (*E. News*). For the second wooing scene the lighting perfectly captured 'the atmosphere of long hot afternoons in early summer, with sunlight filtering

through the forest to dapple the stage with refreshing shade'
(*Warwick Adv.*), and for Orlando's nocturnal publication of his
verses 'the mysterious shadows cast on a moonlit night are as
perfectly suggested as the glow filtering through to clearings and
thickly wooded tracts on a summer's day' (*Morn. Adv.*). (One
occasionally needs to remind oneself that the set consisted of one
far-from-naturalistic tree on a mound.) 'By the end of the evening',
wrote Bamber Gascoigne in the *Spectator*, 'I was in no doubt that,
from Epping to the Schwarzwald, this was the knoll where I would
pitch my ideal picnic.'

The atmosphere of summer afternoon picnics that the
production finally created came slowly, however, and arrived late.
Reviewers are clear, and the television film confirms this, that this
was by no means a sentimentalized Arden. Winter and rough
weather lingered long and the sense of the Duke's followers as tired
men struggling for a living is strong in the film version. This mood
seems to have been intensified when the production transferred to
the Aldwych. Irving Wardle thought Paul Hardwick's Duke was 'a
brooding forerunner of Timon' (*Observer*) and W.A. Darlington
sensed that his followers 'were thoroughly fed up with picnics'
(*D. Telegraph*). The setting of 'Under the greenwood tree' (in
Elizabethan style to lute accompaniment), to which they listened
so patiently, leaves little room to doubt that most friendship *is*
feigning and most loving mere folly.

The production's final reminder of the unsentimental harshness of Arden came in the deer-killing scene (4.2), which becomes
the object of widespread critical comment for the first time in post-
war Stratford productions. As yet unconnected with the emotional
development of Celia (see chapter 3), the scene revealed what
Bamber Gascoigne called 'a streak of savagery' in the foresters
(*Spectator*). The television film follows the stalk, the shooting, the
shouting, the hacking off of the antlers and the trussing up of the
body. Jaques watches the hunters, appalled, as they make their
chanting exit. J.W. Lambert wrote vividly of the scene:

> Shakespeare must have written that strange little scene of the
> foresters, the slaughtered deer, and the brooding Jaques with
> something more in mind than filling another five minutes. By
> staging the stalking of the prey and its killing amid bestial cries from
> men momentarily turned wolves, Mr Elliott gives point to Jaques's
> wincing – and suggests a reason for his folly, the old nightmare of
> the horns.   (S. Times)

When *As You Like It* returned to the Stratford stage in David
Jones's 1967 production, there was very little green about
Timothy O'Brien's wood of Arden, though some thought that
the two huge tree trunks (partly visible in Figures 21 and 28)
alluded to the main item of the exiles' diet: 'The forest swings
majestically into view, its great spreading branches also suggesting
by their forms the antlers of the deer who live there' (*SA Herald*).
The 'swinging' is explained in B.A. Young's review (though with
another animal analogy):

> the forest set is two vast dead trees, pivoted high up offstage, whose
> roots come questing slowly out of the upstage gloom like the heads
> of two grazing dinosaurs to take root in a variety of alternative
> positions while appropriate boscage descends from the flies.   (*FT*)

His colleague on the same newspaper, John Higgins, reviewing the
Aldwych transfer, was reminded of 'gigantic stick insects ... or a
pair of predatory brown lobsters', and a further biological
comparison came from a local reviewer: 'two huge lopped trees
on pivots; at times they hover like huge dragonflies over the
actors' heads, at others they swing to earth to form a resting place
for tired travellers and lost lovers' (*Leam. Spa Cour.*). My own chief
memory of their ponderous rising and falling is of the way their
immense size and cumbrousness dominated the space, placing the
actors in an environment that reflected the hugeness and
indifference of the forest; even the apprehension that something
might go wrong with the lifting and pivoting mechanism thus
became, in a curious way, part of the experience of the play, a
reminder of the vulnerability of those who try to survive in Arden

to the mood changes of their forest world. For the actors, of course (as Figures 21 and 28 reveal), the tree trunks provided climbing, and hiding, and prominent sitting places that were keenly exploited – mostly with the endorsement of the characters they were presenting, although it is clear from his face that climbing on tree trunks does not rate high with Roy Kinnear's Touchstone among ways of having a nice day out.

Arden in 1967 was again dark and wintry in the early stages. 'Not until the second half do the stern clouds roll back and the trees burgeon', noted Felix Barker (*E. News*), as if about to grumble about it; but he merely records without opining, so that, for the first time at post-war Stratford, a director's attentiveness to Arden's changing seasons was accepted by reviewers without complaint.

'Thus must I from the smoke into the smother', says Orlando (1.2.277), and that seems to have reflected Ronald Bryden's sense of the movement of the 1967 production from its black-walled court to 'a winter forest in whose glooms fur-jacketed outlaws raven bloodily after venison' (*Observer*). For here again the deer-killing scene, with a deerskin and horns required by the promptbook and the foresters smearing blood on their faces – and 'leeringly' too (*SA Herald*) – was given uncompromising treatment. To this potentially violent bunch of hunter-gatherers, the Duke's homily was delivered, observed Irving Wardle, 'in dead earnest, while his followers freeze – and then respond with boisterous sycophancy' (*Times*). Michael Billington, watching the same moment when the production was revived in 1968, was amused by the Duke 'dispersing free advice to his shivering fur-wrapped followers like the leader of an Arctic expedition trying to boost morale' (*Times*).

In the 1967 production the banished Duke drank from a silver goblet at the forest repast while his followers had much humbler vessels – an indication, perhaps, of that powerful sense of hierarchy which the Duke evinces most clearly as he regains his power, promising those who have endured exile with him a share in 'the good of our returned fortune, / According to the measure of their states' (5.4.173–4). In the modern-dress Arden of Buzz

Goodbody's 1973 production there were, for the meal interrupted by Orlando's famished arrival, elegant wine glasses all round, a lace tablecloth, and waiters in attendance. Michael Billington was surprised to see them all 'tucking into an excellent meal, washed down with an amusing little Burgundy' (*Guardian*), and other reviewers noted the armchairs, the 'grouse-moor hats and jackets' (*New States.*) and the 'smart casuals in the country after the evening dress at court' (*Listener*).

The 'forest' of Christopher Morley's set was a collection of steel poles lowered from the flies (discernible in the background of Figure 29), not unsuggestive, with the help of the lighting designer, of trees receding into the distance. Predictably, however, they found little favour with reviewers – 'a forest of stalagmites' one called them (*Coventry E. Tel.*) – though it was their juxtaposition with a real log, carried on for some of the forest scenes by stage staff, and offering a surely deliberate counterpoising of the abstract and the realistic in design terms, that provoked most complaint. The insistence of earlier directors on the bleakness of Arden had so thoroughly done its work by 1973 that its absence (see Figure 10) caused unease. Irving Wardle was puzzled not to be able to tell whether life in the forest was hard or not (*Times*) and Michael Billington missed any sense of a 'bleak' Arden and felt that, with the exception of Jeffery Dench's 'gnarled' Corin, the foresters 'looked like refugees from an urban rock festival' (*Guardian*). The problem of what to do with the 'native burghers of this desert city' (2.1.23) – Corin, Audrey, William – is one that modern-dress productions, offering a surreal or abstract Arden (such as Adrian Noble's a dozen years later), often find difficult to resolve. I remember feeling in 1973 that Corin must have wandered in from an altogether different production of the play. Tony Church's mellow Duke, leader of his group of 'elegant, high-born drop-outs' (*Spectator*), 'pipe-smoking and mercifully unembarrassed by his own pro-nouncements' (*Observer*), was particularly hard on the desire of Richard Pasco's remarkable Chekhovian Jaques to 'cleanse the foul body of th'infected world' (2.7.60), the fierceness of his rebuke

FIGURE 10 In this modern-dress version of the arrival in Arden, Touchstone (Derek Smith, in 'Max Miller' suit) is seen with Celia (Maureen Lipman, seated on ground) and Rosalind (Eileen Atkins), their hats and luggage suggesting that they have in mind a short country holiday. (2.4, 1973)

about Jaques's libertine past opening up an area clearly painful to both of them and adding depth to Pasco's greatly admired performance. Peter Thomson remarked on the 'tensely loving' relationship between them and on the fact that 'whilst liking to hear Jaques talk, the duke is always nervous of his tongue' (*SS*, 150).

From the modern unreality of Buzz Goodbody's Arden, the stage of the Royal Shakespeare Theatre moved four years later, in designs by John Napier, to the studied artificiality of Trevor Nunn's, 'a dotty fairyland', wrote John Peter in the *Sunday Times*, 'of toy bridges, painted brooks with round holes for fishing, and daintily gartered shepherds' (as Figure 38 shows). After all the satin and lace of the court, the foresters' garb of cream linen was in the strongest contrast, and following the more hospitable climatic conditions of 1973, this was an Arden where winter lingered for a long time: there was a sledge for the arrival of Rosalind and her companions, earmuffs were a wise precaution, and we were invited to imagine icy conditions as late as the fourth scene of Act 3, for the promptbook records Celia's skating (clockwise and anti-clockwise), with her hands behind her back, and even spinning, as she teased Rosalind about the truth (or lack of it) of Orlando's love. In keeping with the metatheatrical artificiality of the whole production, however, the snowflakes made no pretence not to be paper – and nor, as spring came, late and with a vengeance during the penultimate scene as 'It was a lover and his lass' was sung, did the petals later on. Corin, fishing through a hole in the ice, packed up his fishing tackle, and the hole he'd fished through, when asked to 'go off a little' (3.2.155).

Oliver Ford-Davies's Duke Senior, observed Gareth Lloyd Evans, betrayed 'a certain impatience at times, as if he is trying to put down resentment at being where he is, but he achieves this without losing the sense that he is a kind of orchestrator of good fellowship in the forest' (SA Herald). His success in developing that sense of fellowship has already been noted in the preceding chapter: there was, through the evening, a steady influx to his team of defectors from Duke Frederick's court, including Charles and Le Beau. B.A. Young admired the moment when the Duke revealed his identity to Orlando, causing 'a halt in his chat, a swing round to have a closer look, then a dutiful bending of the knee' (FT).

The Arden winter of 1980 was economically created in Farrah's design by recycling the sheepskin wall-coverings of Duke Frederick's court to represent a snowbound forest floor, the court walls flying out in a real 'transformation scene' to reveal the tall bare poles that several reviewers saw as redwoods. (They are visible, if not quite botanically identifiable, in Figures 23 and 31.) Gareth Lloyd Evans thought that the arrival of Rosalind and Celia in Arden looked like 'a sepia illustration of a clearing on the way to the American frontier, with Rosalind as intrepid buckskinned guide' (SA Herald); Michael Billington was struck by the same moment, describing Rosalind's reaching 'a forest filled with sky-seeking birches and vulpine howls, through a haze of mist, like one who has endured a long journey' (*Guardian*). Dry ice and angled lighting produced, as I vividly recall, some memorable misty-morning effects from those poles in the first half of the play. After the interval, colour came to the set, with the snow fleece replaced by greensward, creepers trailing from tree trunks, flowers sprouting with increasing profusion and the stage ending in a blaze of colour with red swags of cloth looped across it for Hymen's arrival. The 'garrulity' of Duke Senior was 'playfully tolerated' by his followers, thought Michael Coveney (*FT*, writing of the Aldwych transfer). Other reviewers were less tolerant (or playful): to Robert Cushman the Duke seemed to 'lecture his followers with an oily self-righteousness that would be scary if it wasn't so entertaining' (*Observer*), while Benedict Nightingale thought him 'a moralizing bore ... an amalgam of donnish ecology buff, busybodying bishop, and ra-ra scoutmaster' (*New States.*). The question of how to take a deposed duke who calls his followers 'mates and brothers' (2.1.1) when he needs them to catch his dinner for him, but later promises them reward 'according to ... their states' (5.4.174), was growing more complex as the half century wore on.

Which may partly explain why Adrian Noble and his designer Bob Crowley decided, in 1985, for the first of a number of occasions in this sequence of productions, to double the role with that of his younger brother Frederick. Joseph O'Conor played both parts, and at the beginning of 2.1, still wearing the white tie and tails of his court persona, he threw a cloth over his shoulders and stepped down through the enormous mirror that stood upstage and began to address his 'co-mates and brothers in exile' (2.1.1). A few moments before they had stood behind him as he exiled Rosalind; now they were downstage, cloths over their evening dress too, dutifully listening to his homily. At the end of the evening Jaques would step back up through the mirror, the grandfather clock would start to tick again – for 'there's no clock in the forest' (3.2.295–6) – and the Arden excursion would be over.

As if one Lewis Carroll allusion were not enough, Rosalind, Celia and Touchstone made their entry into Arden through what had seemed, in the preceding scene of Orlando's decision to flee with Adam (2.3), a big blue upstage moon, but which now turned out to be a large round hole (rabbits, perhaps, for the use of) through which they could step and descend to the darkened stage. They were dragging behind them a huge white silk which draped itself over all the court furniture, clock, mirror, gilded chairs, like a white blanket of snow settling in drifts and undulations on the world they had left behind. It was on this 'glacier', as Michael Ratcliffe called it in the *Observer*, that Celia, somewhat surprisingly, decided to begin her new career in sheep-farming and on which Duke Senior took his meal, his table (as may be seen in Figure 11) a veritable block of ice. Here, though, silver salvers were set, so that the event seemed 'like a meal in a Victorian club' (*Oxf. Mail*). The sound of a howling gale, with a wind machine rippling the silk into drifts and waves, created the blizzard for the arrival of Orlando and Adam, Orlando's decision not to leave his old retainer 'in the bleak air' (2.6.15) prompted by the sight of him disappearing under the billowing silk snow.

As the second half of the evening began, the silk had been hitched to wires reaching up into the flies and it was on them (there being nothing else on offer) that Orlando hung his verses. He then climbed onto this little totem and the whole thing began to ascend, so that he was hoisted to the flying rig himself (usually to a round of applause from the audience, whether cheap or not let the forest judge). Thus the silk became (as may be seen in Figure 39) a tall, thin tent – a 'palanquin', thought Martin Hoyle (*FT*), 'a sort of maypole', decided Jack Tinker (*D. Mail*, reviewing the Barbican transfer) – in which the actors could hide, or around which they could chase, or which Rosalind could use to wrap around her legs as a skirt in the wooing games, and which finally spread and lifted again to form something resembling a huge bridal veil for the appearance of Hymen (see Figure 44). The court mirror and chairs, and stationary grandfather clock, making their

FIGURE 11 On Bob Crowley's silk-draped set, Orlando (Hilton McRae) jumps onto the 'ice' table at the exiled Duke's forest meal and threatens death to anyone who eats any more; Jaques (Alan Rickman) responds by walking deliberately to the table and taking and biting an apple. (2.7, 1985)

second-half reappearance from under the silk, were now green, like the floor. The invitation to believe that we were still somehow inside the ducal palace, transformed merely by the power of the imagination into a green and cheerful world of light and birdsong, was slightly complicated, however, by the appearance of a downstage watercourse, canal-like in form, not a remembered feature of the palace scenes. This was soon to demonstrate the truth of Corin's 'philosophy' that the 'property' of water 'is to wet' (3.2.26), as actors (or their director) found falling into it irresistible. Arden, in short, became a sort of adventure playground until the exit of Jaques signalled the end of the game.

The way to Arden in John Caird's production of *As You Like It* in 1989 was, as we have seen in the preceding chapter, through the floor of the stage. The destruction of the court set with which the production's designer Ultz had replicated the art deco public areas of the Royal Shakespeare Theatre was begun by Duke Senior and his followers and completed by Rosalind. It was she who pushed open the great marquetry-panelled doors, splitting the clock in two (see Figure 12) to pass into the forest's timelessness. In a swirl of mist and falling leaves, and to the sound of rooks cawing and the wind blowing, she entered Arden (alias that space behind the proscenium arch where, as the theatre was conceived, the public areas ended and the playing began). Strongly backlit, the first unlikely inhabitants of this magical region approached: 'a young man and an old in solemn talk' (2.4.18). And, as in 1985, departure from this fabled region was marked by replication in the exit of Jaques of the moment of arrival: having delivered his verdicts on the quartet of copulatives, Jaques opened another door, far upstage, and, strongly backlit just as the arrival had been, passed through it in quest of another play.

The response of reviewers to the extraordinary moment of arrival in Arden was largely enthusiastic. Michael Billington may represent his colleagues: 'When the central doors of the wood-panelled set finally part to reveal a smoky, chilly, leaf-billowing world ... we get a sense of Arden's strangeness' (*Guardian*). There were a few dissenting voices, however, John Peter's the most disgruntled of them: he thought the moment of the opening of the panelling 'one of those stunning but ultimately quite mean-ingless *coups de théâtre* which, in such productions, stand in for imagination' (*S. Times*). The Arden scenes, he went on, 'seem to take place in the débris of the court – an image that deftly contradicts the central metaphor of the play'. The central metaphor of the *production*, however, was a simple metatheatrical one: that the place where discoveries are made, where time and the everyday are left behind, is the stage itself; the world of Arden has no location, no reality, beyond that simple theatrical fact. Hugo Williams clearly responded to the metaphor: 'Rosalind and her companions break through from the foyer to the world of the play, a world of mist, autumn leaves, dreamtime, where they can

FIGURE 12 Sophie Thompson's Rosalind, having just pushed open the great door in the back of the set to break in two the replica of the foyer clock and reveal the way through into Arden, turns to encourage her weary companions, Celia (Gillian Bevan) and Touchstone (Mark Williams), to follow her through to this new, if somewhat forbidding, world. (2.4, 1989)

make their desires come true' (*S. Corresp.*). Adrian Noble had taken us to an imagined Arden through a mirror; John Caird offered us a route by means of entering a stage. Many other routes to Arden have been, and will be, tried.

The Arden that Rosalind and her companions found in 1989 was an unalluring tract of territory, gloomy, and cold, with the Duke and his followers huddling together for warmth in what Peter Kemp thought 'an ecological disaster zone' (*Independent*) – a slight exaggeration, in fact, for a few clumps of bluebells did make their appearance in the treeless landscape in the later stages. Arden was cold and foggy, thought Katherine Duncan-Jones, 'with nothing to recommend it except the beneficence of its duke and the companionability of its inhabitants' (*TLS*) – 'precisely', one can imagine its director responding.

Those who wanted a landscaped Arden had their wishes fulfilled beyond their wildest dreams in Johan Engels's set for David Thacker's 1992 production. All the court scenes having been brought together at the beginning of the play, the Jacobean-tragedy court world was then flown and trucked out, with a series of impressive instructions in the promptbook involving several flying and many electrical and musical cues, sliders, a ramp, a new floor-cloth, and much more. To the accompaniment of romantic horn and woodwind music, and a big drum roll, the lights went up on a steeply sloped stage, rocks and hummocks and moss tumbling down to the front row of the stalls, a little rustic bridge over an audible stream, and the leafless twigs of a great tree silhouetted against the sky. Figure 25 shows the bridge, the mossy bank, and the tree in its summer foliage; the production in fact went through the full seasonal cycle, the final scenes taking place in autumn. Was it, one wondered as those lights went up, still 1992, or had we, during that little musical interlude, slipped back through several theatrical decades?

The return to naturalism in Arden was by no means without its enthusiasts. It provided, thought Jack Tinker, the appropriate setting for the romantic energies of the play, 'fairly throbbing', as he saw it, 'with rampant nature' (D. Mail). So naturalistically detailed a set, however, like some of its predecessors in similar vein, had its problems: 'the unnegotiable green of the sward causes the Ardenites to trip and sweat' observed Plays and Players, and the representational naturalism of it all inevitably provoked the question 'why this small bit of woodland is so crammed with assorted lovers' (TLS).

Although there was a distinctly old-fashioned quality about the set, the climatic conditions of more recent Stratford Ardens were still being observed. The exiled Duke and his followers who hunt this particular stretch of Arden's acres were first encountered huddled around a smoking fire and cowering beneath old blankets and manky furs. Jeffery Dench's 'unvaryingly placid' Duke struck Charles Spencer as very lucky indeed to get away with the umpteenth version of his homily on the life 'exempt from public haunt' (2.1.15): 'only loyalty prevents them from wringing his neck' (*D. Telegraph*). Martin Hoyle thought him 'patently off his rocker as he burbles on ... while the forest folk bitterly sing "This life is most jolly"' (*Times*, reviewing the Barbican transfer). The hospitality of these miserable exiles was real enough, however. The interval was marked by an exhausted Orlando gratefully embracing an exhausted Duke Senior, and a group of foresters just about managing to bring Adam back from death's door.

Four years later those forester lords failed in similarly devoted efforts. Steven Pimlott's 1996 version of the forest, designed by Ashley Martin-Davies, goes down in theatre history as the first Stratford Arden to sacrifice a victim to its wintry harshness. Carried in by Orlando after his collapse in the most hostile of several snowstorms to hit that year's Arden – the imitation snow lay thick on the stage, showing the tracks of the little sledge with which Rosalind and her party travelled – Adam lay wrapped in blankets at the end of the ducal table with attentive foresters trying in vain to feed and revive him. At the end of the song the Duke walked over to Adam, utterly failing to notice how critical was his condition. 'Support him by the arm', he said (2.7.202), and escorted Orlando, who was quite unaware of his servant's state, from the stage. As they strode off arm in arm poor old Adam breathed his last, the first half of the comedy ending (perhaps a little dubiously in terms of genre) with his death – providing a 'big moment' for the interval, its downbeat quality to be balanced by the upbeat of the ending of the second half. During that second half there was a huge mound of earth, with daffodils strewn over it, upstage centre. No one ever behaved as if it was anyone's grave (it was big enough, indeed, to have contained a dead horse or two), but as Silvius and Touchstone, Ganymede and Orlando, ran round and over it, it was difficult not to think of Adam lying at peace below. Steven Pimlott is on record as saying that the notion of its being Adam's grave was an unlooked-for, but not unwelcome, addition to his idea that it should suggest an ancient and sacred place in the forest (Pimlott, 18).

The cold and snow which proved too much for Adam provided an interesting moment in Duke Senior's homily to his co-mates, which became here 'the merest self-delusion' (*TLS*). To demonstrate his own hardiness – and to give a new slant to sentiments they had clearly heard too often before, for they turned their backs when he started – he took off his boots and paddled barefoot in the snow to prove that he knew as well as they did what it was to 'shrink with cold' (2.1.9); the demonstration over, however, he was very quick to snap his fingers and have one of his followers kneel and put his boots back on for him. Benedict Nightingale thought he looked like 'a bedraggled scoutmaster doggedly cheering up a troop snuffling miserably in the pelting snow' (*Times*). His gang were to find considerable animation, however, in the deer-killing scene, when they revealed themselves as 'ecstatic hunters, dragging onto the stage a deer's carcase and daubing themselves in its blood' (*TLS*); a similar 'blooding' ritual had been used in 1992, both productions determined that the brutal realities of forest existence should not be forgotten.

To the design of a ribbed metal box for the court were added for the Arden of 1996 metal poles (visible in Figures 26 and 45), flown in in varying numbers and configurations. So abstract a background for the very precise Elizabethan costumes gave the forest a curiously distanced quality, making it, in Nicholas de Jongh's phrase, an 'alienating limbo' (*E. Standard*). Under sympathetic lighting the poles might seem like silver birches, but this was never an Arden that turned greener with the seasons and the only flowers that appeared were the daffodils that lay (not grew) on the mound. Neither did Arden's avifauna offer anything to cheer the spirits: the dominant species, it seemed, was the peacock, its wailing, echoing cry often to be heard between scenes.

Kaffe Fassett's design for Arden in Gregory Doran's 2000 production made it, as John Peter put it, 'a playpen for townies' (*S. Times*). It was 'easy', thought Robert Butler, 'to see how, in this

FIGURE 13 Celia (Nancy Carroll, in bicycle cart), Touchstone (Adrian Schiller) and Rosalind (Alexandra Gilbreath) encounter Corin (Barry McCarthy) in Kaffe Fassett and Niki Turner's Arden of 'art nouveau' tree (with giant illuminated leaves) and huge embroidered cushions. (2.4, 2000)

forest of Arden, a man like Anthony Howell's Orlando could fall hopelessly in love with needlepoint' (*Indep. Sun.*). The few square feet of colourful needlework on which Rosalind had been working in the banishment scene had, it appeared, taken over the stage, banishing the great monochrome tapestry of the court scenes; and her uncle (he of the Genghis Khan helmet) had become, in Ian Hogg's doubling of the roles, the grey-haired, softly spoken leader of a group of gentle, and for once fairly respectful, foresters. Was one intended to imagine the whole thing as Rosalind's dream? The stage floor was painted to resemble snowdrifts (but not so closely to resemble them that one was ever intended not to see it as a painted floor), and centre stage was a large stylized tree with huge stained-glass-window leaves, vaguely art-nouveauish, at some of its branches' ends (see Figure 13). With lights behind them they were rather reminiscent of the lights on a Christmas tree. It was clearly winter in Arden, but four more years of global warming on from the last production and climatic rigour was apparently abating.

Spring came to this Arden with a green bank upstage centre, sprouting a climbable tree in generous leaf and a series of enormous needlepoint flowered cushions. The inhabitants of Arden were dressed to match, with thick woollen pullovers and cardigans in the fashionable Fassett style, Silvius and Corin in particular sporting seriously enviable knitwear. Michael Billington's almost too astute 'To Liberty's and not to banishment' epithet (*Guardian*) exposed a problem obvious enough in this Arden, but latent in any production of the play: how are director and designer to respond to the great mixture of information, realistic and utterly unrealistic, that the text provides about the forest? In taking the unrealistic road to a land that was reminiscent of Oz or *Jack and the Beanstalk* Doran had, thought Michael Dobson, given us a world 'where only whimsy could flourish'; the choice of a design that 'highlights the fantastical elements of Arden at the expense of the graphically rustic ones turned out in practice to sabotage much of the play' (*SS*, 272). When the production moved to London it played in the Pit theatre at the Barbican; the greatly simplified setting required by the studio space had a remarkable effect in releasing the relationships between characters into immediacy and directness.

The Forest of Arden may be imagined to the north of Stratford-upon-Avon, or editors may (as in the Oxford *Complete Works*) locate it in the same country as Duke Frederick's court by spelling the name *à la française*, but it will always remain a tantalizing mixture of the imaginary and the realistic. Doubling may suggest that it exists only in Rosalind's dreams, or Duke Frederick's, or the audience's; several of its inhabitants have more to do with the conventions of pastoral literature than any conceivable rural economy, English or French, while others have their hands greasy from handling their ewes and are oppressed by greedy landowners; its vegetation and fauna mix the exotic and native in splendid confusion and its seasons follow no discernible order; it is, as

Steven Pimlott said in the programme for his 1996 production, 'a shape-shifting, metamorphosing place, much easier to present on the bare stage for which Shakespeare wrote with everything left to the audience's imagination, than in a proscenium arch theatre'. The attempts of a dozen Stratford directors to present it in just such a theatre do indeed make clear what a 'shape-shifting' place it is.

3

JUNO'S SWANS

> We still have slept together,
> Rose at an instant, learn'd, play'd, ate together,
> And whereso'er we went, like Juno's swans,
> Still we went coupled and inseparable.
>
> (1.3.69–72)

Although several of the productions with which this book is concerned have shown female attendants at Duke Frederick's court, they have all been silent, for no woman beyond the Duke's daughter and niece is given an entrance in the Folio text, let alone a word to say, during the court scenes of *As You Like It*. Even the confession of 'Hisperia, the princess' gentlewoman' (2.2.10) about the escape of Celia and Rosalind is reported by one of Duke Frederick's lords. The companionship of Celia and Rosalind is thus sharpened and intensified by the harshly masculine world in which it exists, where amusement comes from watching the court wrestling champion break the bodies of his challengers: 'It is the first time that ever I heard breaking of ribs was sport for ladies', as Touchstone aptly observes (1.2.127–9).

How long Celia and Rosalind have been driven together by political circumstances is a question raised but not fully answered in the play. The banishment of Rosalind's father by his usurping brother is the 'old news' according to Charles the wrestler (1.1.98), who also lets us know that the daughters of these brothers 'were ever from their cradles bred together' and that 'never two ladies loved as they do' (1.1.108, 112); but he nevertheless still refers to the 'new Duke' (1.1.100), which seems hardly to suggest that Frederick's régime has been in place for years. Celia, on the other hand, pleading with her father against Rosalind's banishment, says that (at the time of the coup d'état) she 'did not then entreat to have her stay', since she was 'too young that time to value her' (1.3.65, 67), while Duke Senior tries to persuade his followers that 'old custom' has made their exile 'sweet' (2.1.2). Trying to tie Shakespeare down to temporal specifics is a notoriously futile enterprise, but the players of Rosalind and Celia probably need to agree on some sense of the length of time during which court circumstances have thrust them together.

On two other little issues left puzzling by the text, the comparative height and age of the two women, pragmatic decisions according to casting are usually made. The normal solution as far as height is concerned (and it is the solution actually adopted in the text of the Temple Classics edition on which the promptbooks for the earlier post-war Stratford productions were based) is to emend the Folio's 'the taller is his daughter' in Le Beau's phrase (1.2.262) to 'the smaller is his daughter', thus according with Rosalind's description of herself as 'more than common tall' (1.3.111) and Oliver's information that Celia is 'low' (4.3.87); when the casting happens to make Celia visibly the taller (as in the 1967 production) Le Beau's information will be left unamended and a joke made of Rosalind's self-consciousness about her height. As for comparative age, Charles's story of simultaneity in the cradle suggests that casting should aim not to make this an issue. But since the bigger role is, by the nature of things, likely to go to the more experienced actress, an age difference liable to suggest leader and follower may, as we shall see, sometimes be perceivable and seem significant.

The relationship of Rosalind and Celia is one of the most important in the play, its intensity a powerful contrast to the brutality and hatred of Frederick's court. Its displacement by Rosalind's passion for Orlando may easily present the melancholy spectacle of a lonely, resentful and uncomprehending Celia distracting the audience from taking pleasure in Rosalind's happiness. To read, as the author of such a book as this must do, some hundreds of reviews of a dozen and more productions of *As You Like It*, is to be struck by the apparently inexhaustible capacity for surprise of successive generations of reviewers at the importance of the role of Celia. Confident in the belief (true by the end, of course, but not at the beginning) that this is Rosalind's play, they forget the simple facts of the text: that it is Celia who is the heir of the dukedom at the beginning, Celia who has a lot more of the lines before Rosalind's forest meeting with Orlando, Celia who controls Rosalind's moods in their first dialogue (1.2.1–45), who protests to her father at Rosalind's banishment, who thinks of the escape to Arden and plans its practical details (and especially its financing), and Celia who keeps in mind such significant matters as acquiring food, and increasing Corin's wages, when they reach their destination. This seems, then, until quite late in the play, to be a partnership of equals, with a strong Celia an important ingredient in a satisfactory staging of *As You Like It*. Most successful productions have indeed followed that route, though some, as we shall see, have explored a certain inequality or dislocation in the relationship to present an interesting variant reading.

To be cast as Rosalind after playing Celia is a not uncommon occurrence: Sophie Thompson had played Celia for the Renaissance Theatre Company before coming to Stratford as Rosalind in 1989; Janet Suzman played Celia for the RSC in 1967 and took over the role of Rosalind when the production was revived the following year; and Fiona Shaw played Rosalind at the Old Vic four years after her RSC Celia in 1985. Samantha Bond's move in the opposite direction was more unusual: she played Rosalind at Stratford for most of the 1992 season until she went on maternity leave and Kate Buffery took over the role; Bond then moved to Celia, Buffery continuing as Rosalind, for the Barbican transfer. The fact that a move to Celia was judged an interesting possibility by someone who had watched the role from Rosalind's proximity is further evidence that those who allow themselves to be surprised by its significance are misunderstanding, or misremembering, the play. This chapter, then, will consider the role of Celia in the thirteen post-war Stratford productions of *As You Like It*, her interaction with Rosalind at court and in the forest scenes, and her sudden betrothal to Oliver, that shameless (but, as the evidence shows, not entirely unactable) device to resolve the problem of her growing isolation and loneliness.

Joy Parker played Celia in 1946 and the only two mentions of her in reviews offer, in their contrastive responses, a representative barometer of the problem of finding the appropriate balance for this role. For the *Stratford-upon-Avon Herald* her 'delicate youthful charm' and 'willowy grace' were inappropriate for Celia, 'too ethereal for this practical little woman'. The *Leamington Spa Courier*, on the other hand, complaining that too many recent Celias had been 'dowdy', rejoiced that here was one who managed to be 'gentle yet sparkling ... quick-witted yet full of tender attractive charm'. In today's less graceful terminology the proposition seems to be that Celia needs to be pushy enough but not too pushy: it is through the channel between the Scylla of being too 'ethereal' and 'willowy' and the Charybdis of being too 'quick-witted', too much the 'practical little woman', that Celias must sail. Joy Parker, however, had the advantage of the young Paul Scofield as her Oliver and he made his conversion, and his falling in love with Celia, 'as convincing as they can ever be' (*SA Herald*). Angus McBean's photograph (Figure 14), though obviously posed, perhaps captures a little of that intensity. This 'quick-witted' Celia played opposite Ruth Lodge's 'intelligent and thoughtful' Rosalind (*Birm. W. Post*); if one may infer from this that they were an intellectual match for each other (and way ahead of most other persons in the play) then the relationship probably worked as it should.

Six years after reviewers had been surprised to be convinced by the conversion of Oliver, the phenomenon was repeated in Glen Byam Shaw's 1952 production: 'Oliver's conversion is much more

FIGURE 14 Stratford's most enthusiastically reviewed Oliver (Paul Scofield) shares a moment of intimacy (posed, no doubt, for the photographer) with Joy Parker's Celia, presumably at the end of the scene of Rosalind's faint. (4.3, 1946)

convincing than usual', wrote the *Stage* (without reference to its last Stratford manifestation) of David Dodimead's performance. His Celia, cousin to Margaret Leighton's Rosalind, was the young Siobhan McKenna (the first of a trio of notable Irish Celias at Stratford that would later number Sinead Cusack and Fiona Shaw). The performance drew so much critical attention that one begins to wonder if the balance between the cousins was right, but there is plenty of testimony that it was: Celia 'gave notable support' (*D. Telegraph*); a 'bewitching' Celia 'never over-stepped the mark between leader and second' (*Birm. E. Desp.*); they 'play delightfully together, easily and freely' (*Leam. Spa Cour.*). The *Birmingham Weekly Post* was struck by 'the ash-blonde Rosalind' alongside 'the darkling Celia' (see Figure 20) and the *Warwick Advertiser* thought Celia 'vivacious when necessary', but 'reposeful and attentive in the presence of the lovers' – and much of the latter part of Celia's role is indeed about listening. For the rest, it is a litany of delight in a performance of a role that few had expected to be so interesting: 'a kitten of a girl' (*Coventry E. Tel.*), 'a mischievous, friendly fawn' (*Birm. Mail*), 'a warm-hearted little miss ... full of fun and sympathy' (*Stage*). The *Stratford-upon-Avon Herald* even developed a Jane Austen comparison for the partnership, with Celia as 'sense' and Rosalind as 'sensibility', Celia taking 'life as it came, with robust, alert sympathy'.

The Celias of the next two productions (1957 and 1961) achieve much less prominence in the critical record and both seem to have been rather more dominated by their Rosalinds. Jane Wenham, who played Celia opposite Peggy Ashcroft in 1957, was very much younger than her cousin and seemed to one reviewer 'disappointingly colourless' (*Liv. Post*). Cecil Wilson, in the *Daily Mail*, thought that 'melancholy hung rather heavy on the friendship' of the cousins early in the play (which doesn't sound altogether inappropriate) and that Wenham 'was inclined to sing Celia's womanly devotion to Rosalind' (which does). Many reviewers seemed to share Wilson's view that the sombreness of the court scenes (so carefully created by the heavy Tudor costumes and the performance of Mark Dignam as Frederick) was due to directorial inadvertence rather than intention. 'That Mary Tudor number', wrote the *Stratford-upon-Avon Herald* about Rosalind's court hat, 'makes her look rather droopy' – and one can imagine Byam Shaw being delighted by what is intended as a complaint. In this context, the dislocation that emerges between a profoundly melancholy, and mature, Rosalind, slow and 'low-key' (*Man. Guardian*) in these early stages, and a Celia who was youthful, 'an enchanting tease' (*SQ*, 480), and perhaps uncomprehending, seems to have produced an interesting variation on the usual reading of the relationship's mutual interdependency. Certainly the comments on Wenham's 'gay and humorous' Celia (*D. Telegraph*), or her 'pretty laughing little Celia … at every moment directing our attention to Rosalind' (*SA Herald*), do not suggest an easy and equal relationship between her and a melancholy Rosalind. (Nor, indeed, does Figure 35, from later in the play: though posed, Celia's expression seems to suggest admiration, Rosalind's toleration; mutual friendship isn't easy to discern.) Perhaps the most telling remark, partly because it is clearly intended as a compliment, came from the reviewer for the *Warwick Advertiser*, who felt that Wenham's Celia had 'succeeded admirably in being a decorative companion to her cousin' – not, one feels, the sort of praise that most performers of the role would relish, though hardly worse than being told, again by an admirer, that she 'bubbled like a little pigeon on a window-ledge' (*FT*).

We know precisely when Wenham's Celia fell in love with her Oliver. The promptbook records it, in that cryptic way that promptbooks have, at the midpoint of the line 'The rank of osiers by the murmuring stream' (4.3.79), as she is giving the newly arrived Oliver directions to her dwelling. The instruction 'Cel turn see Ol love him' no doubt produced a deeply affecting moment 'in the true performing of it' (as Bottom puts it in describing the emotional charge he proposes to bring to the role of Pyramus); in the assistant stage manager's annotation of the text for the 1957 production, however, it reads tersely indeed.

There was nothing about the Celia of 1961 to provoke reviewers into recollections of bubbling pigeons. Here was another production that offered a somewhat dislocated relationship between the cousins. The tall blonde Rosalind of Vanessa Redgrave was as visually contrasted as could be with the short dark Celia of Rosalind Knight (see Figures 15 and 42). Here was a Celia 'content to be a foil' (*E. News*), but content (or so it seems in the television film version) only from a sense of deliberate self-restraint. There is a sharp, perhaps slightly dark, intelligence about the film performance that explains some of the comment on the

FIGURE 15 Rosalind Knight's Celia looks on questioningly, and perhaps a little anxiously, as Orlando (Ian Bannen) takes Rosalind (Vanessa Redgrave) 'for wife'. Rosalind's cap imprisoned the golden hair whose moments of freedom impressed many reviewers. (4.1.129, 1961)

stage version: a 'piquant' and an 'impish' Celia (*SA Herald, Oxf. Times*), a Celia who is 'a mischievous witch' (*Tatler*) and who demonstrates 'pointed mockery' and 'shrewishness' (*Morn. Adv., S. Times*). Robert Speaight remarks that her voice had 'a quality of pure deflation that was in perfect contrast to Miss Redgrave's verve' (*SQ*, 434). Caryl Brahms, writing in *Jack O'London's Weekly*, thought the contrast too great and believed Knight to be simply unsuited to Celia: 'her intelligence calls for a satiric casting' – which would certainly be true if the intention was to present an easy, reassuring friendship between equals. But an interesting variation on that usual relationship derives here from the sense (and again I am judging from the film version) of a Celia who may be a split second quicker on the uptake than her cousin, and whose dark, shrewd eyes have a slightly guarded quality, in contrast to the eager, trusting, and therefore vulnerable, impetuousness of Rosalind. (One is aware in Figure 15 of this sense of Celia holding back.) It is as though Celia recognized from the moment of Rosalind's meeting with Orlando that it was now foolish to continue her previous emotional commitment to her cousin and needed to withdraw a little and observe, carefully though affectionately. The text, as we have seen, offers no information on the comparative ages of the two: in 1961 there was no doubt that Celia was the elder, watching, a little wryly, and with studied self-possession, the emotional turmoil of a Rosalind of whom such phrases as 'youthful zest' and 'schoolgirl high spirits' are all over the critics' responses.

This Celia was, as several reviewers remarked, much more at home in the court than in the forest, and at court she was very much 'the Princess', and Rosalind 'the companion', an impression reinforced by an accent just a notch more upper class than her cousin's. Almost uniquely among this series of Stratford Celias, she kept her seat for the interview with Orlando before the wrestling. As she played second fiddle in the forest scenes the observant self-restraint made one wonder, just occasionally, if her patience was really inexhaustible. But the sense that there was the possibility of tension in this relationship did not mean that one ever discerned its presence: 'her loyalty and capacity for affection can never be questioned' (*Morn. Adv.*). Knight's Celia had her feelings too closely under control, and was too fond of her noisy, open-hearted cousin for that. 'Dark, pert, and loving', wrote J.W. Lambert, she 'never fails to make a point, and never tries to steal a scene' (*S. Times*, reviewing the Aldwych transfer) – not even, indeed, the scene of Rosalind's faint at the bloody napkin. So many Celias here 'change eyes' with their Oliver in a way that reads to the back of the gallery, but even in the film version there is no discernible moment of self-commitment in Knight's performance and the news of her betrothal is left to be broken by Rosalind at her next meeting with Orlando.

From two pairs of Juno's swans not quite indulging in synchronized swimming, and offering interesting alternative readings of the relationship in their two very differently positioned Celias, the pendulum swung the other way in 1967, when so much critical attention went in the direction of Janet Suzman's dark and beautiful Celia that reviewers started wishing that she, rather than Dorothy Tutin, were playing Rosalind – a wish fulfilled the following year when the production was revived. Reviewing its first season in the *Times*, Irving Wardle moved unerringly to Suzman's performance as the saving grace of what he thought the muddle of the court scenes, 'an enchanting combination of self-mocking dignity and sheer fun', while B.A. Young spent more time in his review on Celia than on Rosalind, finding her 'just as gay and hoydenish' as Rosalind 'and never retreating into nonentity' (*FT*). The evidence of other reviewers, and indeed my own memory of the production, is that Young was slightly understating the case. This was 'a mocking, languorous, eloquently silent Celia' (*S. Telegraph*), who used 'the mobility of her face to its wittiest advantage' as she watched the wooing scenes (*SA Herald*). She spent 'half her time reclining on a tree trunk, and everyone wants her to speak' (*New States.*), and her eyes 'in her long silences … speak, and the body declares that here is another Rosalind' (*Guardian*). She gave the impression 'of virtually going to sleep some of the time', noted Gerard Fay, which was (and the fatal word appears) 'the most subtle way I have seen a Rosalind upstaged by a Celia, but it worked' (*Queen*). That may be an exaggeration, but the danger represented by Celia's silent presence to Rosalind's loquacious love-making is very real. If 'watch out for your Iago' is famous advice to any actor contemplating the role of Othello, 'watch out for your Celia' is equally pertinent for would-be Rosalinds. It only needs an eyebrow flickered at the audience at the wrong (or the right – according to one's point of view) moment, and tragic hero, or comic heroine, can be sunk.

In many dozens of reviews of the 1967 *As You Like It*, the word 'upstage' appears only once. For most, the energy and watchability of Suzman's Celia was a bonus to, rather than a distraction from, Tutin's performance of Rosalind. Celia stung Rosalind 'only as lightly as the midsummer midge', thought Peter Lewis in the *Daily Mail*, evincing either a subtly sarcastic spirit or the fact that he had never found himself in Wester Ross on a humid midsummer evening. Gareth Lloyd Evans admired her 'mocking affection that suggests envy without rancour' (*Guardian*) – a mood perfectly caught in the expression of her eyes in Figure 16. She was certainly the ironically detached observer, but the observation was always affectionate and supportive. Her practicality over getting jewels and wealth together before setting off for Arden (1.3.130) was, thought John Higgins, 'the cry of the well-equipped girl who is not prey to ill-considered decisions' (*FT*, reviewing the Aldwych transfer). The same reviewer enjoyed her spying on the long wooing scene (4.1) 'like a madame purring over a particularly successful coupling', and the feline metaphor returns in the description of her 'lazily stretching, cat-like watching, long tresses tossing, pushing, urging, teasing, needling' (*Nott. Observer*, again on the Aldwych transfer). She was, pronounced W.A. Darlington when the production reached London, 'the best Celia since Siobhan McKenna' (*D. Telegraph*). Her falling in love with Oliver was not as heavily signalled as some Celias have made it – not a single reviewer comments on it, indeed. The promptbook records her sitting up quickly on 'Are you his brother?' (4.3.133), rising and taking a pace towards him as he declares his conversion and the two of them joining hands behind Rosalind's back at the end-of-scene exit.

When Suzman moved to the role of Rosalind in the 1968 revival, her Celia, Rowena Cooper, was the first at post-war Stratford to use a later recurrent, and rather schoolboyish, joke over the fainted Rosalind: her 'there is more in it' (4.3.159) was provoked by Oliver's move to undo Ganymede's shirt to help bring him round. Cooper's Celia was 'coolly blonde and teasing' (*D. Mail*), 'lively and level-headed' (*Oxf. Mail*), and in spite of attracting far less critical attention, proved, as nearly every Celia

FIGURE 16 Janet Suzman's watchful, thoughtful Celia plays 'priest' to Michael Williams's Orlando and Dorothy Tutin's Rosalind as they make their vows to each other. (4.1.117, 1967)

seems to need to prove all over again, that 'the role of shrewd observer is more of a gift to the actress than is generally supposed' (*D. Telegraph*) – but, not, perhaps, quite so much of a gift as Suzman had made it.

And yet again a production with a very prominent Celia was succeeded on the Stratford stage by two in which the role drew much less attention – surprisingly so in 1973 at least, when the part was played by Maureen Lipman. The main focus of critical attention in 1973 was, inevitably, on the modern setting and its effect on the play's narrative and relationships: 'I do not believe that modern-looking girls like these would be in the least frightened about fleeing to the country' (*Nott. Guardian*) is a fairly typical reaction. Lipman's Celia was thought to be 'coolly and elegantly stated' (*Jewish Chron.*) and 'the stronger of the two in the duos' (*Times*), while the photograph of the wedding scene (Figure 22) nicely catches that splendid Lipman expression of amused and quizzical knowingness. It is clear, however, that the modern setting left less need for the usual mutual protectiveness between Rosalind and Celia, though that aspect of the relationship certainly emerged in the banishment scene, as Figure 3 makes clear. Here their bedroom has been invaded by the dark-clad Duke Frederick, with his black eye patch and his henchmen, while the cousins stand, frightened and disbelieving, in their white nightdresses, the clothes they have just taken off on view over the screen, their place of feminine privacy invaded.

Lipman's Celia was also notable for being the first to dream the deer dance: 4.2 was presented 'as a kind of fertility dance' (*Listener*) around Celia as she lay asleep in her hammock, the play's first female Stratford director being first to launch this apparently innocuous little scene on a career which would give it a place of increasing significance in Celia's psychological, and sexual, development.

Judith Paris's Celia in 1977 made Stratford history by appearing to skate on the Arden ice during her teasing conversation with Rosalind in 3.4 – a very 'swan-like' bit of behaviour from one of Juno's swans if the young lady commentator on the Christmas skating at Dingley Dell is to be believed (*Pickwick Papers*, chapter 30). (As the production was directed by Trevor Nunn, the skating was, perhaps, a little forerunner of some rather more elaborate ideas on these lines in a later musical.) Once again reviewers seemed to need to be 'reminded of what a good part this is' (*Oxf. Times*), but here, as in the preceding production, Celia was little noticed and Rosalind drew all the critical attention. Paris was thought 'unusually grave but still perky' (*SA Herald*) – a difficult combination to achieve, one would have thought – 'notably alert' (*Oxf. Times*), and 'impish' (*Coventry E. Tel.*), but in the picturesque world of Nunn's baroque operatic treatment of the play little of the reviewers' attention was drawn to the relationship between the cousins.

The production was notable for Celia in one way, however: she and Oliver came on stage for the singing of 'It was a lover and his lass' (5.3.14ff.), which thus came to 'accommodate, very touch-ingly', their courtship (*Observer*). Earlier he had, the promptbook tells us, brushed her hair from her face as she turned to look at him when describing 'the rank of osiers by the murmuring stream' (4.3.79). Later he wrapped her in his cloak (which Rosalind had rejected after her faint) and they left the stage together, hand in hand behind her cousin.

From two somewhat inconspicuous Celias we move in 1980 and 1985 to two of the most prominent, and most noticed, in the history of the play at Stratford. Picking up from Siobhan McKenna thirty years earlier, Sinead Cusack (1980) and Fiona Shaw (1985) brought an Irish sense of mischief and energy to the role that once again lifted it to prominence. That Cusack's Celia regarded herself from the start as a direct sexual competitor for Orlando there was no doubt. In the interview with him before the wrestling the promptbook has several directions for her to push in front of her cousin each time she addresses him; Michael Billington described her as 'man-hungry' (*Guardian*, reviewing the Aldwych transfer) and Irving Wardle thought that she evinced enough eagerness for Orlando at the beginning 'to justify being poleaxed by Oliver at the end' (*Times*). Benedict Nightingale, providing the statutory expression of reviewer surprise, felt that she 'did much to bring an unrewarding part to life by suggesting that she too fancies Orlando, is jealous of, if good-humouredly resigned to, his preference for Rosalind, and doesn't altogether relish her role as gooseberry at the flirtations' (*New States.*).

The reviews, and my own memory, are full of delight at the way Cusack found 'every possible ounce of humour and sensibility in the part' (*Plays & P.*) and at her face expressing 'sustained eloquence in itself' (*Birm. Post*). 'From the first', wrote Nightingale (*New States.*), 'one feels that the girls' friendship is a genuine thing', and this emerged vividly as the laughter and excitement of the plotting of their escape grew out of the grief of the banishment, the director again juxtaposing young women in white nightdresses to the male threat of a dangerously unstable

Duke Frederick and his followers. The remarkable energy of Susan Fleetwood's Rosalind (see chapter 4) needed a big performance of Celia to balance it, and Cusack, with her 'wide-eyed loyalty, warmth and prettiness' (*D. Telegraph*), provided it. 'As a listener', wrote J.C. Trewin, 'Miss Cusack has one of the most expressive faces in the classical theatre' (*Birm. Post*, reviewing the Aldwych transfer); Figure 23 corroborates this. Charles Spencer, writing at the time for the *New Standard*, and also commenting on the Aldwych transfer, caught something of the joy, and the pain, of the role: 'One of the show's chief delights is Rosalind's relationship with Sinead Cusack's Celia – who clearly dreads losing her companion to John Bowe's Orlando and who succeeds in converting the love scenes into a duet for three.'

Not surprisingly, this Celia's nubility had an instantaneous effect on Oliver. He made a beeline for her – 'as if she combined the qualities of Helen of Troy and the Holy Grail' as an unlabelled review in the RSC press cuttings collection puts it – and delivered his story adoringly to her, with Rosalind standing by, almost disregarded (see Figure 17). The promptbook records an embrace at 'committing me unto my brother's love' (4.3.144) and a kiss on 'doth call his Rosalind' (4.3.156). When Rosalind tried to get back to the subject of the bloody napkin he snapped her head off with his 'by and by' (4.3.138) and continued to address his besotted attention to Celia. He got his hand slapped for trying to assist the fainted Rosalind by unbuttoning her shirt.

Five years later and Fiona Shaw's Celia and Bruce Alexander's Oliver were ready to build on their predecessors' demonstration of love at first sight. Michael Billington, indeed, thought that their 'exchange of instant glances' was 'the one igniting spark of passion' in an otherwise frigid evening (*Guardian*). The 'glances' were, as Oliver entered, certainly instantaneous, but also momentary. It

FIGURE 17 (*opposite*) Rosalind (Susan Fleetwood, right) is left altogether in the cold as Celia (Sinead Cusack) and Oliver (Jonathan Hyde, the bloody napkin in his hand) become more and more obsessed with each other. (4.3, 1980)

was not until Rosalind fainted that their eyes locked and they stood gazing at each other, mesmerized until recalled to reality by a shift of position from the supine Rosalind. The easy laugh was taken on 'there's more in it' as he started to loosen Ganymede's shirt, and then came another long, adoring stare at the exit, only broken by a very sharp 'Will you go?' (4.3.182) from Rosalind.

Fiona Shaw's Celia had altogether dominated the relationship in the court scenes. Irving Wardle thought that Rosalind seemed 'very much the house guest of Fiona Shaw's sharp-eyed Celia' (*Times*). The phrases that other reviewers found for Celia all reinforce this sense of her intellectual dominance: 'mature and acerbic' (*D. Telegraph*); 'Mitfordesque' (*Guardian*); 'a sparky deb with a sharp tongue, an even sharper sense of style and, eventually, a comprehensible weakness for a similarly upper-crust Oliver' (*TES*). Nicholas Shrimpton particularly enjoyed her 'heroic but horrified declaration "I'll put myself in poor and mean attire" [1.3.107], spoken like a duchess contemplating a visit to an Oxfam shop' (*SS*, 200).

Two decisive stages in the relationship are passed, as Shaw and Juliet Stevenson make clear in their penetrating essay on it, in the banishment scene (see Figure 18). This begins with Celia confronting that 'feeling of impending isolation that a girl experiences when her best friend's passions are diverted to the opposite sex and suddenly a gulf gapes between them' (Shaw and Stevenson, 61) and continues with Celia, in spite of this, defying her father and allying herself with her cousin:

> This is a crucial point in the play for Celia – her love for Rosalind seems to intensify because it has now become a sacrifice; there is cost and loss in it now, she has sunk everything into it and the stakes are higher. (62)

Once in the forest the gulf widens, but Shaw's Celia refused to languish. Irving Wardle was impressed by the way the 'sharp-eyed, spinsterly tease' changed into 'the gypsy once she settled in Arden' (*Times*) and Michael Coveney enjoyed the energy and

FIGURE 18 The 'Mitfordesque' and dominant Celia of Fiona Shaw protects her cousin Rosalind (Juliet Stevenson) from the anger of Duke Frederick (Joseph O'Conor) while other courtiers, in evening dress, look on. At the end of the scene Duke Frederick and his followers will throw sheets over their formal attire and be metamorphosed into the court in exile. (1.3, 1985)

decisiveness of the arrival: '"I like this place" [2.4.92], says Celia, with all the nervous defiance of any crisp upper class girl choosing a plot on a glacier whereon to build and cultivate her cote' (*FT*, reviewing the Barbican transfer). Shaw and Stevenson write of the problems for Celia in the forest wooing scenes:

> As Rosalind becomes increasingly in possession of her powers, Celia is left powerless, drawn into a game which is not of her making, and dazzled by a friend who is now barely recognisable ... What *is* Celia's attitude to it all? Wonder, horror, amusement, rage, confusion, isolation, jubilation, fear, or all of these? ... Rosalind draws strongly on Celia's presence; to show off, outrage, seek refuge in, and silently confer with ... Celia, whether she likes it or not, becomes a sort of chaperone-cum-referee.   (66–7)

By the end of the second wooing scene (4.1) 'Rosalind has now abandoned all sensibility in relation to her cousin, and Celia is alone' (69).

It was at this point that the little deer-hunting scene took a further large step in the direction of the symbolic. 'And I'll sleep' (4.1.208) said Celia sulkily, and tucked herself up in the folds of the great silk tent hanging centre stage. In came Jaques with a long, bloody sheet which he trailed solemnly across her sleeping form; the drums and horns of the hunt followed, the huntsmen chasing her, one of them shooting her as she ran for cover in the folds of the tent, the others following, lifting its skirts in pursuit of her. (She emerged unscathed a few moments later to begin 4.3.) This was clearly not a case of what Arthur Sprague calls 'deficiency doubling' (Sprague, 12), for Shaw made no attempt to convince us that she was a deer; the episode was offered as a sexual initiation for Celia in anticipation of her meeting with Oliver. But why it was Jaques (with whom she never exchanges a word in the play) who dragged the sheet was something over which the audience was left to puzzle – and the reviewers, several of whom thought the scene depicted a gang rape. The dividing lines between the thought-provokingly mysterious, the portentous and the pretentious are fine indeed in the world of directors' Shakespeare, and this was a classic example of the form. Curiously Shaw and Stevenson are silent about the episode in their otherwise comprehensive essay, remarking only that the arrival of Oliver is precisely timed to coincide with the moment of Celia's complete isolation: 'If our loves are informed to a great extent by our situations, then Celia is now available, and readiness is all' (69).

The sense of an equal intellectual partnership between the two cousins, so impressively achieved in 1985, receded again in the next two Stratford productions of *As You Like It*, both Gillian Bevan in 1989 and Phyllida Hancock in 1992 presenting Celias who appeared to be much more dependent on their Rosalinds as well as seeming simply younger. Where Fiona Shaw's Celia had been described as 'Mitfordesque', the word that reviewers reached for when describing Gillian Bevan's was 'schoolgirlish'. Christopher Edwards was rather cross about it: 'There is too much schoolgirlish gushing and larking about … and not enough poise, grace and wit' (*Spectator*). Poise, grace and wit were clearly not the intention; energy, excitement, youthful joy were what was aimed at and Rex Gibson's 'Bisto Kids' epithet for the cousins (*TES*) aptly sums up the relationship.

In spite of her ability to look so very young in her baggy shorts, one was never in any doubt that Sophie Thompson's Rosalind was always one move ahead of her more naive cousin. In the opening dance sequence Rosalind's low-cut evening dress and Celia's rather more covered-up appearance seemed immediately to suggest the comparative levels of sophistication in the relationship (see Figure 5); Celia even cried childishly in pleading with her 'sweet Rose' to 'be merry' (1.2.21–2). They were still in their dance dresses for the banishment (night attire would return a couple of productions later) and Duke Frederick's possessiveness towards his little daughter was clearly signalled when he whispered 'she robs thee of thy name' (1.3.76) as a secret aside to her.

Celia's idea of escaping to Arden had something of the quality of a teenager's 'dare', and that idea of a couple of kids having a wonderful adventure was a not inappropriate aspect of the earlier forest scenes of this production. The sense of increasing pathos about Celia that it induced as the forest scenes progressed was remarked on by several reviewers: 'she sulks at her cousin's increasing indulgences' (*S. Times*); she follows 'a nicely plotted route from princess to farmer to gooseberry' (*TLS*); she shows 'a growing psychological dissatisfaction with her supporting role' (*SA Herald*). This last emerged clearly in the first of Rosalind's forest scenes with Orlando (3.2): for the first half of it Celia stayed close, trying to join in; then she gave up and went and sat disconsolately on her own, the kid who had been left out of the game and who now revealed 'a powerful sense of isolation and loneliness' (*SS*, 162). She played the wedding scene 'in a ruminative melancholia', thought Nicholas de Jongh (*Guardian*, reviewing the Barbican transfer), quite unable to watch the kiss that ended the ceremony, and her 'And I'll sleep' (4.1.208) was extremely tetchy.

The deer-killing scene, with a dance again suggesting a fertility rite, was less portentous than it had been four years earlier, but with Celia on stage throughout it was undoubtedly intended to be taken as 'a dream while Celia slept' (*SA Herald*). Once again a point was made of the exit after her meeting with Oliver: Rosalind, who had been about to bustle off leaving Celia and Oliver gazing into each other's eyes, turned back, interrupting an almost-achieved kiss. 'Will you go', she asked briskly (4.3.182) – and the situation somehow made one remember Celia's returning after a similar half-exit (after the wrestling match) to awaken her cousin from the same state of hypnotic concentration on Oliver's younger brother, and with the same 'Will you go?' demand (1.2.245). The echo signalled the distance Celia had travelled, and her readiness, now, to join the rest of the country copulatives.

Phyllida Hancock's Celia in 1992 came in the same season as her ardent, youthful, charmingly naive Perdita in *The Winter's Tale*, and the fact that the same player was to be seen in both these roles tells us something about the way Celia's relationship with Rosalind worked here. Michael Coveney wrote of the 'simple girlishness' of Celia offering a foil to Samantha Bond's 'smart and snappy' Rosalind (*Observer*); David Murray described her as 'pleasant upper middle genteel ... but without that astringency that sharpens the best Celias' (*FT*). 'One of the most moving moments of the evening', wrote Charles Spencer of Rosalind's confession of her fathomless love, 'is Celia's realization that her friendship will now take second place' (*D. Telegraph*). Others were less generous to a reading of the role that they found 'pliant', 'bland', 'curiously understretched' (*D. Mail, E. Standard, Times*), but which seemed to me to derive from a deliberate decision to be self-effacing, searching for the sort of personality that might explain those long and patient silences while Rosalind takes over the play.

FIGURE 19 Amused by Monsieur Le Beau (not visible), Rosalind (Samantha Bond, left) and Celia (Phyllida Hancock), in their dark silk dresses in Elizabethan–Victorian style, sit with Anthony O'Donnell's Touchstone on the stool of the grand piano which Rosalind had earlier been playing. (1.2, 1992)

In the first court scene, where the cousins were discovered at a huge black grand piano, Rosalind playing a melancholy little tune (see Figure 19), one observed a Celia full of admiration for her older cousin, very much the adoring friend. She seemed at a loss, in the banishment scene (where they still wore their tight-laced, full-skirted silk dresses), to know how to help Rosalind in her outburst of grief. In the forest scenes she was much more still than some Celias have been, sitting mostly upstage, even hiding under the little rustic bridge (see Figure 25), watching anxiously, conveying her sense of the gulf widening every moment between herself and the friend she loved. For the wedding scene there was none of the angry embarrassment that many Celias have evinced on 'I cannot say the words' (4.1.121); one felt that Celia was out of her depth, bewildered and saddened, anxious to withdraw again into the upstage shadows. 'You have simply misused our sex in your love-prate' (4.1.191–2) seemed to be said with pretended rather than real anger and her intention to sleep was expressed at the end of the scene with quiet resignation.

The deer-killing had, for once, no part in Celia's dreams, nor were there meaningful glances at Oliver's entry with the news of his brother's injury. Oliver spoke to Rosalind and Celia's attention was focused, it seemed, entirely on the story, and then on her anxiety about her fainting cousin. Not until the end of the scene, when Rosalind withdrew the hand that Celia and Oliver had both solicitously been holding, leaving Celia's hand in Oliver's, did she seem conscious of the young man's attractions. (Whether Rosalind had deliberately or inadvertently so symbolically joined their hands one was left, intriguingly, to wonder.) Then came the long, eye-locked gaze, interrupted only by Rosalind's 'Will you go?' (4.3.182). Two more occasions were then found in this production to explain the young couple's presence in the final dance: they came on (along with most of the rest of the cast), wrapped in each other's arms, for the choric treatment of 'It was a lover and his lass'; and when Rosalind hurried from the stage in the final scene to 'make these doubts all even' (5.4.25) she had to come nipping back for Celia who, oblivious to everything in Oliver's embrace, had clearly forgotten that they had an appointment to keep with Hymen.

When David Thacker's production moved to the Barbican, Samantha Bond, who had handed Rosalind over to Kate Buffery two-thirds of the way through the Stratford season, returned from maternity leave to play Celia opposite Buffery's Rosalind. And the reviewers' attention was immediately attracted to Celia in a way that had not happened at all at Stratford. She was now 'joyously comic' (*E. Standard*), 'pert and ardent' (*D. Express*), a 'creature of shine and shimmer' (*D. Mail*). 'Usual moves?', an older generation of actors used to be able to enquire when moving into an existing Shakespeare production, but what a world of difference is made by the personality of the actor, however similar the moves.

The cousins' relationship has continued to yield interpretative variations in Stratford's two most recent productions. There was less of an age difference in the friendship in 1996 and it took on a rather serious complexion. 'Celia declines all chances of wryness', thought John Mullen, 'and Rosalind avoids all playfulness' (*TLS*). When Charles the wrestler gave a nasty, knowing laugh as he told Oliver that 'never two ladies loved as they do' (1.1.112), audience attention was inevitably heightened when Rachel Joyce's Celia said that she and Rosalind had always 'slept together' and that she could not live out of her company (1.3.69, 82). Celia stayed seated (the first Celia to do so since 1961), very much the Princess, for the interviews with Orlando either side of the wrestling, and there was not the least sense here (in contrast with some earlier productions) of her being interested in the young man for herself. At the beginning of the banishment scene they were on the floor in their white petticoats, Rosalind's head in Celia's lap, Celia's arms around her cousin; their position on the stage was precisely that at which, a couple of hours later, Celia would, so unwillingly, have to pretend to marry her cousin to the man who had taken Rosalind away from her.

The growing estrangement between Celia and Rosalind had been clear in Celia's frown and flounce of annoyance at Rosalind's references to the 'giddy offences' of women (3.2.341), and she was clearly winding Rosalind up in the conversation (at the beginning of 3.4) about whether or not Orlando is in love. By the second wooing scene she had withdrawn into complete isolation, reading a book and skulking in the 'trees' upstage (see Figure 26) from where she came, unwilling and bad-tempered, to 'say the words' (4.1.121) over the lovers. Celia was, for a change, offstage for the deer-hunting but her meeting with Oliver was still subject to the mysterious influence of the forest, for, as he came in and stood on that upstage mound that may or may not have been Adam's grave, a strange high-pitched sound echoed around the theatre as their eyes met – the forest's electronic equivalent of a wolf-whistle, it seemed, though referred to in the promptbook as 'magic bird'. The agitation of the two of them in the ensuing dialogue found relief at Ganymede's faint: over her cousin's prostrate form she and Oliver lent immediately into a passionate kiss and made their exit hand in hand.

In the tapestry world of the 2000 *As You Like It* it was inevitable that one more variation on the cousins' relationship should be considered: the possibility that it might be rather artificial. Alexandra Gilbreath's Rosalind was 'very tense and cautious at court ... as if anything spontaneous might be dangerous' (*S. Times*); this, set against Nancy Carroll's 'cut-glass' and 'prickly' Celia (*Indep. Sun., D. Telegraph*), created a certain brittleness about a friendship 'wreathed in whalebone-corseted melancholy' (*Guardian*). And a black dress with white on it, and a white dress with black on it (see Figure 7), though they may visually complement each other, obviously tell very different stories about their wearers. There they sat in their first scene, some feet apart, divided by the width of the monochrome tapestry, which we should later perceive had provoked Rosalind (but not, it appeared, Celia) into her own, much more colourful, needlework efforts. The moment Rosalind saw Orlando she was 'reduced to open-mouthed adoration' (*Guardian*), so that Celia's 'And mine to eke out hers' and 'Your heart's desires be with you' (1.2.185, 187) were merely desperate attempts to break the eye contact between her cousin and the young man. Here, as in 1989 and 1992, was a Celia who was younger, and much more immature, than her companion. Rosalind seemed partly to live in a secret world from which Celia was excluded. This appeared not just in her escapist needlework, but in the miniature of her father which she pulled from inside her bodice in the banishment scene, forcing Frederick to look at it as she insisted 'my father was no traitor' (1.3.59). As they planned their escape (and one hears this clearly on the archival video), Celia was sharp and clear, busy about the practical arrangements (especially getting their jewels together) while Rosalind's voice was quieter, more detached and solemn, and with a crack in it that threatened the possibility of tears. The sense of girlishness about

Celia was further emphasized by giving her a little cart, propelled by Touchstone's pedalling (see Figure 13), in which to ride to Arden – the 'weaker vessel' indeed (2.4.5).

In Arden one watched her realize, slowly, that she was on her own. There was still enough warmth in the relationship for her to embrace her cousin after giving her the news that Orlando is in the forest 'with a chain, that you once wore, about his neck' (3.2.178), but by the end of that first wooing scene she was scowling and storming off alone. She assessed the trustworthiness of Orlando's love (3.4.1ff.) in a poised, rather business-like way, reducing Rosalind to sobbing in her lap with her reference to the man's ability to break vows 'bravely' (3.4.37–8), and she sat so far upstage for the second wooing scene that one wondered if she could hear (or even wanted to) – she did hear, though, about Rosalind's 'coming-on disposition' (4.1.107) and gasped audibly. She almost shrieked her inability to 'say the words' (121) of the marriage and strongly emphasized the demonstrative adjective as she asked Orlando whether he would 'take to wife *this* Rosalind' (123–4), as though contrasting the present fake with the absent reality in the hope of stopping him from going through with it. After the exchange of vows, it was the pressure of Celia's hand on his shoulder that seemed to force Orlando to lean backwards in evasion of Rosalind's attempted kiss, and the fierce contempt with which she referred to Rosalind's 'love-*prate*' (191; my italics – or Celia's) provoked the power and emotional depth of Rosalind's explanation of 'how many fathom deep' she was in love (196).

Rosalind's tearful exit left Celia alone to sleep for only the first moments of the deer-hunting scene. She awoke to watch a deer-dance of naked-torsoed men, highly balletic and not a little sadistic in its chasing and catching and throwing about of the victim, but so homoerotic as to seem a puzzling way of provoking in her the heterosexual energies that propelled her irresistibly, in the following scene, into partnership with Oliver. Her directions to him for finding the house were remarkably eager, she stared longingly into his eyes as he described 'the thing I am' (4.3.137) and totally absorbed his attentions thereafter. Neither of them at first heeded Rosalind's 'Will you go?' (4.3.182), so intense was their gaze, though the anticipated kiss remained in their imaginations.

'Never two ladies loved as they do' (1.1.112) is a powerful description of a friendship for the players of Rosalind and Celia to try to realize. Over the past half century at Stratford the attempts have taken many forms, the partnership seeming sometimes equally balanced, sometimes very uneven. The play charts the emotional journeys of Celia and Rosalind, beginning in their love for each other and ending in their commitments in love to the brothers de Boys. In terms of language, Celia moves from fluency, loquaciousness even, to silence – the silence of those long, mesmerized gazes into Oliver's eyes that so many productions have shown as her journey's end, a 'love silence' altogether unlike the 'love-prate' (4.1.191) of Rosalind that so appals her. Rosalind's journey is in the opposite direction, from lacking a word 'to throw at a dog' (1.3.3) to her conviction that 'you shall never take her without her answer, unless you take her without her tongue' (4.1.162–4). It is to that journey's presentation, in the performances of thirteen Stratford Rosalinds (and Orlandos), that I now turn.

4

WOO ME

Come, woo me, woo me; for now I am in a holiday humour and like
enough to consent. What would you say to me now, and I were your
very very Rosalind?   (4.1.65–8)

osalind's is by some way the longest woman's part in
Shakespeare, and since *As You Like It* became a more or less
constant presence in the English theatre repertoire in the
first half of the eighteenth century most major classical actresses
have been seen in the role, some over many years. There have,
however, been some notable omissions: Ellen Terry, for example,
never played the part and in a book about the play at Stratford over
the last half century or so it is perhaps surprising not to be writing
about Judi Dench's, or Harriet Walter's, Rosalinds, as one would be
about their Violas, or Imogens, or Beatrices. Like the first two of
those other roles, and several others besides, the part requires its
player to spend much of the evening pretending to be a boy, a
disguise required by the convention to be impenetrable to everyone
on the stage and to no one in the auditorium. Unlike those other
male disguises, however, Rosalind's Ganymede spends most of his
time pretending to be a woman, producing a level of sexual
ambiguity unequalled in Shakespeare, though operating in the
modern theatre at only three-quarters of its original complexity, for
the earliest performances of the role would have been given by a boy
pretending to be a girl pretending to be a boy pretending to be a girl.

For a girl to pretend to be a boy in the modern theatre inevitably brings with it the danger of seeming like the 'principal boy' in a pantomime, with all the arch knowingness and metaphorical – if not actual – winking at the audience that that implies. When Rosalind's disguise as Ganymede drifts into that area, self-destruction threatens; and yet our awareness of her constant oscillation between her adopted male persona and her feminine self is a crucial part of our delight in the role, paralleling our sense of the tension between the vulnerability of her emotional commitment and the sharpness of her intellectual control. How 'convincing' should the disguise be? A recurrent complaint in the critical response to this sequence of Stratford productions is that Ganymede was so obviously a girl that it was impossible not to think Orlando a fool for being taken in. That is partly a literal-minded reaction to a convention common in sixteenth- and seventeenth-century drama but encountered regularly in the modern theatre only in a handful of Shakespearean comedies, but it is more significant than that. The all-male productions mentioned in the Introduction were one way of moving beyond the issue; both, interestingly, could afford to be in modern dress. Eileen Atkins, Stratford's denim-jeans Rosalind of 1973, confided in an interview many years later her belief that the part is unplayable for a woman in modern dress and that at one point during the rehearsal period she felt so anxious that she acquired a pair of false sideburns – never, one learns with a sense of happy escape, seen in performance (Hemming).

Nor, it may be reported with equal relief, has any of these Stratford productions tried that other literal-minded solution to the problem of a disguise that convinces Orlando completely and us not at all: to play a patronizing Orlando only pretending to be taken in and humouring the little woman by going along with her game – for then one bids farewell to the play. Like Proteus, and Orsino, and Posthumus, and Bassanio, it doesn't occur to Orlando that his disguised beloved is a woman for the very simple reason that she is wearing 'doublet and hose' (3.2.215–16) – or whatever equivalent the director and designer's chosen period may offer. A production has to find a way of making a modern audience accept that proposition without dismissing Orlando as a fool. It also needs to find a way of preventing an audience from feeling that Orlando, inarticulate, shy, a little gullible, doesn't 'deserve' to marry the brilliant Rosalind. In a rigorous and unmerciful appraisal of comparative intellectual and moral merit none of the Shakespearean husbands or husbands-to-be I have just listed comes off very well alongside his betrothed; and one could take that proposition further – except that it might be in danger of coming too close to home. That Rosalind loves Orlando is sufficient, within the play's formal comic structure, to confer desert upon him, though in performance, of course, the player of the part needs to show us some of the reasons for her doing so.

The tensions and counterpoises in the role of Rosalind offer an extraordinary area of choice to the performer: emotional commitment and sincerity swing to detachment and self-mockery, wistfulness and regret to ebullience and laughter, the girl hopelessly in love switches instantaneously to the woman aware of her folly for being so. 'What's lovely to play in Rosalind is the range she goes through', said Samantha Bond in an interview when she was rehearsing the part in 1992 (Grimley). She went on to discuss the mixture in the role of 'great sadness, elegance, charm and wit' and suggested that 'unless you go for the darkness ... you don't get the full beauty of the play at the end. It's a difficult balance.' One constant in that range and that variety of choice – 'brave, vulnerable, optimistic, honest', as Bond put it – is the absolute need of the audience's sympathy and affection; without that the play falls through the floor. How fully was this realized by the thirteen Stratford Rosalinds of the last half century, what were their choices among the role's range of options, and how was the relationship with Orlando explored, particularly in the two big wooing scenes in Arden? To these issues I now turn.

The general consensus of reviewers in 1946 was that Ruth Lodge's Rosalind was underprepared – a particular danger at that period when a range of productions opened very close together at the beginning of the season. She was, thought T.C. Kemp, 'too cautious, when she should soar' (*Birm. Post*); it was 'a well-planned sketch', but it needed more 'personality' (*Times*). Alan Dent thought her performance would develop but that at the press night she had been 'arch and coy ... leg-conscious and doublet-and-hose conscious' (*News Chron.*); the *Stage* seemed to point to similar problems when it suggested that in avoiding the 'principal boy' hazards of the role Lodge had remained too much 'the genteel young lady'. Myles Eason's Orlando, in the opinion of some reviewers a 'fine figure of a love-shaked sonneteer' (*Times*) and 'amusingly love-sick without being irritating' (*Warwick Adv.*), seemed to others 'not happily suited' to the role (*Berrow's Worcs. J.*) and an 'embarrassment' (*News Chron.*) – the sort of variation that provides a useful reminder of what a subjective business the response to theatre performance is. A thoughtful review in the *Evesham Journal* (yet another indication of how interesting some of the local press coverage was at this time) admired Lodge's 'easy grace and wit' but missed the 'flamboyant enthusiasm of a young woman in love' and then went on to explain, perhaps, why no account of the production offers a word on the relationship between Orlando and Rosalind: Eason's Orlando, it suggested, 'was better as the sympathetic companion to Adam than as the ardent admirer of Rosalind'. The promptbook records the removal of the passage (4.1.159–67) about 'your wife's wit going to your neighbour's bed' – a victim, like Celia's remark on having Rosalind's doublet and hose 'plucked over' her head (4.1.192–4), of contemporary morality – but offers us nothing more on the wooing scenes. The most interesting aspects of the 1946 production seem not to have lain in its presentation of the relationship of Orlando and Rosalind.

There can have been nothing underprepared about Margaret Leighton's 1952 Rosalind in the first of Glen Byam Shaw's productions, for she had played the part to great acclaim at Birmingham Repertory Theatre a few years earlier. Both she and her Orlando, Laurence Harvey, with their film as well as theatre reputations, were what one might call 'star casting'. The critical response was extraordinarily enthusiastic – 'the finest Rosalind for years' (*D. Herald*) and an Orlando who had 'looks, innocence, single-mindedness – all the qualities proper to the role' (*Times*). What comes up again and again in responses to Leighton's performance is its ardour and commitment alongside its energy, joy and sense of mischief ('elfin' is a much-used term): it combined 'passion, pulse-beating sincerity, throat-catching charm' (*Man. D. Desp.*), and 'gaucherie, grace, archness and gentility with a radiant hoyden humour' (*D. Mail*). She was 'roguish, enchanting, yet bringing one near to tears by the quality of her love' (*E. News*) and 'sparkling with the joy of life yet wistful at its absurdities' (*West. D. Press*). That scintillating quality of mood-change is enormously important in the role, particularly in the big Act 4 wooing scene as Rosalind moves between passionate commitment and wry detachment, and the accounts of Leighton's performance certainly suggest that she achieved this: 'grave, mischievous, tender, sprightly' (*Birm. E. Desp.*); 'railing deliciously, moping forlornly ... as capricious as April, and as sweet' (*News Chron.*) – the epithets of infinite variety roll out.

There were, however, some hesitations. Where most reviewers admired the fact that 'no one ever gave the lass a more delicate air ... tall, blonde, slender as a wand' (*D. Express*), others found her an 'underfed *gamin*, not the sturdy English adolescent the role requires' (*SA Herald*), or 'paler and thinner' than she should be and, as Ganymede, 'too short in the coat, too long and flimsy in the leg. What an actress she could be if she could be persuaded to transfer her reverence from Stanislavsky to steak and kidney pie' (*S. Times*). (It is moving indeed to find a reviewer taking so personal an interest in his subject's dietary needs; Figure 20 will allow readers to assess the relevance of the prescription.) Her speaking, too, had its detractors, and there were inevitably comparisons with the past: she lacked 'the bubbling gaiety' of Edith Evans (*S. Times*), 'the poetic cadences of Peggy Ashcroft' (*E. Standard*) and the

FIGURE 20 'Good day and happiness, dear Rosalind': Orlando (Laurence Harvey) greets Rosalind (Margaret Leighton) who punishes him for his lateness by concentrating her attention on Celia (Siobhan McKenna, right); the much-remarked-on blonde/brunette contrast is very clear here. Michael Hordern's Jaques crumples against the palm tree before the onslaught of blank verse. (4.1.28, 1952)

'aristocratic sense of comedy of the greatest Rosalinds' (*Man. Guardian W.*). Such comments are, however, very much in the minority: 'complete mastery and understanding of the language' (*Man. Guardian*), 'a voice of crumbling tenderness' (*News Chron.*), 'the grasp always sure, the lines beautifully spoken' (*Birm. Post*) are much more representative comments. It was a performance, W.A. Darlington concluded, that showed that 'Rosalind is one of the great romantic comedy parts in dramatic literature' (*D. Telegraph*).

Laurence Harvey's Orlando, 'young, virile and handsome ... declaring his love with an engaging frankness and spirit and in good round tones ... for once matched Rosalind' (*Warwick Adv.*). That sense that this was a convincing and believable partnership pervades the critical response, and it is as a mixture of such qualities as 'hearty, natural manliness' and 'fresh, honest simplicity' (*Birm. Mail*, *Coventry Sta.*) on the one hand, and 'touching devotion' and 'moonstruck adoration' (*News Chron.*, *D. Mail*) on the other, that his performance is described. (Some of these qualities may be discernible, perhaps, in Figure 20.) It was above all his voice that focused admiration: 'powerful but controlled' (*Coventry E. Tel.*), a 'baritone that thickens with emotion' (*Man. D. Desp.*), it combined, for Ivor Brown, with his 'charm and presence' to 'give the excuse of irresistible romance' (*Observer*). And hardly a reviewer on this occasion raised the issue of his failure to recognize Rosalind, the 'lanky boy' of Leighton's Ganymede seeming to W.A. Darlington a perfectly plausible disguise (*D. Telegraph*). The promptbook, indeed, records that at her 'will you go?' at the end of the first wooing scene (3.2.422–3) he pulled her back by the seat of the trousers and, with proper deference to the lady, ushered Celia from the stage first. The promptbook also records that the lines about Rosalind visiting her neighbour's bed and having her doublet and hose plucked over her head (4.1.159–67, 192–4) were still considered unsuitable to be uttered from the Stratford stage.

That was still the case in Byam Shaw's second production in 1957 when Peggy Ashcroft, almost fifty, came to Stratford to play, opposite the young Richard Johnson's Orlando, the role she had last performed at the Old Vic in 1932. Inevitably there was a sense of the critics gathering almost ghoulishly to watch middle age endeavouring in vain to present youth. Most saw no such thing, though a substantial minority raised doubts: she was not too old to play Rosalind, but 'too experienced' (*Star*), she played too much on 'one note of feverish intensity' (*Times*), and was 'too hurried, too anxious to achieve the required vivacity' (*West. D. Press*). Milton Shulman thought that she achieved 'every nuance but that of tender passion' and evinced an 'instinctive control of abandon that gave her romantic gusto a slightly over-refined edge – as if love were something not quite "done"' (*E. Standard*), a point reflected in the *Liverpool Post*'s remarking of 'a nimble wit rather than an ardent heart'. The *Stage*, too, discerned 'a sense of strain' in the performance, and admired Johnson's Orlando in all his scenes except those with Rosalind (which is a back-handed compliment if ever there was one).

Most, however, saw things very differently. Muriel St Clare Byrne thought Ashcroft's performance was 'quiveringly alive' and 'exquisitely light-hearted' (*SQ*, 480); Derek Granger found her 'thrillingly spontaneous' and 'light of touch in her gaiety and youthfulness' (*FT*); W.A. Darlington admired her 'miraculous gift of youth' (*D. Telegraph*); and Cecil Wilson enjoyed the 'trim and jaunty' Ganymede disguise that was 'gay without being hearty, roguish without being arch' (*D. Mail*). There is (and it makes a welcome change) a good deal of comment on specific moments in the performance: the 'shades of fancy and wonder' that 'cross her face at the moment of falling in love' (*FT*); the 'glint in the eye' when she invents her 'old religious uncle' (3.2.335–6) and the 'guilty pause' as she mentions the 'fringe upon a petticoat' (3.2.330) (*Birm. Post*); the 'new beauty behind the yearnings' as she describes 'how many fathom deep' she is in love (4.1.196) (*Yorks. Post*); and the 'spin round in sudden ecstasy' at 'what talk we of fathers' (3.4.34) (*Illus. Lon. News*). The 'peculiar silver charm' (*New States.*) of Ashcroft, her ability to 'inspire more immediate affection than any other actress on the English stage' (*Illus. Lon. News*), had worked its magic on the critics.

And with the one exception quoted above, most witnesses suggest that it had the same effect on Johnson's Orlando, a 'subdued' performance 'brought to glowing life' in her presence (*Oxf. Mail*), so that 'the wooing scenes come off as likeably as they have ever done' (*Man. Guardian*). Rosemary Anne Sisson admired the moment of troth-plighting 'with Rosalind sincere, Orlando ignorant, and Celia half-dismayed at this sudden seriousness' (*SA Herald*). Byam Shaw's casting of Richard Johnson as Orlando elicited very much the response that Laurence Harvey had received in the same role five years earlier (and a repeat of the business of hauling Rosalind back at the 3.2 exit). Johnson evinced 'solid romantic sturdiness' (*FT*), was 'virile alike in wrestling and in yearning' (*D. Mail*), 'a fellow of character and exceedingly likeable' who preserved his humour even in love-sickness (*Punch*) and 'so unaffected and sensible that the poetry came through almost as if it were being improvised' (*Time & T.*). The love scenes thus received a 'lyrical and lucid' performance of 'perfect candour and eagerness' (*Man. Guardian*).

This was a hard act (or perhaps two acts), to follow, then, for Michael Elliott's production four years later. It rose to the challenge impressively. There is such a plethora of eulogistic comment on Vanessa Redgrave's Rosalind that what follows has to be even more selective than usual. There was no question here, obviously, of needing to act youth: Redgrave, in her first season of leading roles at Stratford, possessed it – personified it, indeed, in the opinion of many reviewers. 'Sunlight' was what reviewer after reviewer perceived in the performance. Unlike most Rosalinds she did not cut her hair short for the Ganymede disguise and wear a wig for the 'Rosalind' scenes; instead her hair was tucked into a linen cap (see Figure 15, and cover photograph) which she could snatch off when the disguise was no longer needed and 'shake sunbeams out of her hair' (*Birm. Mail*), or, in J.W. Lambert's more ornithological metaphor, allow it to 'tumble like a flock of goldfinches into sunshine' (*S. Times*). From some seventy reviews of Redgrave's performance in its Stratford and London versions the following must serve as a sample of the quite extraordinary critical response:

> her enthusiasm, the bubbling joy, the breathless love of life and the urgency of her passion for Orlando force the pace ... this tall, fresh whirl of a girl with the honeysilk voice has the lot – the sweetness, courage, dignity, high spirits, wit and radiance. Can there ever be a better Rosalind? (Edmund Gardner, *SA Herald*)

> Above all enchantment – oh wonderful, wonderful, most wonderful, and after that out of all whooping ... a creature of fire and light, her voice a golden gate opening on lapis-lazuli hinges, her body a slender supple reed rippling in the breeze of her love. The naturalness, the unforced understanding of her playing, the passionate, breathless conviction of it, the depth of feeling, the breadth of reality – this is not acting at all, but living, being, loving. (Bernard Levin, *D. Express*)

> Her performance is a triumph ... Her Rosalind, very properly, is mewed up in court clothes. As soon as she gets into the forest she throws her arms wide in the air and frolics up and down Negri's hill like one of Corin's long-legged lambs ... Between leaps she pants out Rosalind's euphuistic conceits with all the excitement of someone who has just found that she too can play the game of fashionable wit ... Once or twice my tight English soul winced at the exuberance, but the lines cry out for this interpretation ... She has thrown herself so fully into her role that if it goes wrong she will look merely foolish. It goes right. (Bamber Gascoigne, *Spectator*)

To watch the television film of the production is to catch something of the mood of this response to the energy, commitment and sheer rapture of Redgrave's performance – though not, one trusts, to be infected with the same self-indulgences in prose style. The joy on her face, the long, loving look and the momentary inability to speak when Orlando tells her that he 'would not be cured' of his love (3.2.413), the passionate anxiety with which she asks him 'how long you would have her, after you have possessed her' (4.1.135–6), and the sighing cadence of her voice in the total, almost pathetic, commitment of her confession of 'how many fathom deep' she is in love (4.1.196) are intensely moving. Reviewers of the theatre performance picked out other moments: the poignant effect with which 'the cry of "excellent young man" [1.2.201] is torn from her during the wrestling' (*D. Express*) when one saw the moment she falls in love and begins 'to walk on air . . . as her wit and her self-possession were shaken by her heart-beats' (*New States.*); the uninhibited 'flinging herself backwards before Orlando when "in a coming-on disposition"' (*E. News*, reviewing the Aldwych transfer); 'the conviction with which she says "I cannot be out of the sight of Orlando" [4.1.205–6] that stops one's heart in its tracks' (*New States.*, also reviewing the Aldwych transfer); and, in the Act 4 wooing scene, 'her investing what is most serious to her with the charm of an exquisite frolic' (*Times*), so that 'we understand her love and its sincerity' (*Birm. Post*). There were a few less enthusiastic responses (including, inevitably, the odd unfavourable comparison with Edith Evans), the most significant, perhaps, a twice- or thrice-repeated suggestion that Rosalind's wit had been rather eclipsed by the huge youthful energy of Redgrave's characterization. But J.W. Lambert discerned in her performance 'a silver note unheard on our stages for years, a note which sings of radiance without effort' (*S. Times*), Felix Barker thought her 'the best Rosalind I have ever seen or ever expect to see' (*E. News*, reviewing the Aldwych transfer), and Robert Speaight, admiring (with a professional's respect) the way in which 'she was so passionately concerned with what she was doing that the words sprang to her lips with the spontaneity of a mountain stream', pronounced Redgrave's 'a magical performance' and added that 'earth has not anything to show more fair than a production of this quality at Stratford' (*SQ*, 433–4).

To play Orlando to a Rosalind with whom several reviewers confessed themselves to have fallen in love was clearly to court envy, and Ian Bannen did not escape a few harsh comments, mostly directed at his speaking. (A trace of a Scottish accent could cause supercilious comment at a period when 'received pronunciation' was still widely felt to be de rigueur in the classical theatre.) Some felt that he lacked 'romantic glow' (*FT*) or even that he was 'morose and melancholy' (*S. Wales E. Argus*), but the overwhelming reaction is of respect for a performance of Orlando as a 'gentle, modern-looking young man of considerable charm' (*Stage*) who was 'active, ardent and likeable' (*Liv. Post*). A reviewer from Bannen's native Scotland drew attention to 'the fervent manner he brings to his first encounter with Rosalind, showing his first flush of love to the audience but not to her' (*Glasgow Her.*) and thought it 'touchingly natural'. The same reviewer, alluding to the perennial question of Orlando's failure to recognize Rosalind, pointed out that Redgrave had carefully avoided presenting a Ganymede 'so seductively feminine as to make Orlando seem blind'. J.W. Lambert thought Bannen's Orlando 'a love-lorn wanderer ... strangely haunted, like all Mr Bannen's heroes' (*S. Times*), Geoffrey Tarran admired the way in which he had shown 'the roughening influence of peasant upbringing' through which shone his 'innate honesty and chivalrous quality' (*Morn. Adv.*) and Caryl Brahms enjoyed his ability to be 'passionate', but 'with humour played over it' (*Jack O'L.*). She also remarked, interestingly, that he 'gave us no time to recognise what a fool he is not to recognise Rosalind' – and there is no better way to describe how that non-problem needs to be dealt with in performance. The recurrent note is of his strength and ruggedness of disposition, a strength that he 'manages to sustain even in the most moonstruck moments in Arden' (*SA Herald*). The *Times*, reviewing the Aldwych transfer, summed up the performance (and perhaps the requirements of the role) in calling him 'handsomely romantic, and marvellously slow on the uptake'. Yet again the alleged imbalance of the relationship had been resolved. And there was no queasiness here concerning jokes about neighbours' beds and plucked-off doublets: those traditional cuts disappeared, and have not returned.

After a slightly longer gap than usual, Rosalind came back to Stratford in 1967 in the person of Dorothy Tutin, who brought the legacy of her own considerable successes as Juliet and as Viola on that same stage to provide some sort of counterpoise to the Leighton, Ashcroft, Redgrave trio of Rosalinds that it was her fate to follow. Her Orlando was Michael Williams, 'tough, teasing, with a twinkling of humour' (*Guardian*). He was clearly not conventional romantic casting, but that eager, perky, rather puckish quality that I well remember in this and so many other roles made him immensely likeable. The critical response was here and there a little dubious – 'a plain, beefy fellow inclined to boom' said Peter Lewis rather disdainfully (*D. Mail*), and B.A. Young, snootier still, thought him 'a bit of a hobbledehoy', though he conceded that he was 'maybe the kind of person this Rosalind would fall for' (*FT*). Mostly, however, the directness and honesty of the performance were enjoyed: 'sturdily attractive in voice and gesture' and 'the embodiment of unaffected goodwill', it was difficult not to like this 'warm-hearted, tousle-headed Orlando' (*Guardian, S. Wales E. Argus, Oxf. Mail*, all reviewing the 1968 revival). The *Yorkshire Post* admired the way in which he remained 'conscious of his peasant upbringing', so that he 'approached love fearfully', and John Higgins thought he was right 'not to turn Orlando into too fluent a lover' (*FT*, reviewing the Aldwych transfer). The chemistry with Tutin's Rosalind worked excellently, these two rather stocky figures, similarly dressed in dark trousers, white shirts and leather boots and jerkins – though Rosalind had a broad-brimmed hat that made her 'look like a Mexican bandit' (*Sun*) – evinced a complementary mixture of energy and of hesitancy that worked 'charmingly together' (*D. Telegraph*). Figure 21 catches something of this – as well as showing the Mexican hat.

Certain moments in Tutin's performance attracted attention: the 'gruff bark, hat pulled down over her eyes' with which she accosted Orlando at their first forest meeting (*Times*); 'the gauche walk, the awkward movement of her hands into her trousers pockets, the timorous way in which she bunched a fist' in the second wooing scene (*E. Standard*); 'her pleasure when she phrases something neatly' in the improvisation on Time (3.2.202–27), or

FIGURE 21 Dorothy Tutin's Rosalind describes the realities of marriage to Michael Williams's earnest, eager Orlando as they sit on the giant swinging tree-trunks of Timothy O'Brien's Arden. (4.1, 1967)

the 'moment of enchanted emotion when she says "I do take thee Orlando ..."' (4.1.130–1) (*Birm. Post*). It was, however, the hesitancy, the timidity almost, of Tutin's Rosalind that was distinctive (and memorable) about it and that drew most critical attention. 'One feels', wrote Herbert Kretzmer, 'that her reserves of strength are severely limited' and that 'her helplessness ... calls for our protection and concern' (*D. Express*). She was 'a bit short of strength in the Arden adventure ... too much in need of protection', commented the *Bristol Evening Post* disparagingly – inadvertently catching the very point of the performance. Tutin's Rosalind was

> a sensitive, romantic creature whose spirit and imagination drive her to a role she can barely sustain: the swoon at the sight of blood is the clue to this Rosalind. She may be the one who wears the trousers, but her survival in the forest ... is due to Celia's down-to-earth common sense and Touchstone's instinct for self-preservation.
>
> (*Leam. Spa Cour.*)

Her face was 'a mirror in which the fleeting anguish and agonies of young love are wondrously reflected' (*Bristol E. Post*) – and the 'anguish' was of fear of the possibility of love being lost. Ronald Bryden described her as 'a small figure of choirboy bossiness and cheek ... for ever climbing rocks to lecture her elders on love, then collapsing into femininity within an inch of Orlando's arms' (*Observer*); to Alan Brien she was 'starry-eyed' and 'breathlessly improvising her lessons in female psychology, unconvincingly trying to swagger, or to bunch a male fist' (*S. Telegraph*); and Peter Lewis was much impressed by the 'sighing maiden' discernible beneath the 'breathless tomboy' exterior (*D. Mail*).

That sense of tremulous vulnerability, of its all being very precarious, was at its most vivid in the wooing scenes, which she 'managed to play as an enchanting game' while exposing to the audience 'the full range of her underlying feelings' (*Times*). The rather sparsely annotated promptbook records her laying her head on Orlando's chest at 'Not out of your apparel' (4.1.83), then moving quickly away again. She was 'mistress of everything but her own passion', 'emotionally full, yet emotionally starving', and her 'desperate attempt to ingratiate herself with Orlando as a cheeky boy' had a 'touch of pathos beneath the surface humour' (*FT, Time & T., D. Telegraph*, all reviewing the Aldwych transfer). She was, thought J.C. Trewin, 'a windflower' where Redgrave had been 'a lily' (*Birm. Post*, reviewing the Aldwych transfer).

When the production was revived in 1968 Janet Suzman moved from Celia to Rosalind, answering a wish expressed by a number of reviewers – several of whom now thought her imagination had been 'cramped' by watching Tutin night after night (e.g. *Stage, SA Herald*). The vulnerability of Tutin was not repeated: there was less of the girl, more of the 'young woman of enormous intelligence and sensitivity who falls head over heels in love' (*Oxf. Mail*). Michael Billington admired the 'nimbleness of wit and ecstasy of spirit' (*Times*) and Barry Norman and J.C. Trewin, too, responded to the 'wit and zest' and 'quick-witted enjoyment' (*D. Mail, Birm. Post*). B.A. Young (*FT*) found her 'a little too gay ... when she is excited she squeals away at high, over-prolonged syllables, like a musical comedy actress leading up to a song' and thought her at her best when most restrained, as in '*nearly* tucking Orlando's poem into her bosom, then suddenly remembering and putting it into her pocket'. Gareth Lloyd Evans, who had so admired her Celia the previous year – 'here is another Rosalind' (*Guardian*) – now thought that, in comparison with Tutin, 'trickiness replaces winsomeness, coquetry ousts romance' (*Guardian*). The balance of emotion and intellect in Rosalind is the most difficult aspect of the role – even the extraordinary success of Redgrave had left some doubts here – and there were few who thought Suzman had fully achieved it, though even in noting its lack of romance, Robert Speaight hugely admired the intelligence of a performance that he found 'utterly feminine, unflaggingly resilient and broadly humorous' (*SQ*, 371).

When Eileen Atkins played Rosalind in denim jeans in 1973 Robert Cushman, in the *Observer*, thought that this ought to have

FIGURE 22 Celia (Maureen Lipman), the hammock in which she spends much of her time in Arden empty behind her, looks on quizzically as David Suchet's Orlando seems about to kiss Eileen Atkins's Rosalind, the modern-dress denim jeans of the lovers reducing, in the opinion of many reviewers, the sexual ambivalence of the scene. (4.1, 1973)

been 'the perfect solution to Rosalind's disguise – she could just as easily be a boy as a girl'. The problem, though, he felt, was that 'she could just as easily be a girl as a boy, and I have never felt less inclination to suspend my disbelief'. Jeremy Kingston, too, felt that the wooing scenes went 'for nothing in terms of sexual ambiguity, since Eileen Atkins looks exactly like a 1973 woman' (*Punch*). Michael Billington thought the 'fringed blouse and crotch-hugging jeans' made a 'minimal attempt' to disguise Atkins's femininity (*Guardian*); J.W. Lambert (*S. Times*) felt they positively emphasized it; and to B.A. Young she 'never for a moment looked like a boy' (*FT*). (Figure 22 presents the evidence for or against these views.) Inevitably, therefore, the old problem raised its head: Orlando seemed 'entirely foolish' when Rosalind looked 'no more boyish in trousers than she did in a dress' (*Spectator*). For many this vitiated the experience of this aspect of the play; my own memory is of its being an experiment I was pleased to have seen (and of a certain amount of relief that there were other more satisfactory aspects of the production). In an interview some years later, Eileen Atkins recalled Peggy Ashcroft's saying to her 'My dear, you can't play Rosalind without a hat and a tree'; Atkins goes on to confess to the false sideboards (mentioned above) and to recall how much happier she was in the role a few years later in a production in the United States in Watteauesque style (Hemming).

The aspect of the performance that was interesting, however, was its presentation of Rosalind's sceptical intelligence. Atkins, thought Robert Cushman, took 'complete possession of just *one* corner of Rosalind ... the mordant satirist of romantic attitudes' (*Observer*). Richard David thought her 'self-doubting, ironic, inward, almost sly', a young woman with 'a highly alert intelligence combined with a quick and passionate sympathy and a sense of the comic all the more bubbling for the fact that, for much of the play, the lid must be kept firmly clamped upon it' (David, 138). She was, John Barber remarked, 'a girl of deep feeling, introspective, horribly dashed by Celia's perceptive teasing ... Her intensity risks tearing the fabric of the comedy' (*D. Telegraph*). Irving Wardle thought the tearing had occurred: 'with her swivelling eyes and sceptical cadences she expresses the wary defensiveness of someone who has seen too much to have Rosalind's emotional confidence' (*Times*). For others the balance (or the fabric) survived the scepticism: Jack Tinker thought her 'mercurial and bewitching ... full of fiery wisdom, uncertain confidence and droll insight' (*D. Mail*); Jeremy Kingston admired the 'quicksilver ... oscillation between laughter through tears and sorrow in smiles' (*Punch*); and Wendy Monk found her 'wistful, mischievous and at rare moments transparently in love' (*Stage*).

Her Orlando was David Suchet, near the beginning of his distinguished RSC career and in fact taking over during the rehearsal period the role he was only understudying when Bernard Lloyd, the principal, had to withdraw. There were a number of trite remarks from traditionalist reviewers about the impossibility of his looking romantic in denim jeans, but Richard David thought that Suchet brought a 'blunt honesty and directness' to the role (138) and there was much respect for a 'vigorous, confident Orlando' (*Observer*), 'boyish and loveable' (*Malvern Gaz.*), and 'tender' (*D. Telegraph*). J.W. Lambert felt that the love scenes were played 'with a nuanced delicacy making nonsense of all the laborious psychologizing lavished on their ambiguous exchanges' (*S. Times*). The promptbook makes it clear that although Orlando kissed Rosalind's hand at his 'So adieu' exit (4.1.188), the kiss that seems imminent in Figure 22 was never achieved. Nor, indeed, was the moment that Benedict Nightingale apparently spent his evening anticipating, when the 'covert sexuality' of Atkins's Rosalind would erupt and she would 'clutch Orlando by the buttocks and kiss him' (*New States.*): so much for the unattractiveness of denim jeans.

Between 1973 and 1977 *As You Like It* moved from denim jeans to seventeenth-century elegance (with a continuing absence of any recorded buttock-clutching), and to Kate Nelligan's Rosalind in Trevor Nunn's baroque-opera version of the play. Where Tutin had emphasized Rosalind's vulnerability and Atkins her satiric intelligence, Nelligan, responding, no doubt, to the rather tongue-in-cheek pastiche mood of the production, explored the energetic happiness of the role, though with glimpses of a less confident interior. She was a 'joyous, urgent, waiting-to-be-loved Rosalind' (*SA Herald*) who 'bubbles over with warmth and fun' (*E. News*). John Barber thought her 'sparkling', laudably free of coquetry and archness, and 'disgracefully, shamelessly smitten' at the first sight of Orlando; in the forest scenes, he wrote, 'she teases him with so much mischief, laughs at him with so much delight, brims over with so much fun, that her whole being becomes a frolic of happiness which it is impossible not to share' (*D. Telegraph*). 'Wholehearted' was Irving Wardle's word for her: 'she practically bursts her whalebone when she first falls for Orlando' and in the later wooing scenes she mingled 'tears with ecstatic laughter, never relaxing for an instant' (*Times*).

Beneath this ebullient surface, however, John Peter discerned 'a girl who doesn't quite feel at home with emotions and observes her own with uneasy joy' (*S. Times*), and Michael Billington thought the 'nervy wit' existed only as 'camouflage' for the true feelings of a young woman in emotional turmoil, 'a cat on hot bricks, for ever thumping Orlando with her tiny fist' (*Guardian*). Others were much less convinced and felt that the apparent spontaneity of it all was a pretence. J.C. Trewin thought the calculation was Nelligan's: 'she drives towards Rosalind's heart, but the drive is still too closely plotted, the spontaneity calculated' (*Birm. Post*). Frank Marcus, on the other hand, took Rosalind (not Nelligan) to be the plotter: he discerned 'blatant calculation' in her behaviour after the immediacy of her decision that 'Orlando is her man' and concluded that 'her rapture is cerebral – intelligence shines from her eyes' (*S. Telegraph*).

Marcus also perceived, through the forest wooing, a 'dignified assumption of womanhood' after the 'girlish screeches' of the early scenes. What to Roger Warren (*SS*, 146) was a lack of 'vital erotic charge' in the wooing scenes seemed to B.A. Young a 'burgeoning friendship' with Peter McEnery's Orlando, a lean and nervous young man whose 'country burr' betrayed his upbringing (*FT*). My own memory, too, is of a discernible growth of confidence and trust through the Arden wooing scenes; this gave a sense of increasing stability to the central relationship that provided some basis in emotional reality for the theatrical ostentation of the final scene, with its masque-like descent of Hymen. McEnery's raw and nervous Orlando, intelligent but very vulnerable, was an interesting creation, 'lean and tense ... a gauche country boy barely past his adolescence and a trifle unstable' (*S. Times*). Jack Tinker thought it 'a performance of high romance, seldom attempted and never equalled these days' (*D. Mail*). Even at the end McEnery remained serious, and a little anxious, in response to the radiance and authority that Nelligan's Rosalind finally assumed. Once again this curious relationship had demonstrated its theatrical versatility and fascination.

For his Orlando in the 1980 production John Bowe was similarly anxious to emphasize a rustic upbringing – 'ill-educated, and condemned to a life of servitude' in comparison with Rosalind's courtly sophistication. 'The interaction of their backgrounds serves as an education for the two lovers', he goes on, for although Rosalind 'mocks the uneducated Orlando's verses . . . she learns much from his simple faith and sincerity' as he 'learns sophistication from her' (Bowe, 68–9). The reviewer for *Plays and Players* thought him 'a raw energetic force . . . a "nature's gentleman" . . . a worthy suitor to Rosalind'; the *Yorkshire Post*, too, admired his 'eager virility' and 'sweetly judged love melancholy'. There was for some, however, a danger that this 'warm, sympathetic Orlando' (*SS*, 149) would be 'completely submerged' (*Birm. Mail*) by the remarkable energy of Susan Fleetwood's Rosalind.

If 'vulnerability' might have been one's choice if allowed only one word to describe Tutin's Rosalind, and 'wholeheartedness' to describe Nelligan's, 'restlessness' would certainly have been the choice for Fleetwood's. Michael Billington thought she had 'looks, presence and nimble intelligence' but that she was forced in the wooing scenes into such 'an orgy of leaping, skipping, jumping, pushing and kicking' that he found himself wanting to say 'cool it' (*Guardian*). Much the same response came from Gareth Lloyd Evans, who admired Fleetwood's 'verve . . . breathless charm . . . pleasurable excitement' but 'longed for her to be still a little'; Rosalind's language has its own life, Lloyd Evans goes on, and 'doesn't need thrusts and pulls and nods and wallops from the actress' to illustrate it (*SA Herald*). For Robert Cushman, Fleetwood's inability to relax meant that 'the heart of both the character and the play is by-passed' (*Observer*). It was certainly one of those performances that are so committed and energetic as to be in danger of causing some members of an audience to switch off. Returning to it in the Aldwych transfer, Cushman wrote that Fleetwood 'spills herself vocally and physically full-length across Rosalind' (*Observer*); Irving Wardle, watching her performance at Stratford, thought that she personified 'the speed and emotional generosity' of the production (*Times*) – the phenomenon remained the same, only the reactions differ. John Barber confessed that he had anticipated that Fleetwood, 'with her great vulnerable countenance and passionate expressiveness fashioned by nature for tragic parts' would endow Rosalind 'with too much emotion altogether'; in the event he found her performance 'superb' (*D. Telegraph*, reviewing the Aldwych transfer). J.C. Trewin, too, was won over and thought her 'the most persuasive Rosalind I have known in four decades' – which goes back to Edith Evans – 'fathoms deep in love' and 'ruling her Arden with a gaiety' that he found irresistible (*SQ*, 164). B.A. Young, on the other hand, annoyed early on by Rosalind's stealing Le Beau's hat and capering about with it, complained that she 'doesn't make Rosalind a serious girl at all' (*FT*). And so the divided response continued.

It was in the wooing scenes that the energies of the performance were at their most flamboyant, with Rosalind 'positively aching for love and for life' (*Oxf. Mail*) and 'in such a breathless coming-on disposition that she itches to get her hands on her pupil', Orlando (*D. Telegraph*). Roger Warren discusses Fleetwood's changes of mood in the scene of Rosalind's first forest meeting with Orlando:

> After 'love is merely a madness' [3.2.388], for instance, she and Celia collapsed on the floor in gales of laughter; but in seconds Rosalind has modulated to a rapt, still 'yet I confess curing it by counsel' [392–3]; she held the mood as she described her love cure, dissolved into mockery again at 'sound sheep's heart' [411] and then reverted to a still, infinitely tender delivery of the line 'I would cure you, if you would but call me Rosalind …' [414], contrasting with Orlando's brash gaiety and Celia's alarm and concern. (*SS*, 150)

John Bowe describes Terry Hands's prescription of 'circles' for the wooing scenes: 'histories and tragedies have straight lines, comedies and romances have circles. If you had a map of our footprints in the two major scenes of the second half, you would have a picture of spirals all over the stage' (Bowe, 73). The mood of the second wooing scene, Charles Spencer thought, was 'at times positively randy' (*New Standard*, reviewing the Aldwych transfer), an allusion, no doubt, to the moment when Rosalind, having borrowed Celia's shawl, wrapped it round her waist like a skirt and then let it fall to the ground. 'Orlando ... so involved in the game ... imagines he sees his love's body. This is too much, the game must cease and he must leave, but Rosalind torments him and makes him promise to return' (Bowe, 74). The shawl had earlier been used, following the wedding, as a blanket in a 'pretend' game of a married couple in bed, squabbling over shares of the bedclothes (see Figure 23) and had also done duty as a toreador's cloak in a mock bullfight chase around the upstage trees, two of his poems, rolled up, making Orlando's 'horns' (4.1.57) – 'so much movement and effervescence ... the abiding impression is of children enjoying themselves on an afternoon in the forest' (*Country L.*). The promptbook records that on 'Come, woo me' (65) Rosalind 'picks a flower' and 'puts it between her teeth'; at 'like enough to consent' (66) she 'lies on her back' and 'opens her legs'.

Beneath all the exuberance, however, there was danger. Michael Billington, returning to the production at the Aldwych, wrote of Fleetwood's 'wild, ardent' Rosalind conveying 'a real sense of frightened excitement' in the presence of Orlando (*Guardian*); Charles Spencer (also at the Aldwych) described her voice switching 'from the ludicrously butch tones of her disguise to the trembling vulnerability of a woman lost for the first time to the wonder of love' (*New Stand.*); and Irving Wardle (at Stratford) described the 'drugged adoration' with which she kissed the ground where his feet had stood after his exit (*Times*). John Bowe picks up these ideas when he writes that Orlando, too, 'has been

FIGURE 23 In front of the towering tree trunks of Farrah's Arden, Celia (Sinead Cusack) watches in appalled disbelief as Orlando and Rosalind (John Bowe and Susan Fleetwood) fight over their shares of the 'blanket' (Celia's shawl), one of the games of joking premonition of married life that followed their exchange of vows. (4.1, 1980)

wounded deeply' by Rosalind's game-playing, yet at their next meeting (by which point he has been wounded physically too)

> she goads and teases him about his love until he can bear it no longer: 'I can live no longer by thinking' [5.2.50]. We felt that it was at this point that Rosalind and Orlando learn their greatest lesson. He realizes that to dream is no substitute for reality and she realizes that it has been very wrong to play with Orlando's emotions.
>
> (Bowe, 74)

From here the play therefore moves rapidly to the quartet in which 'they intone their devotion to each other' (Bowe, 74) and to

FIGURE 24 Rosalind (Juliet Stevenson) encourages Orlando (Hilton McRae), both of them dressed androgynously in white, to examine his own reflection, and hers, in the downstage watercourse. A moment later she will move away, leaving him to lament the absence of Rosalind. (5.2, 1985)

Rosalind's return as herself – which are the subject of later chapters.

'I can live no longer by thinking' was a decisive moment also in the 1985 production. The promptbook records Orlando's kneeling downstage centre as he said the line, Rosalind behind him with her hands over his eyes. She then removed her hands and stood behind him. Both of them looked at their reflections in the downstage watercourse during a long pause (see Figure 24) –

another manifestation of the production's pervasive concern with the search for identity – before she skipped away to leave him bewildered and isolated. Roger Warren described him glimpsing 'through eyes dimmed with tears, the features of Rosalind, not just of Ganymede', so that his later cry 'why blame you me to love you' (5.2.106) powerfully caught 'the underlying emotional intensity' of the situation (SQ, 117). Many thought that emotional intensity had been a long time coming in this production. Michael Billington remarked that there was never any sense that Juliet Stevenson's Rosalind had been 'poleaxed' by Orlando from the start, as most recent Stratford Rosalinds had; she was 'edging her way into a relationship' and not until 'I cannot be out of the sight of Orlando' (4.1.205–6) 'did one hear the true voice of passion' (Guardian). Identically dressed in loose-fitting androgynous white suits (hers with red braces and cummerbund), Stevenson's Rosalind and Hilton McRae's Orlando explored in their courtship scenes the Jungian concepts of 'animus' and 'anima' and the search for each in the other. Nicholas Shrimpton thought Stevenson 'touching in her vulnerable moments but desperately unsure when she was required to be witty, flirtatious or high-spirited' and wondered whether 'the psychological lumber she was required to carry in this production was too much' (SS, 200). Many other reviewers reacted similarly. Nicholas de Jongh thought there was 'too little sense of erotic love breaking bounds and surprising Rosalind' (Guardian, reviewing the Barbican transfer), Michael Coveney (also at the Barbican) wrote of a 'blithely intellectual reading of Rosalind' (FT) and Michael Ratcliffe referred to the 'cerebral chill' of the evening, with Stevenson's performance 'selflessly concealed behind a mask of reticence until later than is customary' (Observer).

This was, of course, precisely the intention. Stevenson herself writes (with Fiona Shaw, her Celia) of the importance and the intensity of Rosalind's friendship with her cousin. It is a long time before this is fully displaced by her love for Orlando, and there is pain and some sense of guilt in the process. The division between

the cousins is not really clear until their dialogue at the beginning
of 3.4, by which point Rosalind, wholly taken over by 'the agony
and vulnerability of the lover', is no longer 'picking up on Celia's
wit and word-play', while an uninvolved Celia 'resorts to under-
cutting' (Shaw and Stevenson, 68). It was not, therefore, until the
second forest wooing scene that a Rosalind fully committed to her
love for Orlando was observable. Here she was

> free to articulate her own doubts and fears, and to discover and
> challenge all Orlando's preconceptions and resistances on the
> subject of women, sexuality, and marriage ... pushing him to limits
> so dangerous that he is forced to extract himself from the scene, and
> departs.   (Shaw and Stevenson, 69)

Of the erotic charge in this dialogue there was no doubt. Irving
Wardle writes of Stevenson succumbing 'to an erotic spell that
comes over in great waves of musky intoxication' (*Times*). He is
here describing the Barbican transfer; at Stratford earlier he felt
that he had never seen this scene 'played with more erotic force, or
... the mock marriage take on such sacramental qualities' (*Times*).
The promptbook records Rosalind and Orlando rolling on the floor
together after 'woo me, woo me' (4.1.65) and leaning together 'as
if to kiss' on 'take thee Orlando for my husband' (130–1); but
instead they turned to look up at an increasingly embarrassed and
exasperated Celia, her presence justifying Stevenson's remark that
without it 'Rosalind might not be able to trust herself alone with
Orlando' (Shaw and Stevenson, 67). (The only kiss in the scene was
in fact a shy little peck at Orlando's departure.)

The kiss aborted, a little dance took its place, the promptbook
recording Orlando's taking Rosalind 'in a "Come Dancing" grip'
and swinging her round in a little waltz on 'For ever, and a day'
(137), with a sharp change to a 'tango throw' when she says that
'the sky changes when they are wives' (141). Samuel Crowl
remarks on the juxtaposition of 'the romantic waltz and the jarring
tango' as 'a perfect physical expression' of Rosalind's realization, in
this moment of 'most intense romantic awareness', that 'life is not

always ... to be lived at such heights of rapture' (Crowl, 139). The same sorts of mood-swing had emerged in the earlier dialogue, with Rosalind's remembrance that 'men have died from time to time ... but not for love' (101–3) profoundly touching in its intensity of regret. Irving Wardle wrote of the larger dance structure of the scene, with Rosalind 'continually breaking away from Orlando to repeat the process of approach. Choreographically it is brilliant ... emotionally it is spell-binding' (*Times*, reviewing the Barbican transfer). The production had delayed the emergence of Rosalind's full romantic commitment, but from this scene onwards, even the rather dubious Michael Ratcliffe conceded, Stevenson 'gloriously took command of all the other characters and, as Rosalind should, of the entire play' (*Observer*).

From the restlessness of Fleetwood's Rosalind and the reticence of Stevenson's, Stratford moved in 1989 to the breathless adolescence of Sophie Thompson's. Her disguise as Ganymede began as a cap, waistcoat, and scruffy trousers (see Figure 12) but was later a pair of baggy shorts and a T-shirt (both too big for her), a pair of pumps and a Christopher Robin hat. The outfit gave her a waif-like air and an aspect of youthfulness that had most of the unsympathetic reviewers reaching for the epithet 'schoolgirlish'. Michael Billington, adding to his *Guardian* review in *Country Life*, put it down to the direction of a 'hyperactive' production: 'she is forced to deliver every line with a festive sportiness as if she were the life and soul of the Arden Junior Lacrosse team'. Peter Kemp thought her 'a gamesome oddball in short pants, visually reminiscent of the Clitheroe Kid' (*Independent*) and Nicholas de Jongh, reviewing the Aldwych transfer, called it a 'larkish, gamey performance' that ran the 'gamut from bawling declamation to doleful quaver' and made it understandable that Jerome Flynn's 'morose' Orlando 'would rather be elsewhere' (*Guardian*).

There were more sympathetic voices, however. Hugo Williams thought that Thompson, 'short, knock-kneed, Chaplinesque', 'triumphs by radical conviction and wholeness'. 'She uses up the stage like an excited child, circling and mocking the men in her ungainly outsized clothes ... Orlando is wise to stand still and take his medicine with a good grace'. And, he concluded, 'though never luminous, she is finally lovable' (*S. Corresp.*). Michael Coveney thought Thompson's performance 'a personal triumph for a Stratford début' and praised the 'darting radiance' and 'quixotic charm' of 'a blazing comic personality' (*FT*), while Christopher Edwards was struck by the 'great presence ... packed into her tiny frame' and the energy of this Rosalind's desire to 'laugh, send people up, take the mickey' (*Spectator*). It was the quality of excited and risky improvisation that I remember most clearly about the performance. As Thompson herself wrote:

> I think the audience should see clearly that Rosalind does not know what will happen. But she does see that she has undreamt-of opportunities – and suddenly it all comes flooding into her mind. She's playing a dangerous game: not only can she discover things about his love, but her own as well. (Thompson, 81)

The 'lack of poise' in comparison with the 'self-assured' Celia of Gillian Bevan, about which John Gross complained (*S. Telegraph*), derived from precisely this conception: there was something almost hopelessly committed – 'difficult not to like and trying a little too hard' I put it at the time (*SQ*, 493) – about this Rosalind as she rushed around Jerome Flynn's simple, still, slightly bewildered Orlando. One reviewer called her 'querulous' (*Yorks. Post*), which doesn't seem quite right to my memory, though anxiety and tension, and perhaps something occasionally near to desperation, were certainly discernible. Stanley Slaughter caught the mixture of attributes well when he wrote of her as 'in turns cajoling, over-confident, street-wise, and with child-like vulnerability' (*Birm. Post*, reviewing the Barbican transfer). That sense that it was all rather precarious is important. Thompson describes a kiss that occurred in the discussion of orators (4.1.70–4): 'He kisses me ... We were up against the left-hand side of the proscenium arch, and we wanted it to be somehow dangerous, with Rosalind cornered and her cover in jeopardy' (Thompson, 82).

In contrast, the gentle little kiss, of which she was in charge, that followed the wedding promises (during which Orlando had presented her with a bunch of flowers) seemed to suggest that the risks had been passed and that plainer sailing lay ahead. For much of the evening, however, this had been a Rosalind playing with emotions over which her control was extremely fragile.

The childlike, anxious Rosalind of 1989 was followed by the much more poised version of the role presented by Samantha Bond in 1992. With her 'trousers cut to emphasize her femininity' and her 'brief bursts of breathy ecstasy', this was a Rosalind who seemed to David Murray altogether unconvincing in her Ganymede disguise; Orlando 'would have to be a fool to be taken in' (*FT*). Charles Spencer's assessment of the disguise was precisely the reverse: Ganymede, for once, he thought, 'really does look like an adolescent boy', so that it was possible to 'understand why Orlando fails to recognize her' (*D. Telegraph*). Kate Buffery took over the role late in the Stratford season and played it during the Barbican transfer where Peter Roberts thought she translated 'so perfectly' into a boy that 'she misses out on that quality which the truly great Rosalinds like Vanessa Redgrave had of the mask slipping and femininity coming through' (*Stage*). These three comments nicely capture the impossible problem for the player of Rosalind/Ganymede: to please all of the critics all of the time you must be very convincing indeed – but not, of course, too convincing. Lindsay Duguid summed it up in a description of Bond's Rosalind as 'wholesome and pert with her slightly husky actress's voice and her gamine gestures (legs apart, arms akimbo, hands in pockets, and so on). The English actress playing Rosalind is a gender all her own' (*TLS*).

Samantha Bond, as Jack Tinker said, 'is an artist of power, wit and daring' (*D. Mail*); he, and many others, were 'bewitched' by her Rosalind. Benedict Nightingale admired her 'self-mocking wit and intelligence' (*Times*) and John Gross thought her 'intelligent and deeply appealing' (*S. Telegraph*). It was the movement between a jaunty exuberance and an introspective seriousness that I found most striking (*SQ*, 348): 'delightful comic flair with a lovely quality of pensiveness', Paul Taylor called it (*Independent*); 'the right mixture of playfulness and sudden glimpses of deep feeling' was Charles Spencer's phrase (*D. Telegraph*); the ability to 'mock her own unfolding sensuality while trying to understand it' was John Peter's formulation (*S. Times*).

For many, however, the performance lacked the appropriate context – or as the *Birmingham Mail* more simply put it, the 'strength and depth' of Bond's acting was the only worthwhile thing in the production. There was something a little less than magical about the relationship with Peter de Jersey's Orlando – certainly Nicholas de Jongh was not alone when he missed a 'sense of ecstasy' between 'this slightly earthbound couple' (*E. Standard*) and wondered whether the elaboration of the set in which they had to perform demanded an 'ardour' which they could not supply (see Figure 25). Benedict Nightingale enquired (a little sardonically) whether Rosalind's passion for Orlando 'could perhaps be stronger' (*Times*) and Garry O'Connor watched the two of them 'tug on their braces, but fail to ignite mutual attraction' (*Plays & P.*). John Gross, however, discerned a 'tender eroticism' in the wooing scenes (*S. Telegraph*) and Terry Grimley a 'moving immediacy and simplicity' about them, 'poetry floating on a reservoir of scarcely concealed emotion' (*Birm. Post*). Even these more positive comments, though, suggest something discreet, if not underpowered, and Paul Lapworth was surely right when he decided that Bond's 'best moment' was 'her gentlest', when, as Orlando tells her that he can 'live no longer by thinking' (5.2.50), 'she realizes the game is no longer bearable and she must hazard her real self again' (*SA Herald*); from this the production moved into what Peter Holland saw as its revelation of the 'pain and sadness' of love (*SS*, 180) in the quartet of 5.2 (see chapter 6).

If there was a certain lack of charge between Bond's Rosalind and de Jersey's Orlando, there was rather less when Kate Buffery took over. This was a Rosalind of cool grace, seemingly always in control of her own emotions and of the situations in which she

FIGURE 25 'I will speak to him like a saucy lackey': Rosalind (Samantha Bond) crosses the little rustic bridge that was a feature of Johan Engels's Arden, while Celia (Phyllida Hancock) hides beneath it and Orlando (Peter de Jersey) lies, dropped-acorn-like, beneath a tree to which one of his poems is still attached. The photograph makes clear the high degree of naturalism of the steeply raked set. (3.2.290–1, 1992)

found herself. Suave and elegant, she suggested to Jack Tinker, when he went to see the Barbican transfer, a 'sly intelligence' that contrasted curiously with the 'impetuosity' he remembered from Bond's performance (*D. Mail*); no one, rightly in my memory, now remarked on Rosalind's vulnerable emotions being glimpsed under the Ganymede disguise. In the same production (and with the 'usual moves') it was instructive (yet again) to be reminded of the breadth of the interpretative options.

The kisses which, in immediately preceding Stratford productions, had become more or less inevitable in the second wooing scene (4.1) were eschewed in 1992; they were back in 1996 when Niamh Cusack and Liam Cunningham played Rosalind and Orlando. There was almost a kiss on 'How if the kiss be denied' (4.1.75), Rosalind kissed Orlando, briefly and to his mild surprise, when she took him for her 'husband' (131), and there was a long, mutual kiss (marked as a 'snog' in the promptbook) on 'if thou wert indeed my Rosalind' (186–7). Russell Jackson noted that 'in the early performances there did not seem to be any suggestion that he might be more than momentarily puzzled to find himself kissing a boy. Later in the run a "take" was inserted to register his confusion' (*SQ*, 209).

It is conceivable (though changes in response to reviews are rare) that this change was effected, directly or indirectly, by the widespread sense that the production had failed to respond to the sexual ambiguity of the scenes. With her long blonde hair and Elizabethan pantaloons (see Figure 26), Niamh Cusack remained 'obstinately in female terrain' (*E. Standard*), 'unequivocally feminine' (*Guardian*), a judgement with which Russell Jackson concurred. One reviewer even went so far as to suggest that Liam Cunningham's Orlando was 'ahead of the game' (*What's On*, reviewing the Barbican transfer), a mistaken (I'm sure), but perhaps understandable, perception. For here again was a version of the relationship between Rosalind and Orlando that not everyone found satisfactory. Many reviewers thought Cunningham rather too old for Orlando. David Murray (*FT*) found his range too

FIGURE 26 Celia (Rachel Joyce) observes – as she lurks among the upstage metal poles that represented trees in Ashley Martin-Davies's Arden – the efforts of Niamh Cusack's Rosalind to make Orlando (Liam Cunningham) share her awareness of the complexities of love. (4.1, 1996)

limited and Robert Hanks thought he didn't 'learn anything' in the wooing scenes (*Independent*) – which, according to Russell Jackson, was not his fault, since Cusack played 'Rosalind's delight in her own freedom to be in love, rather than some more tentative and testing game of "educating Orlando"' (*SQ*, 208).

The discontent, however, was far from universal. Karen Harbridge found Cunningham's Orlando 'proud, exuberant, energetic' (*E. News*); Charles Spencer thought Cusack's 'a beautifully warm, vulnerable, heart-catching performance' (*D. Telegraph*); and for Michael Coveney she was 'the sweetest and most unselfishly sexy Rosalind in ages' (*Observer*). My own response, too, was largely positive, both to Cusack's 'splendidly vital, unselfconsciously sexy, intelligent, and touchingly vulnerable' Rosalind and to the 'manly dignity' of Cunningham's 'amiable' (if 'more mature than the text really supports') Orlando (*SS*, 205). The individual performances were excellent; to watch them again on the archival video, however, is to reinforce a memory that there was something about the relationship between Rosalind and Orlando that made it seem just a little short of emotional charge.

That was again the case when Alexandra Gilbreath and Anthony Howell played the lovers four years later. Michael Dobson formed the impression that Rosalind 'might tire of this stooge-like and faintly prudish Orlando, handsome though he was, a good deal sooner than he of her' (SS, 273) and Paul Taylor missed any sense of 'erotic charge' between the couple; instead, he thought, Gilbreath played a relationship with the audience, 'tipping the wink that the character's in a tried-and-trusted theatrical convention' (*Independent*). The problem was only partly that there was 'no sexual electricity whatever' between Rosalind and Orlando (*S. Times*); more important was the fact that the set and costumes (see chapter 2) so dominated attention that excessively demonstrative playing was required. Gilbreath thus 'fell back on trying charm' (*Indep. Sun.*) and was driven to 'pummelling and winking' (*Observer*), to 'doing laps around the stage' (*SQ*, 109) and to kissing tree trunks and biting cushions 'to convey her headlong ecstasy' (*Guardian*). This was immensely frustrating and disappointing, for here, potentially, was a splendid Rosalind from a 'naturally endearing actress' (SS, 272), and post-war Stratford has never (as we have seen in the Introduction) given a second chance in the role. It was, thought John Peter, as if 'she had been brought to the edge of the magic forest called dangerous love and then not been encouraged to go any further. Knowing her work in other plays I wonder if she felt as cheated and frustrated as I did' (*S. Times*).

It was not, of course, entirely disappointing – there was too much energy and infectious joy about Gilbreath's performance for that – 'refreshingly frank' Peter J. Smith called it (*Cahiers Elis.*, 79). Benedict Nightingale admired her 'wickedly witty ... responsiveness and volatility', her 'leaping and whooping' up the tree on which Orlando has carved her name, then 'collapsing in a vulnerable heap when he fails to keep a date', and wondered whether she might not be 'the most delightful and touching

Rosalind since Vanessa Redgrave' (*Times*). He also praised her success 'in the trickiest task – to convince you that, though fly and flighty, she is also "fathom deep in love"' (4.1.196). That was, indeed, a powerful and moving moment as she confessed her love to the cousin who was now so conscious that their friendship would never be the same again, the catch in Gilbreath's voice and the nearness of tears giving it a remarkable emotional rawness. John Gross, for whom hers was the only performance in the production that 'really touches the heart', thought that she might here be 'almost too powerful, as if she were acting in a tragedy' (*S. Telegraph*). My own feeling was that the situation, and the emotional breadth of the performance, absorbed the moment easily.

'She could afford to relax', Michael Billington had said of the Stratford performance (*Guardian*), and the energy with which she kept sidling up on those enormous Fassett cushions to Howell's reluctant Orlando, the number of occasions on which she came close to kissing him (though their lips never in fact met), the utter commitment of her 'coming-on disposition' that had Celia gasping with apprehension, did often give the impression of an actor working overtime to counter the world she had been given to play in. Things were better when the production moved to the Barbican's studio theatre, the Pit; here relaxation became possible as most of the set was lost and the space was left, as theatre spaces must be, for the players to dominate. Gilbreath's performance now swept 'all objections before it' (*Guardian*) as she rode 'the switch-back of Rosalind's quick-change emotions ... by keeping a tight hold on the unexpected, even unrealised, fervour of her love for Orlando' (*FT*). In this new environment changes of pace and opportunities for introspection became possible, and a 'warmly winning' performance, full of 'moments of repose and romantic reflection' (*What's On*) emerged. What had promised so much in Stratford became indeed 'utterly delightful' (*FT*) – and so took the place that it deserved in this remarkable succession of performances of Shakespeare's most substantial, and in many ways most challenging, woman's role.

5

O THAT I WERE
A FOOL

> O that I were a fool!
> I am ambitious for a motley coat.
>
> (2.7.42–3)

aques's energetically expressed desire for a career in fooling links him with Touchstone within the play in a way that reflects the very obvious external link between them. For these two figures are Shakespeare's principal additions to the extensive gallery of characters he found in Thomas Lodge's *Rosalynde*, his main narrative source for *As You Like It*, and like so many such additions to well-defined source stories (Antonio in *Twelfth Night*, for example, or the Countess in *All's Well that Ends Well*) one seeks in vain in their contributions to the plot for the reasons why the dramatist felt the need to add them.

Both Touchstone and Jaques bring an anti-romantic voice to the highly romantic matter of the play. As Helen Gardner (citing an earlier essay by Harold Jenkins) pointed out long ago, in a lecture to the Theatre Summer School in Stratford on the occasion of the 1957 production (Gardner, 28; Jenkins, 48), Touchstone has a splendid way of reducing matters to a level of commonsense physicality that cuts through swathes of romantic posturing. It is his 'legs' that are weary on arrival in Arden, not his spirits (2.4.2); he could imitate Orlando's rhyming indefinitely (and he proves it), but would not be diverted in so doing from 'dinners and supper and sleeping-hours' (3.2.94–5); arriving at the wedding scene that ends the romance he brings things firmly down to basics by describing himself as joining 'the rest of the country copulatives' (5.4.55); and looking at his watch and responding to the ripening passage of time, he reflects that the destiny of himself and everyone else in the play is to 'rot, and rot' (2.7.27). That sense of human life as a physical process of eating and sleeping, procreation and decay, is no doubt the source of his remarkable allure for Jaques, whose most famous speech offers a similarly loveless physical progression from puking infancy through belly-filled middle age to shrunken and decrepit senility.

Jaques's enthusiastic response to Touchstone lasts the play through, from his arrival at the Duke's table with a triple announcement of his meeting with him and his new scheme of joining Touchstone's profession (which leads to a prolonged altercation with Duke Senior about the role of satire in society), to the final scene when he introduces him proprietorially as a protégé whose career development he is anxious to further: 'Good my lord, bid him welcome ... Good my lord, like this fellow ... Is not this a rare fellow, my Lord?' (5.4.40, 51–2, 103). The reasons why Jaques has so enthusiastic and (as it sometimes appears) so naively committed an interest in Touchstone, who can't even remember his name (3.3.66), are not immediately apparent and need to be considered carefully by the role's performer. The first reference to Jaques labels him 'melancholy' (2.1.26) but too literal and unvaried a response to that epithet (especially in its modern sense) may eclipse, or make inconsistent or incredible, this genuine, and enduring, enthusiasm for the foolery of Touchstone.

Important though the connections are between these two characters, however, the differences that lead one to join the final dance of copulatives and the other to walk out of it, and out of the play, are considerable. For all his mockery of romance, Touchstone is remarkably quick to find himself a partner in Arden and, however carnal his motives may be, he is also the first of the play's lovers to propose marriage. The sight of Silvius's love pangs immediately induces memories of his own: 'I remember when

I was in love I broke my sword upon a stone, and bid him take that for coming a-night to Jane Smile ... We that are true lovers run into strange capers' (2.4.43–5, 51–2). The innocence of his stories of the peascods and the cow's dugs that 'her pretty chopt hands had milked' (2.4.47), even if they are all fictions, could not be more strongly contrasted with what we learn from the Duke about the sexual past of the contender for his motley coat:

> For thou thyself hast been a libertine,
> As sensual as the brutish sting itself,
> And all th'embossed sores and headed evils
> That thou with licence of free foot hast caught
> Wouldst thou disgorge into the general world.
>
> (2.7.65–9)

The syphilitic imagery of that, the shock it administers about the possible origins of Jaques's attitudes and behaviour, and the fierce energy with which he and the Duke debate the question of the satirist's right to criticize his fellow sinners, take the role of Jaques in a direction altogether different from that of the 'motley-minded gentleman' (5.4.40) he so admires.

In an interview for the programme of his 1996 production Steven Pimlott insisted on the importance of a serious age difference between Touchstone and Jaques. 'Faith the priest was good enough, for all the old gentleman's saying', insists Audrey (5.1.3–4), and although this may be explained away (as it is, for example, in Agnes Latham's footnote in the Arden edition) as just a matter of comparatives for the youthful Audrey, a sense that Jaques has a long, puzzling and, in part at least, murky past can certainly add an important dimension to the role in performance. For it is possible to push these two Shakespearean anti-romantic inventions symbolically very far apart indeed, with Touchstone as a youthful life force driven by the copulative urge that gives 'man ... his desires' (3.3.72) and Jaques as an aged memento mori figure, preying on that same life force 'as a weasel sucks eggs' (2.5.12), thwarting Touchstone's desire to be married, insisting on the inexorable progress to senility and decay, and incapable of joining the dance of life and community that ends the play. Only Pimlott's production offered a committed version of that reading, but others have certainly been influenced by it. There is a sense, therefore, that the comparative weight that it gives to its Touchstone and its Jaques is a measure of a production's position on the scale of romantic optimism. *As You Like It* is, in the end, Rosalind's play, but Jaques tries hard to pull it his way and very strong casting of the role may seem to increase the likelihood that he will do so, or give his exit (discussed in chapter 7) from the party she has arranged, and at which Touchstone has been such an enthusiastic presence, so deflating an effect as to seem to undermine the entire enterprise. More particularly, it is possible, and the last half-century at Stratford provides the evidence (particularly in Richard Pasco's performance of the role in 1973), for Jaques so to dominate the attention of reviewers and audiences that even the apparently uncontentious proposition that this is Rosalind's play becomes questionable. A very dominant Jaques may therefore require a particularly energetic Touchstone to provide the counterweight for Rosalind. The post-war Stratford sequence of productions of *As You Like It* offers many variations on these issues.

There were a number of complaints from reviewers of the 1946 production that the Jaques of Julian Somers was understated. The *Stratford-upon-Avon Herald* thought he seemed 'ashamed of his own voice' and the *Stage* felt that he had lost the impetus of the 'seven ages' speech by going 'hiking' in the middle of it. The expectations, sanguine or gloomy, that one takes to the theatre emerge tellingly in the sigh of disappointment from the reviewer for the *Warwick Advertiser* that he 'might have been slightly more amusing' and the sigh of relief from W.A. Darlington that there was about him 'a welcome absence of fantastication' (*D. Telegraph*). It seems clear that this was a performance that avoided the stereotypes for the role: 'his melancholy was not quite an affectation ... he was clearly viewing himself objectively' (*Leam. Spa Cour.*) and he achieved in the process 'a philosophic gravity and eloquence' (*Birm. E. Desp.*) with 'a keen edge' (*Birm. Post*).

The Touchstone admired by this understated (but, it would appear, hardly misstated) Jaques was played by Hugh Griffith. Figure 8 shows him, 'oddly like a magpie in appearance' (*D. Telegraph*), arriving in Arden in traditional fool's costume, the 'cheerful cynicism and comic detachment' admired by one reviewer (*Birm. Post*) perhaps discernible in his facial expression, even in a posed photograph. (Or is one too apt to read in memories of this actor's later performances?) The *Times* enjoyed a Touchstone that seems precisely to have caught the reason Shakespeare added the role to the play, 'blurting out with the air of a ruffled cockatoo those plain facts which it is the whole purpose of romance to refine away'. His 'manner and make-up' gave a 'saturnine' quality to the performance, thought another reviewer: this was thus 'an uncomfortable fool ... perhaps they were less romantic in those days than we like to think' (*Leam. Spa Cour.*). To provide that 'uncomfortable' quality is a function of both characters in the play; it would seem that it was there, perhaps to an extent not everyone enjoyed, in 1946.

Michael Hordern and Michael Bates were the Jaques and Touchstone in Glen Byam Shaw's 1952 production. Hordern's Cavalier costume, with feathered hat and lace-topped boots, may be seen in Figures 20 and 40, the 'Knight of the Rueful Countenance' as one reviewer dubbed him (*Coventry E. Tel.*). This was clearly a rather mellow version of Jaques: when Anthony Quayle took over the role towards the end of the year for an overseas tour his 'suave, supercilious' presentation seemed 'altogether different' from the 'kindly' figure that Hordern had portrayed (*Stage*), transforming it into a Jaques 'in a drawling, casual, who-cares West End style' (*Leam. Spa Cour.*).

That word 'kindly' chimes through many of the accounts of Hordern's performance. He had, thought the *Birmingham Post*, 'quietly but surely revealed ... the full beauty of the character' of Jaques. (It is difficult to imagine 'beauty of character' being among the qualities that one might list for some later interpretations of the role.) For the most part this reading was warmly welcomed: 'a gentle, never bitter melancholy edged with swift, good-tempered wit and grace of speech and movement' (*SA Herald*) and 'dry-humoured but never extravagantly melancholy' (*E. Standard*) are typical reactions. Some, however, wanted a sharper edge. Philip Hope-Wallace regretted that Hordern had missed 'the sardonic, self-accusing note' (*Man. Guardian W.*) and the reviewer for the *Birmingham Evening Despatch* thought the performance 'subdued – the weight is there, but not quite the nimbleness of mind'. 'Mr Hordern', reported *Time and Tide*, 'neither threw away Jaques, for which we were grateful, nor pointed him up with the sardonic wit, for which we were sorry. He was too anxious not to steal the show.' That curious back-handed compliment seems very much to catch the Hordern style; so too does the description of the 'sad, gentle music' of his performance of the 'seven ages' with its 'slight, knowing gesture, the pause, the softening of the voice as he uttered the last words ... a thoughtful and touching masterstroke' (*West. D. Press*). There was much favourable comment on Hordern's delivery of this famous speech, on the 'emphatic authority' that made it seem 'full of brand new wisdom' (*D. Mail*), as though 'we have never heard [it] before' (*Spectator*). Fundamentally it was the humanity beneath the melancholy that attracted attention, 'giving the *poseur* an inner conviction that at all times overlaid and underrode the pose' (*Solihull N.*). To the *Stage* he did not seem 'a man apart from his fellows' – the implication that he might be is itself interesting – 'rather an impartial, curious observer, occasionally retiring within himself to draw his own conclusion'.

Against this humane and wistful Jaques Michael Bates's Touchstone could afford to be 'more frail than usual', his cynicism 'gentle' and his opportunism 'engaging' (*SA Herald*). One reviewer likened him to 'an elderly Edwardian cabby' (*Bolton E. News*); whether this reveals itself in Figure 34 as he accompanies the pages in 'It was a lover and his lass' (5.3.14ff.) – a scene that attracted enthusiastic comment with magnetic regularity – may be left to the reader's judgement. Several reviewers were unconvinced of his courtly employment – 'he looks as if he was born with a straw in his mouth' remarked T.C. Worsley (*New States.*), though the *Stage* thought him 'a sharp townsman, amiable enough to enjoy a good lark with Corin'. Philip Hope-Wallace admired the way Bates 'worked with a will' at the part, but 'did not find much to charm us' (*Man. Guardian W.*) – which recalls Olivia's comment on a 'distempered' response to another member of the fools' union. Others were clearly more susceptible to Bates's efforts: 'a prepossessing pippin of a Touchstone' (*Birm. Mail*) who found in the role 'an unforced note of genial world-weariness' (*D. Mail*).

This makes the widespread critical delight at Patrick Wymark's performance of the role in 1957 all the more remarkable. Terms such as 'charming and untedious' (*Time & T.*), 'actually funny' (*Punch*), 'unusually tolerable' (*Birm. Mail*) are all over the reviews. Muriel St Clare Byrne found him 'a dear man ... the only Touchstone I have ever loved ... no wonder they took him with them to the forest' (*SQ*, 481). The performance clearly made the most of the cheerful energy of the part, giving it a bustling quality of 'russet homespun ... buoyant and hearty' (*Liv. Post*). There were wonderings about whether he would ever have held down a job in court, but the response to the joy and gaiety of the performance is everywhere. Even in a posed, crowd-scene photograph, something of that sense of fun may be discerned (Figure 41). His 'zest and inventiveness', thought Rosemary Anne Sisson, 'electrify every scene', and (like several other reviewers) she picked out as especially funny his 'scantily performed morning ablution in the stream' (at the beginning of 3.2, while the cuckoo called, the promptbook makes clear); it was, she concluded, 'a Touchstone in the George Robey tradition' (*SA Herald*). Even J.C. Trewin, usually apt to evince distemperature about Touchstone, found him an 'amiable buttertub' (*Birm. Post*). All this critical acclaim may possibly have derived from a cunning strategy to flatter the reviewers by actually performing their opinions: Wymark had, thought the reviewer for the *Oxford Mail*, 'discovered in Touchstone the beguiling notion that he realizes that his own jokes are as bad as we have always thought them'.

Whatever the source of Wymark's success, it offers an example of that not infrequent phenomenon of a prominent Touchstone rather eclipsing the Jaques of the same production. Robert Harris played the role in 1957 and gave what the *Sunday Times* thought a 'colourless' performance in comparison with the 'great, daft, proud Jaques of Michael Hordern'. He was 'melancholy enough, but somehow rather flat' (*Stage*), 'wistfully remote and pleasant' (*Birm. W. Post*) and 'strangely unmusical and prosaic' (*Oxf. Mail*). 'Long-haired and grey-bearded' – attributes apparent in Figure 9 – 'he comments cynically on the life around him without for a minute forgetting the humanity of the Shakespearean spokesman', wrote the *Yorkshire Post*'s correspondent, engagingly confident of his ability to identify a 'Shakespearean spokesman' when he saw one. And from the other side of the Pennines the *Liverpool Post*'s reviewer also came south armed with preconceptions about the role: what was lacking, he thought (and perhaps he too was recalling Hordern), in a performance that was 'morbid rather than melancholy', was the necessary quality of 'loveable whimsy'. Rosemary Anne Sisson thought that Harris hadn't decided whether Jaques was 'a cynical commentator or a misguided melancholic' (*SA Herald*), a dilemma that perhaps explains why the profession of schoolmaster was connected with him in a number of reviews. The performance was not, however, without its admirers among experienced reviewers: it avoided the 'operatic' in the big speeches and found the golden mean of being 'dry but not too light' (*Man. Guardian*); it had an 'engaging diffidence' (*FT*) and a 'softly modulated' quality (*E. Standard*); and it was 'wonderfully serene ... and golden of speech' (*Punch*).

The word 'golden' is probably not the first one would choose to describe the unforgettable vocal quality that Max Adrian brought to the role of Jaques in 1961. J.W. Lambert catches something of its quality when he refers to 'the mannered elegance of Mr Adrian's death-rattle voice' (*S. Times*, reviewing the Aldwych transfer). On the television film those rather haughty, rasping tones have a precision and fastidiousness of articulation and a contained exactness and astringency of purpose that demand attention and set him apart from everyone else in the play. (It is so distinctive, indeed, that the forest lord who reports his observations on the stricken deer (2.1.47–57) attempts an imitation.) Every word, every line seem to hit the target with deadly accuracy – and with a wry and indulgent pity for the naivety of those who lack his perception. When he demands 'Which is he that killed the deer?' (4.2.1) one feels the foresters quake in their boots like erring schoolboys caught in mischief by the headmaster. The pleasure in the meeting with Touchstone (and his watch) is relished, the argument with the Duke about the social role of the satirist urgently defended, the tolerant amusement in the absurdities of love in his conversations with Orlando and with Rosalind savoured. This was a Jaques of extraordinary power and intensity, the eyes keen and searching, the beaky nose and little goatee beard seeming to intensify their penetrating gaze (see Figure 27). Had Vanessa Redgrave's Rosalind not been so buoyant and vital the play might have been pulled badly out of kilter; in the event, as Robert Speaight observed, 'his refusal of life was the proper counterpart' of her 'lyrical assertion of it' (*SQ*, 434).

The critical response to Adrian's performance stretched the reviewers' supply of superlatives. His handling of the 'seven ages' was particularly admired: his 'melancholy, cadenced utterance' gave it 'a poignant poetry' (*Oxf. Times*); 'he doesn't nudge us all through it ... but let's it speak for its incomparable self' so that it becomes 'far more profound than usual' (Bernard Levin, *D. Express*); at the end of it he found 'a sudden dreadful insight into approaching senility and the futility of existence' (*Yorks. Post*). On the television film the sadness of it is strongly felt, as though he wishes he did not know it all so well. J.W. Lambert felt he could hardly praise the performance too highly for 'its restraint, its

cankered pathos, its exquisite timing' (*S. Times*). Coming back to it in the Aldwych transfer he wrote of Jaques 'furred like a Muscovite' (as Figure 27 shows) and trailing 'terribly behind him that refusal of joy that is the deadly essence of sloth ... his well-savoured sententiousness never hiding the pain behind the eyes'. That 'Muscovite' appearance led to a number of Chekhovian allusions among the critics, something that looks forward to Richard Pasco's performance of the role twelve years later; but it is Lambert's perception of the way the performance seemed to operate on two levels that catches something of its quality (discernible, too, in the film): 'sad, sad, sad – but a glint of optimism occasionally glistens through the melancholy', wrote Milton Shulman (*E. Standard*, reviewing the Aldwych transfer); and Philip Hope-Wallace enjoyed the 'sardonic, smiling awareness of his own absurdity which marvellously lightens the weight of the part' (*Guardian*, also reviewing the Aldwych transfer). The theatre critic of the *Oxford Mail* kept it simple, but spoke for most of his colleagues, when he labelled the performance 'spellbinding'.

The Stratford Touchstone in 1961 was Colin Blakely, 'surprisingly yet delightfully full of Irish blarney' (*Yorks. Post*), indeed a 'broth of a Touchstone' (*SA Herald*) with 'an impudence that totters on the edge of downfall' (*Middles. E. Gaz.*). Figure 36 catches something of the latter quality in the moment of his splendidly pretentious explanation to Gordon Gostelow's William that 'drink, being poured out of a cup into a glass, by filling the one doth empty the other' (5.1.40–2). The promptbook records him here taking William's hand and putting Audrey's hand into it; then, at 'He sir that must marry this woman' (5.1.45) 'he "pours" Audrey's hand into his own'. The performance was admired for its warmth and matter-of-factness and for its 'mercurial' quality (*Oxf. Times*), but most reviewers eagerly welcomed Patrick

FIGURE 27 (*opposite*) In the furred robes and hat that were part of the generally 'Russian' appearance of the exiled court, Max Adrian's Jaques describes the seven stages of his vision of the human progress from infancy to senility. (2.7, 1961)

Wymark's return to the part for the Aldwych transfer (and the television film). He made Touchstone's 'wholly unfunny' scene with Corin, Philip Hope-Wallace thought, 'not only bearable, but quite charming' (*Guardian*) and gave to the role an 'almost Falstaffian stature' (*Liv. Post*). His arrival in Arden is a wonderful moment on the television film: 'when I was at home I was in a better place' he says (2.4.13–14), with a profound sense that he could say more – a lot more – but knows that at this particular moment that would not be a good idea.

That same moment in 1967 is well caught in Figure 28 – and an unforgettable moment it was too (as I have observed already) as the chubby face of Roy Kinnear's Touchstone expressed a sense of utter disbelief that he had ever allowed himself to be hoodwinked into this absurd, uncomfortable and probably dangerous escapade. And again the swings and roundabouts of the Touchstone/Jaques balance in the play shifted, with Kinnear's Touchstone now attracting most of the attention and Alan Howard's Jaques distinctly less prominent. This was partly inevitable, of course, for Kinnear came to Stratford as a high-profile television comedian and critics were extremely interested in how he would fare in Shakespeare. The performance turned out to be 'a triumph of bonhomie and miscasting' (*SA Herald*) – a frequent verdict and one that D.A.N. Jones in the *New Statesman*, while agreeing that Kinnear was 'very funny', tried to explain: 'his stage personality – a mean, wounded fatso, like W.C. Fields – is quite inappropriate for Touchstone'. Irving Wardle agreed. Touchstone, he suggested, is 'a strong-minded, aggressive clown', while Kinnear is a victim:

> but somehow he manages to recreate Touchstone in the shape of a collapsing stout party ... and scores in nervous approaches to Audrey, in mistakenly patronizing the peasantry, and in ... superb passages of direct address to the audience. (*Times*)

One of these was the long description of the seven degrees of the lie. Hilary Spurling offers a fine account of this moment, and of

FIGURE 28 As he perches precariously on the tree trunks of Timothy O'Brien's forest, the expression on the face of Roy Kinnear's Touchstone makes it clear that he believes deeply that staying at home would have been a much better idea than coming to Arden. Far from trying to help Celia (Janet Suzman, right), as the text proposes, the efforts of Dorothy Tutin's Rosalind, like those of her cousin, are entirely focused on trying to cheer up the jester who was supposed to be 'a comfort' to them (1.3.127). (2.4, 1967)

the performance more generally; the production, she thought, contained 'one masterpiece' in

> Roy Kinnear's madly frustrated Touchstone, perpetually paddling in the rear of his little party as it retreats behind the bushes to peer and snoop and pry; smoothing a grubby cuff with a ponderous courtly flourish to impress the local yokels; summing up the rustic scene – 'Now am I in Arden' – grim stuff – 'the more fool I' [2.4.13]. Best of all is his dissertation on the seven degrees of the lie, from Quip Modest, Retort Courteous, Reply Churlish to a piercing strangled shriek as he flings up his stubby arms in horror at the deadly Lie Direct. Other directors might like to note that if you want to make sense of the gobbledygook of Shakespearean clowns, all you need is a live clown. *(Spectator)*

Reviewer after reviewer points to superb comic timing as the secret of Kinnear's success: 'wickedly accurate verbal timing ... the Touchstone we've often longed for in the long procession of Touchstones with white faces and a secret grief up their motley' (*Guardian*). The performance evoked inadvertent food metaphors in the reviewers: B.A. Young referred to Kinnear's 'recalcitrant pancake hat' (*FT*), J.C. Trewin to 'a face like a crumpling blancmange' (*Illus. Lon. News*), while John Higgins enjoyed the way in which 'retorts drop from his lips like pearls from a fat and blubbery oyster' (*FT*, reviewing the Aldwych transfer). Reviewers' testimony, confirmed by my own memory, celebrates the sheer fun of the performance and its success, sometimes on the lines, sometimes with a sly wink at the audience off them, in setting the house 'on a roar'.

Patrick Stewart took over the role when the production was revived the following year. Respectful mentions of a performance that was 'likeable enough' on its 'note of north-country matiness' (*Times*, *S. Wales E. Arg.*), and that portrayed 'the funny man who is for ever talking shop', 'with a good ear for the dry, throwaway line' (*Birm. Post*, *Liv. Post*), do nothing to disguise the fact that attention had now switched to the second incarnation of Alan Howard's Jaques, those swings and roundabouts between Touchstone and his melancholy admirer again shifting the play's balance. Not that Howard's performance had gone unnoticed in 1967. Ronald Bryden caught something of Howard's tortured Jaques when he described him as 'a white-faced, haunted apparition of walking pain, whose view of the world is amply justified by the Darwinian jungle of slaughter and mating he finds around him' (*Observer*); 'he has', wrote Gareth Lloyd Evans, 'neither the desire nor the energy to tell his thoughts' and is 'sad for lack of real communication' (*Guardian*). This Jaques was far from being an 'old gentleman' (5.1.3–4): Howard was near the beginning of a distinguished RSC career and offered a Jaques 'emerging as the courtier he presumably was, elegant even in rags, young, noble, ridiculously handsome and a far cry from the jumped-up jester to which the character is too often reduced' (*Liv. Echo*, reviewing the 1967 Aldwych transfer). But this was a performance that many found too mannered. Michael Billington described it in the 1968 revival: 'Alan Howard builds up a remarkably complete portrait of a diseased cynic, conceivably suffering from the pox and unable to look anyone squarely in the face'; his 'seven ages' speech became 'an expression of misanthropic disgust ... at times I feel that the part can scarcely support the weight of the interpretation' (*Times*). B.A. Young, reviewing the 1967 Stratford version of the performance, thought he treated the lines 'as if there were a double meaning in every word: thus he says "Signior Love" [3.2.287] with a huge pause between the words, and a long *diminuendo* on the second, giving a suggestion of subtlety quite beyond me' (*FT*). He came back (for the same newspaper) to see the 1968 revival and felt that the 'weakness for slipping king-sized caesuras into his lines at the most unlikely places seems to have grown worse', pointing to a portentous (and in his view meaningless) pause in the phrase 'thy loving voyage / Is but for two months ... victuall'd' (5.4.190–1). Alan Brien, too, thought he seemed to be 'reading into his lines some cryptic interpretation of his own' and dismissed him as 'the most grinning melancholic on record' (*S. Telegraph*). But for every detractor one can find an admirer (Alan Howard's Shakespeare performances were like that), and particularly in the 1968 revival (when the absence of Roy Kinnear had left Howard the Arden world to bustle in) there were many who shared Gareth Lloyd Evans's belief that in its portrayal of a man whom 'fortune has blighted and his own nature soured', this was 'a superbly original performance, disturbing and enlightening' (*Guardian*).

About Richard Pasco's Jaques in Buzz Goodbody's modern-dress production six years later there was no such critical disagreement; here was a performance that came close to Max Adrian's in unanimity of critical acclaim but lacked the earlier production's forcefulness of performance from Touchstone, and from Rosalind, to maintain the play's equilibrium. Jaques thus became the central character of the play – which, as Robert Cushman observed, is odd, 'since he spends his time on the periphery peering at the action with beady distaste' (*Observer*). The Touchstone here was Derek Smith, fighting the uphill battle that Shakespearean clowns often encounter in modern-dress productions. Milton Shulman found him 'a little too determinedly comic for my taste' (*E. Standard*) and Benedict Nightingale felt that the modern dress so exaggerated 'the pitiful nature of his verbal routines' that he became 'an unendurable nuisance' (*New States.*). The reaction of audiences was often very different from that of reviewers, however: his lead singing of the rock version of 'It was a lover and his lass' (5.3.14ff.) was very liable to bring the house down. The check-suited appearance (see Figure 10) recalled the stand-up music-hall comedian – Max Miller came to mind – though there was also a touch of the bookie about him, or of a pantomime Buttons.

What the performance failed to do was to suggest any reason at all why this Jaques should take delight in this Touchstone. 'The mere sight of the amorous Touchstone and Audrey sends a visible shudder' through Pasco's Jaques, remarked Robert Cushman in the *Observer* – and, he added, 'I sympathised; they were played grossly enough for me to contribute a few winces myself'. The adjective that comes up again and again in responses to this Jaques is 'Chekhovian'. Wreathed in cigar smoke he stalked the forest in his crumpled white suit and steel-rimmed spectacles, his greying beard and thinning hair not quite eclipsing the memory of those earlier, more dandyish days (see Figure 29). 'He gazes sourly at the merry-makers', wrote Irving Wardle, 'and delivers his withering lines trembling with something between passion and incipient epilepsy' (*Times*). John Barber thought that the misanthropy of the 'seven ages' had 'never hurt so much: is it an ulcer? drink? a bad love affair? This is a man with one skin too few, for whom the death of a wild animal is painful and the embrace of lovers a living torment. An unforgettable creation' (*D. Telegraph*). Richard David identified 'bitter cynicism fired by disgust with himself' (David, 136) and Michael Billington similarly discerned

FIGURE 29 Richard Pasco's white-suited and bespectacled Jaques, widely regarded by reviewers as a 'Chekhovian' figure, discusses the particular qualities of his own melancholy with Eileen Atkins's Rosalind, while Celia (Maureen Lipman) listens (or perhaps doesn't listen) from her hammock. (4.1, 1973)

'self-hatred that has turned to misanthropy' and found in the 'seven ages' speech 'the repugnant vision of a blinkered cynic' (*Guardian*). J.W. Lambert analysed Pasco's technique in the speech:

> He enriches the Ages of Man speech by making each age a self-contained antithesis, with a twist in the tail. He signals recognition of each predictable folly with a most delicate play of feature, points each deflationary line with a musical accuracy that is a joy in itself.
>
> (*S. Times*)

The accusation of past libertinism from the exiled Duke was deeply disturbing to him, and the bitterness of self-disgust sensed by many reviewers clearly had its origins in a past that gave him constant shame and unremitting pain. Comparing him with one of those 'high-toned derelicts who wander in and out of Graham

Greene', Benedict Nightingale wrote vividly of that moment of confrontation with Tony Church's Duke Senior:

> Half-crazed with old desires and guilts, as contemptuous of himself as of the world, he blinks, twitches, hiccoughs, screws round his shoulders and half lopes, half stumbles across the stage, seizing the Duke by the lapels and scrabbling at his chest ... Words like 'p-pleasure' get sneering emphasis, and every speech is apt to end with a tiny cracked laugh, as if nothing mattered anyway.
>
> (*New States.*)

The 1973 *As You Like It* goes down as the production in which, as J.W. Lambert observed, 'all the laurels are heaped on Jaques' (*S. Times*). But what he judged an 'unqualified triumph' for Richard Pasco left the romantic half of the play with much ground to make up.

There was little question of either Emrys James's Jaques or Alan David's Touchstone pulling the play too much in their direction in Trevor Nunn's baroque operatic version of *As You Like It* in 1977, so dominant was the director's overall production concept. David Nathan found Touchstone 'more melancholy even than Jaques' (*Jewish Chron.*) and Irving Wardle thought that Touchstone was 'lightweight' and that Emrys James 'restricted Jaques to a croaking raven' (*Times*). Touchstone began at court in pierrot mode, silk-pantalooned and white-faced. Michael Billington thought he looked as if he was 'on leave from the *Fol-de-Rols*' (*Guardian*). Leave from court relaxed him somewhat, but the 'sad clown' style was still dominant; Stan Laurel was occasionally invoked in describing the performance, though John Elsom's 'quaint – a harlequin with a dash of Jonathan Pryce' (*Listener*) was an interesting variation on this. Gareth Lloyd Evans thought his performance of the seven degrees of the lie 'a showpiece of intelligent understanding and controlled comic acting' (*SA Herald*). The missing ingredient in most of the responses (and my own memory) is laughter; reviewers are respectful of a serious actor's efforts in the role where ten years earlier they had celebrated a comedian's natural comic qualities.

FIGURE 30 Kate Nelligan's Rosalind sits on the little white stile that was a feature of what John Peter called the 'dotty fairyland' of John Napier's Arden, discussing travel, and experience, and melancholy with Emrys James's Jaques. (4.1, 1977)

Emrys James's Jaques, 'a sardonic Van Dyke cavalier' as John Peter called him (*S. Times*) – and the word 'sardonic' comes up again and again in reviewers' accounts – was strikingly elegant in Arden in his dark velvet suit and lace collar, with a white cloak on occasions (see Figure 30) to add an extra dash. Frank Marcus found him 'strangely malevolent' (*S. Telegraph*); John Elsom thought his pessimism rather 'mannered' than profound (*Listener*). His pock-marked make-up reflected something of the Duke's remarks about 'embossed sores and headed evils' (2.7.67), and a number of reviewers refer to a 'diseased' quality in his appearance and attitudes. He delivered his 'seven ages' speech from right down-stage out into the auditorium as a sort of aria – 'with no suggestion', thought B.A. Young, 'that it has anything to do with what comes before or after' (*FT*, reviewing the Aldwych transfer). One sensed that he was the most cultivated figure in Arden –

taking charge of the music, for example, in 'Under the greenwood tree' (2.5.1ff.) (and conducting Amiens) – but he remained enigmatic and mysterious, 'totally eccentric', as Peter Jenkins put it, in the 'ambivalence of his own world-weary soul, torn between the court and motley' (*Spectator*, reviewing the Aldwych transfer). The same reviewer writes interestingly of his scene with Kate Nelligan's Rosalind (Figure 30): 'instead of mocking him for his explanation of philosophical pessimism, she appears moved by the idea that knowledge and experience could breed such gloom in so commanding a man'. The *Observer* (also reviewing the Aldwych transfer) was far less inclined to take the performance so solemnly, dismissing it simply as 'prototypical Eeyore'. Emrys James's performances were occasionally like that: seeming hugely significant without one ever being quite sure what they signified.

I remember Joe Melia telling me, while he was rehearsing Touchstone for the 1980 production, how dismayed he had been by that first joke about the knight and the mustard and the pancakes: he had, he said, had far better material than that for an act on, I think it was, Yarmouth pier. He made it funny, though, as he made the whole part funny in stand-up, music-hall patter mode, by sheer force of personality: 'brash and likeable' one reviewer called him (*Coventry E. Tel.*), 'professionally funny' another (*SA Herald*); there was certainly an invincible quality to his good humour. He made a sartorial progress through the play from his solemn courtier's garb, complete with tricorn hat (see Figure 4), through degrees of forest informality (in which his increasing lust for Corrina Seddon's uninhibited Audrey was enthusiastically apparent), to finish capering in a grass skirt with sprigs of corn sprouting from his hair for the final wedding scene – 'like a berserk scoutmaster in the forest gang show', as Michael Billington put it (*Guardian*). He flung stones at the dawn chorus for disturbing him, hugely enjoyed needling Corin in the discussion on 'the copulation of cattle' (3.2.78), and turned the scene with William (5.1) into a little 'turn' that delighted a number of reviewers. He looked at Terry Wood's gigantic William (the actor also played Charles the wrestler), then he looked away again 'as if this giant ... were a bad, though quite funny, dream' (*TLS*). When he addressed him it was in tones of abject terror; he finished up on his knees, imploring him to 'tremble and depart' (5.1.56–7); William made a (literally trembling) departure, like a 'bewildered elephant' (*Times*). Jeremy Treglown recalled another piece of comic business (not coming quite so directly off the text):

> He has a good passage of eerie detachment when, having stepped in some Arden Forest sheep-dung and wiped his shoe with one of Orlando's poems, he tears the paper up, scattering the pieces seraphically over the front row, as if he were giving out a limited supply of rare rose petals.   (*TLS*)

At the other end of the spectrum from this ebullience was Derek Godfrey's sombre Jaques, 'a shrewdly calculated, low-key performance ... giving one time to think about this reflective malcontent with the profligate past ... more conscious of his disillusion with the pastoral alternative' (*Country L.*). Michael Billington, reviewing the Aldwych transfer, called him 'an interesting comic Timon, rubbing his hands with glee at the prospect of railing' (*Guardian*). The 'seven ages' speech, an 'engrossing narrative ... round a camp fire at night' (*Yorks. Post*) spoken with 'an impressive dirge-like dignity' (*D. Telegraph*), went little noticed in this performance; it was a piece of business towards the end of his conversation with Rosalind (4.1) that obsessed reviewers (and audiences) and dominated interpretation of the performance. Just before the arrival of Orlando, Jaques opened his cloak, silently inviting Rosalind to come inside it (see Figure 31). She half-succumbed until, as Irving Wardle saw it, 'Orlando arrives just in time and the sound of youthful laughter drives Jaques back into solitude' (*Times*). The promptbook records that at 'good to be a post' (4.1.9) Rosalind moved away downstage from him and he followed; he then forced her slowly to downstage centre and at 'nor the lover's, which is all of these' (4.1.14–15) he 'put his cloak around her with his right arm' and at

FIGURE 31 Derek Godfrey's Jaques attempts to lure Susan Fleetwood's Rosalind inside his cloak. The sexual significance of the moment fascinated reviewers. (4.1, 1980)

the next line brought 'his left arm up, wrapping her in the cloak'. She was pushing herself away from him at 'rich eyes and poor hands' (4.1.23), but was still, as her Orlando put it, 'on the verge of being devoured by Jaques and his cloak' when Orlando arrived, late for his date. 'No wonder she reprimands him', he adds (Bowe, 74). Responses to this moment inevitably focused on its sexual significance and opinions were more or less equally divided: a homosexual Jaques had fallen for Ganymede, and there, in his repressed sexuality, was the explanation for his hidden past and for his melancholy; a heterosexual, and perspicacious, Jaques had seen through Rosalind's disguise and here was his moment of possible awakening. Some stayed on the fence as far as sexual orientation was concerned: 'A semi-retired voluptuary of florid appearance and pronounced paedophiliac propensities', thought Benedict Nightingale (*New States.*); 'a bisexual hysteric who ... makes a prolonged pass at the betrousered Rosalind', decided

Michael Billington (*Guardian*). Robert Cushman was having none
of it:

> Jaques, melancholy cloak outspread, advances on Rosalind in what
> others believe to be an attempt at rape (and who knows whether he
> thinks her a boy or girl?), but which I, in my innocence, took for an
> endeavour to convert her to his own philosophy by enfolding her
> in it.   (*Observer*)

Alan Drury, too, discerned something of 'the manner of a Greek
philosopher' about Jaques's taking 'the boy' to him, though he
thought he was 'much put out' by Orlando's arrival, which
provoked 'a very dignified suggestion of a flounce on his exit'
(*Listener*). It was left to Sally Aire in *Plays and Players* to take the
speculation to its extreme. 'I admit to be being baffled by this
moment', she confessed, 'but I am ... grateful that a positive new
dimension to the play was created by it.' Perhaps, she thought,
'some Hermetic principle was at work ... a welcome into life'. The
portentousness of reviewers, in response to the portentousness (or
even, perhaps, the pretentiousness) of productions, is one of the
little delights of a study of performance history.

In Adrian Noble's 1985 white-silk-dreamland Arden, Nicky
Henson returned to the idea of the white-faced clown essayed by
Alan David in 1977. Inseparable from his umbrella – he emerged
with it from under a dust sheet in the first court scene and carried
it through to the end 'with Astaire-like skill' (*Plays & P.*) – and with
one glove green and one red, he displayed 'dazzling technical skills
of miming and timing' (*TLS*). His 'vaudeville double act' with
Mary Jo Randle's northern punk Audrey was enjoyed by Irving
Wardle (*Times*), and Michael Billington thought that his 'hectic,
manic, white-faced' performance provided the production's 'only
gaiety' (*Guardian*). It was apt to reveal itself in nattily presented
routines, such as the encounter with William (see chapter 6) or
the disquisition on the degrees of the lie. The latter took the form
of a participation game, with the assembled court-in-exile
required to imitate the gestures he created for each degree,

culminating for the Lie Direct in bending over, backs to the audience, and making a loud farting sound. Since this was directed at the auditorium, the delight that audiences took in it always struck me as slightly perverse.

Alan Rickman's 'intelligent, sardonic, even faintly threatening' Jaques (*FT*), rather debonair in his not-of-the-newest dinner jacket (see Figure 11), seemed to Roger Warren to have been 'deprived of either a real court or a real country to rail at' and so to have become 'a mere cipher' (*SQ*, 116). Nicholas Shrimpton, on the other hand, greatly admired the performance and particularly enjoyed the moment when, in response to Orlando's 'He dies that touches any of this fruit' (2.7.99), 'in entire silence he walked steadily from way downstage to the table ... picked up an apple and bit it' (*SS*, 202).

If opinions were divided about the performance overall, so were they over the 'seven ages' speech. Michael Ratcliffe thought it 'left history standing for outrageous contrivance', and imagined Rickman's note to himself: 'speak the most famous lines in the play as slowly as you possibly can to give the impression that you are making them up as you go along' (*Observer*); the *Stage*, on the other hand, felt that 'he had all the necessary surface absurdity of the melancholy man, but, more important, an inner feeling, passion even, always under control, which brings to his "Seven Ages" a special human ... quality'. Discussing his own treatment of the speech, Rickman says that he thought 'there should be occasions during it when Jaques is in real danger of losing control'; describing it as one of the play's 'great arias', he adds 'that's what I went for, anyway, trying also to keep its roots tethered in the scene. Hang on to it and let it go at the same time. A suitably impossible aim' (Rickman, 78). Perhaps the divided response of the critics was inevitable – maybe even welcome. 'It is a speech', Rickman goes on, 'of indelible imagery, shot through with apparent-truths, but it is the speech of an extremist. Seven ages, not one with a glimmer of hope' (78). Jack Tinker (in a phrase not intended as a compliment) described Rickman's Jaques as 'all-seeing, all-knowing, all-wearied' (*D. Mail*, reviewing the Barbican transfer); the qualities seem close, in fact, to the actor's own conception of Jaques as 'very sure of himself and a bit of a mess' (75) of a man who is

> cursed by his own perception ... condemned to wander forever, endlessly trying to relocate some innocence, endlessly disappointed ... [who] starts each scene with his ears pricked and ends it with his tail between his legs ... So you are left with an image of complete loneliness, mirrored, incidentally, by the fact that the actor walks into the wings and twiddles his thumbs while everyone else is dancing. (Rickman, 78–9)

From the languor of Alan Rickman's Jaques in 1985 Stratford moved, in John Caird's metatheatrically driven version of *As You Like It* in 1989, to the dapper sprightliness of Hugh Ross's (see Figure 32). This was a Jaques whose every poised move suggested the actor–manager. With his fedora hat, his cane, and his elegant greatcoat with astrakhan collar and a flower in its button-hole, he stalked through the play condescendingly, sometimes half tearfully, sometimes with a rather acid smile, his crisp articulation contrasting sharply with the regional accents of the Ardenites. The role was doubled with that of a distinctly camp Le Beau, organizer of entertainment at the ducal court, and Jaques's tendency to watch performances in Arden (on occasions from a seat in the front row of the stalls) was one more aspect of the production's commitment to the idea of all the world as a stage. 'Stagily major-domo-ish' Michael Coveney thought him (*FT*); 'not so much a cynic as a ... romantic weeping quiet tears to himself over human ingratitude' was Michael Billington's view (*Guardian*). His version of the 'seven ages', which Peter Holland found 'painful in its acerbity' (*SS*, 163), was notable for taking 'exits and ... entrances' (2.7.141) as cues for a swaggering demonstration of how these things should be done, with an ostentatious sweep from the stage, a long pause, and an elegantly poised reappearance to continue the speech. It was a performance of bravura grace and

dignity, but its studied theatricality offered no clue as to what kind of human being might be hidden within that suave exterior: there was, as John Peter put it, 'great elegance, but not a glimmer of character' (*S. Times*). And that, one felt sure, was the intention.

Mark Williams's Touchstone took his cue from the same theatrically self-conscious source – 'George Robey re-interpreted by Ian McDiarmid', Michael Coveney called it (*FT*). With carrot-coloured hair standing punkily up on end, white spats, an extensive line in mimicry (of others' voices and of farmyard noises) and a liberal stock of red plastic noses (applied to himself and frequently to his interlocutors), he roared through the play with an enormous energy that was spent mainly to suggest the stand-up comedian; here was, the performance was determined to announce, a professional entertainer in a professional entertainment. 'A tour de force of comic frenzy' Paul Lapworth called it (*SA Herald*), though he also found evidence of human contact in what he thought the 'real possessiveness' of his relationship with Audrey.

The move back to a more naturalistic world in David Thacker's 1992 production inevitably shifted its two anti-romantics in the same direction. Michael Siberry (who had played Jaques de Boys in 1980) now presented a Jaques younger and more handsome than usual, fair-haired and tall, in a long dark-blue overcoat kept stubbornly on when all the rest were dressing down for spring. His elegantly gravel-toned voice, moving easily between rasping irony and wistful regret, provided a highly distinctive, idiosyncratic note in the play, cutting through Arden's self-satisfaction. His 'sourness', thought John Gross, 'is the kind that refreshes rather than jars' (*S. Telegraph*), and despite the bitterness that one sensed about him it was clear that life could still surprise him, that he retained glimmerings of an idealism battered and made angry by

FIGURE 32 (*opposite*) At the exiles' forest meal in Ultz's bleak and gloomy Arden, Hugh Ross's elegantly dressed Jaques performs his speech on man's progress through the seven stages of existence to an audience of Clifford Rose's great-coated Duke Senior and other forest lords. (2.7, 1989)

experience. Nicholas de Jongh felt that he had 'far too much flamboyance and vigour to make him seem a natural Monsieur Melancholy', but admired his ability to 'strike discordant notes' in an Arden otherwise too magical (*E. Standard*). David Murray enjoyed his 'connoisseur's delight in Touchstone's fantastications' and thought him 'strong, uncensorious, philosophically detached' (*FT*). The speech on man's seven ages seemed to Benedict Nightingale 'not nihilism, but a reflection of reality ... beautifully staged and finely acted' (*Times*). It was above all the sense that the character had come from somewhere else, had 'gained [his] experience' (4.1.24) to become 'majestically embittered' (*S. Times*) to which one responded. Peter Holland found his anger 'so powerful and neurotic' in its 'isolating desperation' that he was left 'wishing that the grief had been allowed free rein to undercut and trouble further' the world of a production he did not admire (*SS*, 180).

Against a tall, fair, elegantly spoken Jaques there was a round, dark, grumpily Welsh Touchstone from Anthony O'Donnell, beady-eyed and sulky in his forest exile, where his court-jester's costume (see Figure 19) took on a splendid, gnome-like incongruity. 'A surly, officious little Welshman', Nicholas de Jongh called him, 'who sulks his way about the place, glumly fishing and pontificating' (*E. Standard*). As he stood staring grumpily out front on that carefully realistic, actor-unfriendly, green slope of a set, rotund and stubby and distinctly browned off, dark-hair thinning and his hand across his chest, it was impossible not to think of his Arden incarceration (as Michael Billington observed in the *Guardian*) as a bizarrely comic version of a more famous exile on St Helena.

As he made clear in the programme for his 1996 production, Steven Pimlott wanted a real age difference between his Jaques and his Touchstone and he achieved it by casting John Woodvine (who had played Falstaff on the same stage more than twenty years before) as Jaques and David Tennant, making his Stratford début (four years before he would return to play Romeo), as Touchstone. The contrast between them is clear in Figure 33.

FIGURE 33 David Tennant's notably young Touchstone explains to John Woodvine's notably old Jaques his reasons for not wanting to be 'well married'. Susannah Elliott-Knight's Audrey has no option but to wait patiently among the metal-pole trees of the forest. (3.3.83, 1996)

John Woodvine's Jaques, all in black, was a curiously self-contained creature, sulking 'glumly in a void of his own', in Nicholas de Jongh's phrase (*E. Standard*), 'inhumanly detached from the action' in David Murray's (*FT*). He spoke loudly in stern, schoolmasterly, rather know-all tones, without a shadow of doubt about the infallible wisdom of his own opinions. 'All the world's a stage' (2.7.139), he announced, with the added implication 'as anyone with a jot of common sense knows already'. It was tough and clear-sighted and uncompromising, with just a touch of anger on 'mere oblivion' (2.7.165): 'that's the way it is' – and this production's decision to have Adam die proved him (quite unsurprisingly, he clearly thought) right. John Peter admired his 'strong, brooding' quality, but also noticed his detachment: 'he acts on his own and his speeches seem not to be addressed to anyone on stage' (*S. Times*). There was no malice about him, nor any great sense of pain either: this was a Jaques who had come out strongly on the other side of whatever he had been through and who showed himself, in his conversation with Rosalind, genuinely pleased with the 'melancholy of mine own' that his 'experience' (4.1.15–16, 24) had brought him. Charles Spencer referred to his 'lugubrious authority' (*D. Telegraph*) and Benedict Nightingale thought him 'so grimly in love with melancholy that no-one can take him seriously' (*Times*). As well as being the oldest Jaques of this sequence of productions he seemed the most centred, and the least imaginative.

Against the oldest Jaques was set what was almost certainly the youngest Touchstone. Tall and youthfully slender (the very opposite of his immediate predecessor), in a long and extremely elegant motley coat, his Scottish vowels sharp and precise, David Tennant's Touchstone seemed to Charles Spencer 'a manic melancholic who would be quite at home on the alternative comedy circuit' (*D. Telegraph*). In his essay on the performance, Tennant speaks of it in precisely those manic depressive terms, of 'bouncing back' from periods of melancholia (provoked by looking at his watch, for example) to the 'energy of thought … flights of ideas … the inability to shut up' of 'mild mania' (Tennant, 35). Robert Hanks described him as 'lanky, manic, ferociously clever' (*Independent*) and admired his skill in making the jokes themselves really work – something into which Tennant himself had put much effort and in which he took justifiable pride (Tennant, 44). Benedict Nightingale thought his 'corrosively funny' Glaswegian Touchstone, 'tall, swift, obsessively jesterish', the most memorable of recent years (*Times*). The difficult journey to this success, the decision to make him 'mercurial and chameleon-like' if his survival in Duke Frederick's court is to be believable (Tennant, 34), the description of his conversation with Corin as a 'music hall turn' between the 'old pro' and the 'young pretender' in which Corin 'remains splendidly solid and unflappable, arching the occasional eyebrow at Touchstone's excesses' (39), are dealt with in detail in Tennant's essay. Particularly interesting is his discussion of the final scene's dissertation on the degrees of the lie. It is, he thinks, 'an audition: Touchstone, with his new-found wife to support, will need a court to jest in, so the discovery of a benevolent duke in the forest is an opportunity he can't afford to miss out on' (42). His decision not to 'smother' the speech 'with comic business' because 'if an audience were distracted by any gimmickry, it would probably only help to make it sound like so much gibberish' (42) may usefully be set alongside some of the preceding Stratford presentations of this episode.

From an overwhelmingly confident Jaques in 1996 Stratford moved in 2000, in the performance of Declan Conlon, to a Jaques of enormous, and at times rather touching, diffidence. Softly spoken and with a gentle Irish lilt, he offered his version of the 'seven ages' quietly and intimately to his fellow foresters, 'as if sitting on a bar stool' (*SA Herald*); there was something almost apologetic about it, as if he did not want to depress them with its truth. John Peter thought it 'the dullest I have heard in a long and varied life' (*S. Times*), but its unaffected simplicity had its admirers: John Gross thought him 'firm-voiced and strongly etched' (*S. Telegraph*) and Benedict Nightingale admired an appearance that combined 'the New Age ecologist with the Old Testament prophet' (*Times*). 'Yes, I have gained my experience', he told Rosalind (4.1.24), and there was something eager in the way he said it, as though he was content with where he had got and had no wish to upset anyone now he was there. It was an odd reading of the role, and it led to a curiously gentle withdrawal from the final dancing (see chapter 7), but although critics were apt to dismiss it as 'invisible' (*Times*) and 'lightweight' (*D. Telegraph*), it was, in its way, perfectly coherent, and it added another variation to the history of Stratford performances of a remarkably changing role.

Whatever Conlon's Jaques may have been, no one called him 'lugubrious' – the adjective constantly applied to Woodvine's. That, interestingly enough, was the term that was now reached for to describe Adrian Schiller's Touchstone, a figure of 'sheer, dispiriting unfunniness' in Charles Spencer's view (*D. Telegraph*).

Perhaps it was the heavy blow he received from Duke Frederick for a rather clever bit of mimed wrestling (with himself – just before the real thing), that made him so gloomy, but for the rest of the evening his deadpan facial expressions ('Keatonesque lugubriousness' Michael Billington called it in the *Guardian*) and the dispirited tone of his flat 'estuary' accent made it obvious that he was not having a good time in Arden – though it was engagingly clear that Audrey's attractions had their animating effect on him. In keeping with the monochrome of the court, he began in silver and black motley and travelled in this to Arden (see Figures 7 and 13), but by the end of the evening he looked to Benedict Nightingale like 'a cross between a *commedia* Harlequin and your mad granny's patchwork quilt' (*Times*). He got his biggest laugh by screwing up one of Orlando's poems into a ball and 'addressing' it with his shepherd's crook, as though on the first tee at St Andrew's, before driving it impressively into the stalls – an excursion from his lines perhaps partly redeemed by the text-based simplicity of his unfussy (and, indeed, rather lugubrious) account of the inexorable way that disagreements have of sliding from one degree to the next on a slippery progress to the Lie Direct.

Actors over the last half century at Stratford have explored a remarkable range of interpretations and emphases in their portrayals of Jaques and Touchstone, those anti-romantic intruders in the Arden that Shakespeare found in Lodge's *Rosalynde*. Their interaction (and that of the forest's other visitors) with its native inhabitants is the subject of the next chapter.

6

COUNTRY COPULATIVES

I press in here, sir, amongst the rest of the country copulatives, to swear and to forswear, according as marriage binds and blood breaks.   (5.4.54–7)

U nless one indulges in some fairly creative counting at the end of *Measure for Measure* (where every couple one adds to the list seems to increase the irony), *As You Like It* sets the Shakespearean record for the number of couples at the end of a comedy; Lear's wish that copulation might thrive is nowhere more generously answered. Jaques draws attention to the splendidly self-conscious absurdity of it when he decides that 'there is sure another flood toward, and these couples are coming to the ark' (5.4.35–6). Two of the couples come from the world of the court and will return there with the restored Duke; the third couple are 'forest born' and will presumably remain in that literary pastoral corner of Arden where they belong; the fourth, Touchstone and Audrey, offer the play's only example of a pairing of court and forest and are (if Jaques is to be believed – and one not infrequently feels that he isn't) a partnership that is 'but for two months victuall'd' (5.4.191).

As well as Silvius and Phebe, and Audrey, this chapter is concerned with those other forest denizens, William, displaced in Audrey's affections by Touchstone, who was 'born i' th' forest here' (5.1.22), and Corin, who although not personally involved in

167

copulation himself (so far as we discover), is, in Touchstone's wonderful accusation, sinful enough to be getting his living 'by the copulation of cattle' (3.2.78). Beyond this quintet of 'native burghers of this desert city' (2.1.23), and a brief visit from Sir Oliver Martext, 'the vicar of the next village' (3.3.37), everyone on stage in the Arden scenes of *As You Like It* is a visitor to the forest, almost as subject to Jaques's accusation of usurpation as Duke Senior is. Of that other ancient Arden dweller, 'obscured in the circle of this forest' (5.4.34), who has such a powerful influence on the plot by teaching young women magic and converting wicked dukes in the nick of time, performance history must be silent, for he never quite makes it onto the stage; besides, I have written of him elsewhere (Smallwood, 1998).

They are a curious mixture, this quintet, from the high-flown pastoral artificiality of Phebe and Silvius to the down-to-earth agricultural realism of Corin and the archetypal bucolic plodd-ingness of William, and the context they provide for the play's main love affairs has led half a century of Stratford directors of *As You Like It* in many different directions. An obvious question is what to do about accents: are all of them candidates for that theatrical-rural known in the trade as 'Mummerset', or might Silvius and Phebe, in their slain-by-a-fair-cruel-maid artificiality, offer something a little more 'Home Counties' – for Silvius, one recalls, before his head was so hopelessly turned by Phebe, was on the verge of purchasing the 'flock and pasture' from the 'old carlot' who keeps poor old Corin in such poverty (2.4.86). What can seem the hackneyed staginess of 'Mummerset' has led some directors to try the harder sounds of more northerly regions, and a few, examining maps of sixteenth-century Arden, perhaps, and observing that it covered large tracts of what we now call the West Midlands, have taken the plunge and given its natives full-scale Birmingham accents.

There is an obvious temptation to push the lovelorn spine-lessness of Silvius, and the pouting self-regard of Phebe, over the edge along which they hover and down into complete absurdity.

If this is done, however (and it has been, on occasions, in this series of Stratford productions), it will undermine the moment when, just before the final marriage scene, Phebe invites Silvius to tell Rosalind/Ganymede 'what 'tis to love' (5.2.82). The delicately lyrical litany with which he responds provokes a verbal quartet in love's celebration that leads into the pages' sung duet (frequently performed as another quartet with Touchstone and Audrey) on the same theme and prepares the way for the final appearance of the god of marriage himself. These threads are carefully woven into the fabric of the play and need careful treatment, though over the years they have attracted little comment from reviewers, so that evidence of their treatment, particularly in the earlier productions in this sequence, is sometimes sparse.

That is certainly true of 1946, when the only member of this rural quintet to achieve more than passing comment was William, enacted by the young Donald Sinden and more noticed than any William since, most reviewers responding to his 'vivid and effective sincerity' (*Evesham J.*). Muriel Davidson presented Phebe as 'a petulant schoolgirl' and Trevor Barker showed in Silvius 'a fresh sincerity' (*SA Herald*). (Sincerity was clearly in vogue in 1946.) The pages' song of 'It was a lover and his lass' (5.3.14ff.) was 'more closely drawn into the structure of the play ... by the elimination of orchestral accompaniment' (*Leam. Spa Cour.*), an interesting remark in the light of later treatments in both the accompanied and the unaccompanied vein. Touchstone held Audrey in his arms while it was sung – an activity that set a precedent for the future and would be much developed. Certainly not an augury for future Stratford productions, however, was the relief expressed by one reviewer at finding 'a Sir Oliver Martext who was not drunk' (*Leam. Spa Cour.*); this would prove a considerable theatrical rarity.

The pair of catapult-wielding boys (Touchstone's behind among their targets) who sang 'It was a lover and his lass' in 1952, and whose various antics between scenes figure large in the promptbook for the production, drew the attention of reviewers

FIGURE 34 Michael Bates's Touchstone blows himself cross-eyed as he tunes up on the penny-whistle for the pages (Thomas Moore (left) and Derek Hodgson) to sing 'It was a lover and his lass', while Jill Showell's Audrey watches her betrothed's efforts with amused admiration. The scene was ecstatically received. (5.3, 1952)

like a magnet. Figure 34 shows their song, the two of them sitting either side of Michael Bates's Touchstone, who accompanies them on a pipe. These 'two diminutive, cheeky boys ... voices not always dead on the note' (*Birm. Mail*), 'captured the true spirit of springtime' (*Stage*). These pages, together with the 'country sweetness ... all woman, all coquette, clearly drawn and pleasantly delineated' (*Solihull N.*) of Maureen Quinney's Phebe, and the cheerfulness of Mervyn Blake's Corin, with his face 'like a ripe conker' (*Birm. Mail*) and a hat that made him look like a 'senior member of the Home Guard' (*Truth* – and this is years before *Dad's Army*), give a clear sense of the kind of Arden that Glen Byam Shaw was presenting. (The Home Guard hat – hardly Captain Mainwaring's style – is just discernible in Figure 40.) These small parts, T.C. Worsley thought (*New States.*), were all made into stereotypes, 'all *done* rather than acted'; this included Sir Oliver Martext (drunk again, it would lamentably appear), who fell backwards into the stage pond at the end of his little scene. Worsley mentions with pleasure, however, the 'romantic' style of the 'what 'tis to love' quartet (5.2.82ff.); it was the leader of this quartet, when the production was revived in December 1952, who was picked out by the *Stratford-upon-Avon Herald* for particular mention: the young Ian Bannen had risen from the ranks of forest lords to take over the role of Silvius and made him 'rural, romantic and tenderly comic'; his appeal to Phebe, 'Loose now and then / A scatter'd smile, and that I'll live upon' (3.5.103–4), seemed to the reviewer to 'catch at the heart strings with sudden beauty'. Nine years later Bannen would be playing Orlando in Stratford's most celebrated *As You Like It* of the half-century.

Returning to the play in 1957 Glen Byam Shaw unsurprisingly repeated the two-boys-with-Touchstone's-penny-whistle version of 'It was a lover and his lass' and again produced a 'show-stopper' (*SA Herald*). Stephanie Bidmead's 'delightfully vacant' Audrey, twiddling her toes and kicking up her heels during the song, had 'charm much greater than is ordinarily allowed' said the *Liverpool Post*, pointing to a quality that many future Audreys would discover. What *Punch* called Doreen Aris's 'innocently cuddlesome' Phebe (see Figure 35) did not anticipate future performances of the role quite so clearly as Audrey: innocence has not been every later Phebe's most obvious characteristic. Martext's exit on this occasion, the promptbook tells us, was hindered not by water but by one of Audrey's goats, causing him an ignominious flight in the opposite direction. Toby Robertson presented a William who 'gaups and goggles most amusingly' (*Liv. Post*), and J.C. Trewin (and several others) enjoyed 'the falling cadences of the chiming quartet' of lovers (*Birm. Post*) when, in one reviewer's ecstatic response, the 'magic of Shakespeare's music rang with golden tones as Dame Peggy spoke the words with the fervent ecstasy of springtime' (*Oxf. Times*). A little more soberly, Muriel St Clare

FIGURE 35 'I think she means to tangle my eyes': Peggy Ashcroft's Rosalind (centre) turns to Jane Wenham's Celia (right) from the demurely admiring gaze of Doreen Aris's Phebe. Robert Arnold's Silvius stares obsessively at Phebe and Donald Eccles's Corin watches them all with wry amusement. (3.5.44, 1957)

Byrne doubted whether she would ever hear the quartet 'more beautifully rendered' (*SQ*, 480).

The 'charm' admired in Bidmead's Audrey returned with a vengeance four years later when Patsy Byrne received notices such as few Stratford Audreys before or since have enjoyed. 'Beamish ... by Thurber, out of Brueghel' Roger Gellert called her (*New States.*, reviewing the Aldwych transfer), and the adjectives roll out from his colleagues: 'smirking yet coy' (*Liv. Post*), 'picturesquely uncouth without being offensive' (*Glasgow Herald*), 'ripely earthy, genuinely bawdy' (*Oxf. Times*). Her 'cheerfully ugly, immensely mobile face and constantly wriggling body burn with life' wrote the *Leamington Spa Courier*, while the reviewer for the *Warwick Advertiser* was amused by her 'succumbing, with fatuous smiles, to

FIGURE 36 Colin Blakely's Touchstone smirks with a sense of his own intellectual superiority as he uses the hand of Patsy Byrne's Audrey to explain to William (Gordon Gostelow), the 'figure in rhetoric' of drink being poured from a cup into a glass, filling the latter by emptying the former; he first placed her hand in William's, then removed it and put it into his own. (5.1.40, 1961)

the wooing of Touchstone'. Why the performance created such pleasure (a pleasure caught, in part at least, in the television version of the production) was, thought J.W. Lambert, because its 'floppy affection' had about it 'not the slightest trace of comic condescension' (*S. Times*). Figure 36 catches something of its quality, and of the likeable (and frequently noticed) dimness of Gordon Gostelow's William.

Among the rest of the Ardenites in 1961, Peter McEnery's Silvius (another Silvius who would graduate to Orlando: McEnery played the role in 1977) won praise from Geoffrey Tarran for speaking the 'haunting litany of love' in the lovers' quartet 'sweetly and sensitively'; Tarran was also impressed by William

Wallis's Martext, 'a finished study of a worldly, untidy cleric' (*Morn. Adv.*) – he had also, apparently, added poaching to his list of peccadilloes, for the promptbook records his entrance with a dead rabbit. Phebe was beginning her journey away from innocence and 'country sweetness', however: Jill Dixon, thought the *Coventry Evening Telegraph*, had made her 'a nymphette' (a quality perhaps discernible in Figure 37); the *Oxford Times*, more discreetly, found her 'hispanic' and 'exceptionally well spoken'. 'It was a lover and his lass' remained (as the text proposes but not all directors have agreed) an event for two pages, with Touchstone accompanying on the pipe, while Audrey lay in his lap.

Since he gave his Touchstone fresh from success in television situation comedy, it was a surprise to several reviewers to find Roy Kinnear continuing this traditional accompaniment in 1967. 'Roy Kinnear played a most capable penny whistle to accompany "It was a lover and his lass"', wrote Peter Lewis, perhaps a little patronizingly, in the *Daily Mail*. B.A. Young (in the *Financial Times*) enjoyed the performance of his chosen partner, the 'Brummagem Audrey' of one of Frances de la Tour's earliest Stratford appearances – and an early example, too, of one of the many versions of the 'north Arden' accent. Reviewing the Aldwych transfer, the critic for the *Nottingham Observer* was amused by Audrey's 'frustrating sexual spasms' with Touchstone. Susan Fleetwood, a dozen years before playing Rosalind in Terry Hands's production, took over Audrey when the production was revived in 1968 and made her, in J.C. Trewin's words, 'the best and gawkiest of simpletons' (*Birm. Post*).

The modern dress of Buzz Goodbody's 1973 *As You Like It* offered particular challenges in the presentation of Arden's native

FIGURE 37 (*opposite*) Celia (Rosalind Knight), Rosalind (Vanessa Redgrave, kneeling) and Corin (Russell Hunter) watch from behind the tree as Jill Dixon's Phebe, considerably more overt about her sexuality than her immediate predecessors in the role, teases and provokes Peter McEnery's forlorn Silvius. (3.5, 1961)

inhabitants. Silvius and Phebe, in my memory (they go unmentioned by the press reviewers), were rather posh little visitors from the metropolis in pastiche country dress, in sharp contrast to Jeffery Dench's Corin who was, thought J.C. Trewin, 'so oaken-toned that he seems to have got into the wrong wood' (*Birm. Post*) – the remark is intended as a compliment in a very lukewarm review of the production. The *Oxford Mail*, however, liked his scene with Derek Smith's Max-Millerish Touchstone, the two of them sharing sandwiches and 'enjoying each other's jokes like a village wiseacre and a Cockney refugee'. Finding a niche for the 'vicar of the next village' in such an Arden started a move in the direction of high-absurd Martexts that later directors would develop: his 'wedding cakes, "Just Married" signs, and a swinging censer all packed into a white pram' were, Milton Shulman tartly remarked, 'just plain silly' (*E. Standard*).

It was Annette Badland's 'gargantuan' Audrey – as Irving Wardle called her in the *Times* – who drew most of the critical attention as far as Arden's residents were concerned. A 'roly-poly pudding of a girl' (*Berrow's Worcs. J.*), 'built on the lines of a cute heavy lorry' (*E. Standard*), in enormous dungarees for the Martext wedding scene and mini-skirted summer frock for 'It was a lover and his lass', she seemed to J.W. Lambert to sweep away misgivings (about laughing at her) 'by the simple happiness she communicated' (*S. Times*). Kenneth Hurren in the *Spectator* found his misgivings less easily dispersed: 'a bouncing butterball ... determined that we should have fun at her expense. I had none.' It was that kind of production: you succumbed, or you resisted. 'It was a lover and his lass' became a huge rock-and-roll number with a tea-chest bass thudding in accompaniment and a confetti cascade of paper hearts raining down on actors and audience alike. 'We leave in a happy frame of mind, resolved not to put too much weight on such occasional details as left us half-hearted' wrote Herbert Kretzmer in the *Daily Express*: one might add, with Touchstone, 'such a one is a natural philosopher'.

FIGURE 38 'Dresden china shepherd and shepherdess': the begartered and self-pitying Silvius of Ian Gelder pleads in vain with the pert and skipping Phebe of Lynsey Baxter. (3.5, 1977)

From rock and roll in 1973 the play jumped in 1977 to pastiche baroque opera, but still to another big production number for 'It was a lover and his lass', audience participation invited in the 'Hey ding a ding' chorus, 'all the foresters coming on for a knees-up and spring leaves fluttering from the flies' (*Guardian*). The song also gave extra space, 'very touchingly' thought Robert Cushman (*Observer*), for a bit more courtship between Celia and Oliver, something that would be used in later productions as a way of supporting the 'no sooner looked, but they loved' (5.2.32–3) nature of their partnership. After going rather unnoticed in 1973, Silvius and Phebe sailed back into critical prominence in 1977. Dresden china figures was the comparison most frequently made, although Phebe as Little Bo Peep was also favoured. Figure 38 makes clear whence these comparisons come. Ian Gelder's Silvius was said to glow 'from sheer delight in the presence of his perverse lass' (*D. Mail*), though the photographer seems to have caught instead a moment of self-indulgent self-pity. His promise, just before the appearance of Hymen, that he will marry her 'though to have her and death were both one thing' (5.4.17) 'drew one of the biggest laughs of the evening' when the production moved to Newcastle and earned 'a pat on the arm and an understanding look from Orlando' (*Newcastle J.*).

Yet another variation was found for Sir Oliver Martext (whose part must have concentrated a higher percentage of directorial ingenuity into its five lines than any role in Shakespeare). He became, in keeping with the mid-seventeenth-century setting, a singing embodiment of Puritan zeal who gave out religious pamphlets. The promptbook preserves several bits of extra text that were added to his meagre role, including a little wedding hymn in several stanzas, of which the following are perhaps a sufficient sample:

> O God in whom we trust
> Look on these twain with grace
> Who leave their filthy thoughts and lust
> To come before thy face.
>
> Keep them from pleasures vain
> From dancing and from feasts,
> From all adulteries profane
> And filthiness with beasts.

After the prominence of recent Audreys, Ann Holloway's performance of the role seemed 'subdued' (*Oxf. Mail*), partly, no doubt, because it was heavily subjected to the production's constant desire to metamorphose itself into an opera. William, on the other hand, in David Shaw-Parker's performance, seemed to Robert Cushman 'unnervingly confident' (*Observer*). The full-company version of 'It was a lover and his lass' was the occasion for the transformation of the stage to spring, with the prompt-book full of cues for flats and flying pieces (in the production's pastiche seventeenth-century style) of greenery and blossom: 'a species of greenwood-tree transformation scene ... a full-scale showpiece', J.C. Trewin called it (*SQ*, 216).

'What a good actor the RSC has in Tom Wilkinson', wrote the same critic prophetically of the then-unknown young man playing Corin in Terry Hands's 1980 production of *As You Like It* (*Birm. Post*, reviewing the Aldwych transfer). 'A fine figure of grizzled common sense' Alan Drury called him (*Listener*). The player of Corin always has an interesting choice about when that 'grizzled common sense' starts to be a performance of the attribute, with the purpose of winding Touchstone up, rather than its reality; in most performances there is a twinkle in Corin's eye some little while before he solemnly announces his belief that 'a great cause of the night is lack of the sun' (3.2.27–8), and this was certainly the case with Wilkinson.

'Bo Peep' was again a frequent response to Julia Tobin's Phebe, but this was not a Dresden china-doll version of the part but rather 'a spiky little fugitive' from the nursery rhyme (*SA Herald*), 'miraculously susceptible to the charms of Ganymede' (*Country L.*). During her musings on those charms she ran her fingers suggestively up and down her shepherd's crook; later she used it to haul Allan Hendrick's 'gormless' Silvius offstage (*Yorks. Post*). Silvius, too (in the absence of sheep), found other uses for the stage shepherd's standard prop: 'he goes around with his shepherd's crook behind his neck ... holding on to it with both hands as if crucified' (*Observer*). The Audrey of Corinna Sedden returned the role to the enthusiastic sexiness of tradition – 'delectable' John Barber thought her (*D. Telegraph*, reviewing the Aldwych transfer) – with a good deal of scantily clad romping with Joe Melia's increasingly *déshabillé* Touchstone. Terry Wood's physically menacing, gentle giant of a William (doubled with Charles the wrestler) was the feed man for Joe Melia's comic-turn treatment of their meeting (see chapter 5). He obeyed the requirement that he 'tremble and depart' (5.1.56–7) with an exactness that found a laugh in the simple detail of the text, 'disappearing into the gloaming uncontrollably shaking from head to foot' (*FT*, reviewing the Aldwych transfer).

Yet more directorial inventiveness was lavished on Sir Oliver Martext, who was thought by reviewers to be swatting flies with his holy-water brush, though the promptbook records that he was using it to 'fight off an invisible demon'. He rang an altar bell with much energy and scattered confetti frenetically. 'It was a lover and his lass', however, was much simplified in comparison with the two preceding productions; it was sung by two boys in an unfussy setting as part of a cheerful little comic routine with Touchstone and Audrey.

If Arden is just a version of the court to be discovered under the dust sheets and beyond the looking glass, what is a director to do with its natives? That was the question that faced Adrian Noble in 1985. Nicholas de Jongh thought that he had 'failed to find a way of distinguishing between the rural inhabitants of Arden and the visitors' (*Guardian*, reviewing the Barbican transfer), and indeed it transpired that the locals were all stereotypes from a fairly standard repertoire. Corin, 'garbed as a shepherd and speaking rural English, seems to have stepped in from another play' (*TLS*) and Audrey, in the performance of Mary Jo Randle, became a northern punk with stand-up greenish hair – 'the only really funny person on stage ... loping about like a dislocated fell-walker' thought Michael Ratcliffe (whose *Observer* review had little to say in favour of the production). There was something intangibly, but essentially and disconcertingly, urban about Roger Hyams's Silvius – 'more a Petticoat Lane spiv than a rustic' thought Martin Hoyle (*FT*), while Lesley Manville's straw-hatted Phebe, dousing herself with water from the downstage stream to cool her ardour as she recalled Ganymede's attractions, was as caricatured a performance of the role as I have seen, in comparison with which Griffith Jones's Martext, with his portable mini-altar round his neck, was positively restrained. The lovers' quartet, following as it did a particularly intense version of the duologue between Orlando and Rosalind in which the desperation of his 'I can live no longer by thinking' (5.2.50) was almost palpable, was a curious mixture of the rather laid-back twang of

Silvius's 'Petticoat Lane' vowels and the increasing emotional tension of his three respondents, who were, by the end of their litany, actually shouting their lines of unrequited passion. From this the production moved to a rendering of 'It was a lover and his lass' by two young pages, slightly off tune in the old-fashioned manner, with a rather jolly, punky dance from Touchstone and Audrey that, predictably enough, ended with both of them dancing in the stream.

At least Touchstone was there voluntarily; a few minutes earlier, in his scene with William, it had been clear to the audience through the entire conversation that the stream was Touchstone's ultimate destination. William had entered with a huge tree trunk across his shoulder; on several occasions the cue for immersion seemed to have arrived but had then been averted, so that the end of the conversation was reached with Touchstone surprisingly still on dry land. Then, as he was leaving, William turned round to acknowledge Audrey's parting words, the tree trunk swung with him and the long-expected, long-postponed moment came as Touchstone was clipped round the back of the head and propelled inexorably water-wards (see Figure 39). It provoked uproarious laughter, and its timing (on the principle of the 'delayed inevitability' joke) was perfect, but the contrast with the preceding production, where the laugh at the same moment came directly from the play's text, is interesting.

The yokels who lived in the stage area beyond the foyer wall in John Caird's Arden were undoubtedly giving a performance. The director had apparently decided that not even the most heroic efforts by the audience in suspension of disbelief would ever allow them to cope with Silvius and Phebe. Alan Cumming's Silvius was therefore clad in a pair of Marks and Spencer's Y-fronts and Cassie Stuart's Phebe in a flimsy petticoat from the same source, and they danced through their scenes in a falteringly balletic way, implying, as John Peter crossly observed, 'that this part of the play is not to be taken seriously' (*S. Times*). Birmingham accents were used for Corin and William, and for Joanna Mays's 'gleefully

FIGURE 39 Towards the end of his elaborate dismissal of Campbell Morrison's William, Nicky Henson's Touchstone stoops for a moment. A second later he will stand upright, just as William, a huge tree trunk on his shoulder, turns in farewell to Mary Jo Randle's mini-skirted, punkish Audrey; the swing of the tree trunk will fulfil the audience's long-held expectations by clipping Touchstone round the back of the head and propelling him inexorably into the water-course in the foreground of the photograph. (5.1, 1985)

outsized' Audrey (*FT*), her amplitude a return to the dubious joke of the 1973 production and giving Touchstone an easy laugh on his aside to the audience: 'A man may, if he were of a feeble heart, stagger in this attempt' (3.3.42–3). A chorus for their flirting in this scene had been provided by the assembled foresters in boxer shorts bleating in imitation (presumably) of Audrey's goats. Sir Oliver Martext, with whom three little bridesmaids appeared (there were children at the exiled Duke's court), wore long-john underpants and had a little black bib with a white collar. The lovers' quartet featured ostentatious wailing from Silvius and Phebe which gave a distinct aptness to Rosalind's remark about 'the howling of Irish wolves' (5.2.110–11), and though 'It was a lover and his lass' was simply and pleasantly sung by four 'pages' (two boys and two girls), one could not but feel that the virtues of the 1989 Stratford production of *As You Like It* were to be found elsewhere than in its treatment of Arden's natives.

Three years later, and the ultra-realism of the forest set for David Thacker's 1992 production provided a firmer sense of belonging for its denizens. All the natives, including Silvius and Phebe, now had northern rural accents of the kind that conveys (in the theatre, of course) a down-to-earth grittiness; Arden, perhaps, was merging with Sherwood. James Walker's Martext was the most restrained for years, a small, bewildered, slightly camp figure with the refined ecclesiastical tones of establishment Anglicanism, but with wandering hands too: the promptbook records him 'touching up' Audrey (though only on the shoulder) during Touchstone's conversation with Jaques. Phebe wore a little apron over her printed skirt, and had something of that china-doll quality of several recent Stratford Phebes.

Silvius and William wore embroidered agricultural smocks, William's necessarily enormous, for Nick Holder, like so many Williams, doubled the role with Charles the wrestler. He presented Audrey with a flower on his entrance and became increasingly excited, in his engagingly gormless way, as Touchstone, a foot and a half shorter than he, threatened him with several kinds of death. He positively danced off stage, so entertaining had he found his rival's diatribe, and gave Anthony O'Donnell's roly-poly Touchstone a friendly, and congratulatory, pat on the back as he went. It couldn't happen at Stratford again, one thought, but it did, and after teetering on the brink the rotund little jester toppled into the stage pond.

The lovers' quartet was carefully orchestrated, the four of them sitting on the lower slope of the greensward, Silvius's tenor, Phebe's soprano, Orlando's baritone and Rosalind's contralto chiming poignantly together. Love here became, as Peter Holland observed, 'an emotion of great pain and sadness', leaving the four of them 'sprawled in gloomy isolation from each other' on 'a darkening stage' (*SS*, 180). They remained there as 'one of the banished Duke's lords' replaced the text's 'two ... pages' (5.3.5) and the Amiens of David Burt (in the company to play Macheath in *The Beggar's Opera*) led the singing of a lavishly scored version of 'It was a lover and his lass', pastiche Elizabethan out of twentieth-century musical, that finally involved most of the company, sitting in pairs on the stage hillside (among them Celia and Oliver canoodling enthusiastically) and singing their heads off in a way that I'm afraid I likened (in my review for *Shakespeare Quarterly*, 348) to a scene from *Brigadoon*. Such mean-spiritedness needs to be set beside Paul Lapworth's sense that this 'lyrical ensemble' provided 'a paean of praise to the redeeming effect of life in the forest subject to nature and the seasons' (*SA Herald*). The most interesting aspect of this moment, however, was described by Paul Taylor in the *Independent*: 'While all the couples loll around on the mossy bank ... Rosalind, still in disguise, sits downstage lost in wistful consideration by the stream ... Orlando sits and casts wistful glances at his brother and Celia.' It was, he thought, their 'greater complexity' that made them 'look almost excluded from the world of romance'. The magic of the ending was urgently needed.

Steven Pimlott's 1996 version of *As You Like It* has the distinction of having drawn more critical approval to the performances of Silvius and Phebe than any other Stratford production in the second half of the twentieth century. Several reviewers, indeed, expressed the wish that Joseph Fiennes and Victoria Hamilton (that season's Troilus and Cressida) had been playing Orlando and Rosalind. (The wish was half granted when Hamilton appeared as Rosalind in Michael Grandage's Sheffield production (also seen in London) in 2000; Fiennes, in the meantime, had had an enormous success in the film *Shakespeare in Love*.) Nicholas de Jongh expressed a general sentiment:

it is Joseph Fiennes as a chronically love-sick Silvius prone to hysteria – all quavers, swoons, and mooning attitudes – and Victoria Hamilton's entrancing shepherdess Phebe, who discover the play's erotic comedy. What life they would have brought to the play's leading roles. (*E. Standard*)

Hamilton's pertness and Fiennes's grovelling adoration were what made the partnership so funny and produced some splendidly lively writing from the reviewers, as though a new dimension of the play had been revealed to even their vast experience of it. He 'sniffs and muzzles her like a cruelly rejected dog' (*E. Standard*), dashes about the stage 'dementedly wailing "sweet Phebe do not scorn me" ... while the not-so-sweet Phebe ogles and gropes at the disguised Rosalind' (*Times*), 'pants to be lashed by her yet again' (*Time Out*), and 'writhes in ecstasy as if possessed by eels' while she is 'biding her time and twisting the knife with callous precision' (*Observer*). What was remarkable about these performances (and this is still discernible in the archival video) is the way in which their ridiculous exaggeration – she patting him on the head as he stole an unnoticed kiss, for example, while she imagines the 'damask' of Ganymede's lips and cheeks, or pulling energetically, if involuntarily, at his hair as she remembers Ganymede's taunts about her own 'black' eyes and hair (3.5.123, 130) – still managed to convey a sense of real emotion latent beneath its absurd surface. 'I had rather hear you chide than this man woo', she said to Ganymede (3.5.65), and you knew that she meant it, so that she became the victim of the tidying energies of the plot in the final scene, accepting Silvius only grudgingly.

The accents of all the Ardenites (Silvius and Phebe included) were 'stage-rural', and well south of their immediate Stratford predecessors. Susannah Elliott-Knight's Audrey, 'dim but succulent' (*E. Standard*), was an irresistible temptation to the youngest Stratford Touchstone for many years, his inability to keep his hands off her very plain to see. Arthur Cox's Corin, chunky and unflappable, conducted his debate with Touchstone on court and country life as they sat on the front edge of the stage, their legs dangling, Corin's slow, round, rural vowels and Touchstone's clipped west-of-Scotland sharpness (David Tennant used his native accent, as his essay on the role (Tennant) explains) making a pleasant contrast, Corin clearly goading Touchstone a little along the way, and Touchstone slipping into a strong Paisleyite Ulster to tell the shepherd he is 'dommed' (3.2.34). At the end of his encounter with William, played with frantic energy to a totally passive forester, William headbutted him to the ground before making his defeated exit. 'Why', asked John Peter rather literal-mindedly, does William 'then walk off humbly and leave Audrey to him?' (*S. Times*). I think we were meant to feel that, although still capable of silent aggression, William had in fact been verbally pounded into defeat.

The lovers' quartet was more physically active than it had been for a long time, a quality that derived from Fiennes's Silvius. On his second 'And so am I for Phebe' (5.2.89) he grabbed the object of his adoration around the waist, an action that she then repeated to Rosalind on her following 'And I for Ganymede', with the result that the three of them, hanging on to each other in a little row, came down stage and toppled over in domino fashion as Orlando passionately demanded 'If this be so, why blame you me to love you?' (5.2.106). Also physically active were Touchstone and Audrey during the singing of 'It was a lover and his lass'. The original idea had been that the two of them should sing the song themselves (Tennant, 41), but it was later decided that two of the forest lords should do the singing. This freed Touchstone and Audrey to chase around the upstage mound, she flinging daffodils into the air, and then to roll about on the ground, Touchstone succeeding, in the final stanza (and strictly in the literal sense) in 'getting his leg over' – as the colloquial phrase, useful and descriptive, has it. The scene had come a long way from 1946, when it was Touchstone's arm going round Audrey during the singing that had been considered worthy of note.

In the knitted and embroidered Arden of Kaffe Fassett's designs for the 2000 production there was little opportunity for the forest dwellers to offer much sense of a rural world in which the surgery of sheep might play a part. Sheep had no doubt once passed this way, but it was the cardigans and pullovers derived from their passage that now dominated the scene. And like all productions of the play based on a light-hearted demonstration of the fundamental artificiality of the pastoral ideal, the roles placed in most difficulty were those of the native foresters. Their 'Mummerset' accents seemed bizarrely out of keeping with their wonderfully fashionable knitwear – and the dislocation, which one might have hoped would add an illuminating new angle to the Arden world, in fact seemed merely stagy, depriving the characters of a meaningful context. Corin kept his end up well enough in his discussion with Adrian Schiller's deadpan Touchstone, and had clearly seen through Rosalind's disguise, with a heavily meaningful pause between 'gentle' and 'sir' on their first meeting (2.4.68) and a little snort of disbelief on 'my new mistress's *brother*' later (3.2.84–5; my italics). There was a good deal of laughter for Nina Conti's remarkably pretty Audrey as she conducted her first wooing scene with Touchstone while operating her butter churn – a task that required the suggestively rhythmic pushing up and down of its wooden handle and provoked sympathetic stirrings in Touchstone (the promptbook at one point requires that her 'plunging' should 'build to a climax'), but the resort to such business was a barometer of the problem of getting the relationships to work from the language.

Sir Oliver Martext's ample outdoor cloak, when thrown backwards over his head, revealed a cassock and a little altar that failed to achieve horizontality in spite of (or rather because of) all his inebriated efforts. Silvius and Phebe escaped much of this over-inventiveness, and his lovelorn simplicity (in his magnificent floppy pullover) as she patted him on the head while planning her letter, provided a moment of touching humanity. One innovatory little joke that did come from the text was provided by William's answer to Touchstone's question: 'Is thy name William?' 'Will I am, sir' he answered (5.1.20–1). The effective simplicity of the lovers' quartet, four well-balanced voices speaking the lines straight out to the audience, contrasted with a hugely elaborate version of 'It was a lover and his lass'. Two adult singers, their voices miked (as in all the songs in this production), sang Django Bates's soft rock setting of the ditty sitting in a row with Touchstone and Audrey and managing to come between them, and flirt with Audrey, in the little dances that separated the stanzas. Touchstone finally tired of this and signalled the band (which had been visible throughout the evening in a box above the right-hand side of the stage) to stop playing, starting them off again only when he had got his fiancée back. It was funny – and it was hugely popular with audiences – and it epitomized everything about the self-conscious artificiality of this production that had insisted throughout that Arden was a whimsical little world of theatrical fantasy.

If finding an appropriate balance between pastoral convention and rural realism in Arden has sometimes proved something of a theatrical challenge, however, it is a challenge dwarfed by the task of bringing Hymen, god of marriage, to the stage. To the response of half a century of Stratford directors to that task, and to the other events of the play's final scene, I now turn.

7

RUSTIC REVELRY

> Meantime forget this new-fall'n dignity,
> And fall into our rustic revelry.
> Play music, and you brides and bridegrooms all,
> With measure heap'd in joy, to th' measures fall.
>
> (5.4.175–8)

With the exception of Duke Frederick, who is elsewhere in the forest taking religious instruction – unless he is present in the person of his alter ego Duke Senior – virtually the whole cast of *As You Like It* will be on stage for its final scene. Frederick's anonymous courtiers will almost certainly be there in their normally doubled roles as Duke Senior's anonymous forest lords; those of Frederick's followers whose names we know, Le Beau and Charles the wrestler, may have managed to get home early, but even they have occasionally been there among the defectors from the corrupt régime who 'flock' to the rightful ruler (1.1.117). William is often brought on to take part in the pageant, and when a director is determined to outdo the dramatist in multiplication of couples 'coming to the ark' (5.4.36) has even been given a partner in the dance to replace his recently lost love, Audrey. It is impossible to do the scene with fewer than a dozen actors and all the Stratford productions considered in this book have used more, some many more. Even so large a stage as that of the Royal Shakespeare Theatre – large in terms of depth, at least, though narrowed by its inexorable proscenium arch – will seem crowded unless such numbers are carefully choreographed. On occasions, indeed, they have been choreographed with the express intention of achieving a sense of crowdedness, of an exuberant community bursting with life and energy. The scene includes a dance involving at least four couples, but quite possibly everyone on stage; the notable entrance of a new character, called Jaques, completing the trio of de Boys brothers, and the notable exit of an old character, also called Jaques, threatening the fun; it includes a protracted story from Touchstone about the seven stages of the lie (discussed in chapter 5), told twice to cover a big costume change for Rosalind and Celia; and, most significantly, not to say notoriously and ominously, it includes the arrival of Hymen, the god who 'peoples every town' (5.4.142). It is a scene that offers a major challenge to directors.

In an interview with me for the programme of his 1996 Stratford production, Steven Pimlott had this to say about the arrival of Hymen:

> The main issue, obviously, is whether this is a god, or a bit of dressing up. The Folio's 'Enter Hymen' is unambiguous, though some later editors change this to such things as 'Enter a masquer dressed as Hymen' (which is a very different matter) and there is a stage tradition for a recognisable Corin (or even Adam) to present the part. I think one has to take the Folio at its word and see this as a theophany: the god comes to earth, as in several of Shakespeare's late plays. Hymen is the final manifestation of Arden's magic.

Pimlott's response to that manifestation of magic will be considered later. His presentation here of the issue in principle is admirably clear and challenging. His programme duly lists the name of Hymen and gives the name of the player of the role. Of the twelve other post-war Stratford programmes for *As You Like It* five do the same and seven omit any mention of the character. (Curiously, Agnes Latham's Arden edition of the play, from which the quotations in this book are drawn, also omits Hymen from its list of *Dramatis Personae*, though he is given an entrance, in unamended Folio form, at 5.4.106.) There is, as Pimlott says, a stage tradition for Corin to 'present' the part of Hymen. This is not, one needs to make clear, a matter of role-doubling, of the actor who appeared earlier in the evening as Corin now giving us his Hymen performance, but of a recognizable, if dressed up, Corin speaking Hymen's part in whatever version of a rural accent we heard from him earlier – sometimes with a strong suggestion that, like Viola, he 'took great pains to study it'.

Rather surprisingly, the 'Corin solution' has been adopted in only three of the post-war Stratford productions of *As You Like It*, those of 1961, 1980 and 1992, though it was also used in the 1968 revival of the 1967 production. In 2000 Gregory Doran played a minor variation on it by having Adam speak Hymen's lines, a resuscitation of Orlando's old servant to late prominence that (surely not altogether coincidentally) was a conspicuous reversal of the decision of his fellow RSC associate director Steven Pimlott in the preceding Stratford production to kill Adam off before the interval. In one production, that of 1952, Hymen was simply cut. In the remaining eight (those of 1946, 1957, 1967, 1973, 1977, 1985, 1989 and 1996) there was some sort of an appearance for Hymen, unexplained at least initially, though this has more often been tongue-in-cheek than a real attempt to present a theophany. How have these different choices worked, in the context of the final scene as a whole, in this sequence of thirteen productions of *As You Like It*?

The reviewers were silent about the final scene in Herbert Prentice's production in 1946, but the promptbook reveals how the episode was handled. It has the name 'Hymen' deleted from the entry at 5.4.106. 'Corin' was substituted but there was clearly a change of mind and it was erased and, at the scene's initial entry, the name Amiens was replaced by 'First Lord'. The final idea emerges after the singing of 'Wedding is great Juno's crown' (140–5): 'Hymen rushes up ramp [at the rear of the stage]; revealed as Amiens; gen[eral] laugh'. Dudley Jones's Amiens, then, the singer in the company, played Hymen, presumably at Rosalind's request; the promptbook calls for a lute accompaniment for his first speech, which was thus doubtless sung. This is the only production so to 'cast' Hymen (for whom there is no listing in the programme) and the only one to use the rather engaging idea of postponing the revelation of his identity until after his magical work has been done.

In 1952, as already mentioned, Glen Byam Shaw simply cut Hymen altogether. Rosalind had also been cut from earlier in the scene (5.4.5–25), so that her first line became 'To you I give myself, for I am yours' (115). Both of Hymen's speeches, and the wedding hymn, are marked in the promptbook for omission. Angus McBean's photograph (Figure 40 – posed, of course, but no doubt reproducing the stage picture) shows the four couples paired ready for the final dancing and Mervyn Blake's Corin (with his allegedly Home Guard hat) standing at the rear with attendant musicians looking for all the world as though he has just enacted the god of marriage. But if we may trust the promptbook, this was (again uniquely in this sequence) a production that kept Hymen off the stage.

The only comment on this final scene in the reviews provides that very considerable rarity, a notice for the actor of the awkward little role of Jaques de Boys, who has to wait three hours to utter just one speech, a speech packed with highly surprising, yet vital, information. Jerome Willis, we learn, fulfilled the requirements of the role 'with any amount of aplomb' (*Sketch*). The tribute is apposite, for if we are not wholly convinced that the young man believes absolutely in every syllable of his remarkable story, it is

FIGURE 40 (*opposite*) The final scene in Glen Byam Shaw's first Stratford production: Jaques (Michael Hordern) pauses, about to leave, on the mound beside the palm tree; the newly arrived Jaques replacement, Jaques de Boys (Jerome Willis), is below him to his right and Duke Senior (Jack Gwillim) below him to his left, in front of the 'pool'. Corin (Mervyn Blake, with musical assistants) is to the rear right (in 'Home Guard' headgear), looking as if he has just been playing Hymen, though that role had in fact been cut. The four couples (from left to right Celia and Oliver, Rosalind and Orlando, Audrey and Touchstone, and Phebe and Silvius) stand poised for the final dance. (5.4, 1952)

hard to conceive how anyone else in the theatre (on the stage or in the auditorium) will believe it either.

When Byam Shaw returned to the play in 1957 he had changed his mind about Hymen. The programme includes the role and assigns it to Gordon Wright, an actor whose name is not listed against any other part and who was thus presumably making his first appearance of the evening. He entered 'in a farm wain' (*Liv. Post*), with Corin, William and the pages as accompanying musicians (see Figure 41). The critic for the *Birmingham Mail* hated the fact that Hymen 'spoke from a decorated cart', and the photograph certainly seems to capture a certain incongruity in the appearance of Hymen, crowned and robed like a classical god, and the rural humbleness of his mode of transport. The incongruity seems to have been deliberate: to Muriel St Clare Byrne, Hymen was 'patently one of Rosalind's rural neighbours', who had been recruited 'for a simple bit of rustic mummery and drawn in on a little bright blue cart'. Rosalind, Celia and Touchstone, she thought, had 'knocked those verses off overnight' (*SQ*, 482), and although J.C. Trewin enjoyed the 'beautiful serenity' of the music for the wedding hymn (*Birm. Post*), it is clear (as Byrne remarked) that the event was presented more in the manner of the pageant of the worthies at the end of *Love's Labour's Lost* than as any attempt at theophanic masque.

The chorus of critical delight for Stratford's 1961 *As You Like It* continued, for the most part, right through to include the final scene, though there were isolated voices of doubt about the finale:

FIGURE 41 (*opposite*) The final dance in Glen Byam Shaw's second Stratford production: Jaques has already left, but Hymen (Gordon Wright), in his little blue cart, with musical support from the pages (left), William (Toby Robertson, centre) and Corin (Donald Eccles, right), is still there. Duke Senior (Antony Brown, understudying Cyril Luckham) stands rear centre behind Peggy Ashcroft's Rosalind, with Richard Johnson's Orlando to her left. The other three couples are disposed in two groups of three, Silvius, Touchstone and Audrey to the left and Oliver, Phebe and Celia to the right. The abstract delicacy of Motley's set contrasts with their more naturalistic designs for the preceding production. (5.4, 1957)

the *Stage* referred to 'a stylized final tableau, perhaps a little long-drawn-out' and the *Stratford-upon-Avon Herald* thought it 'a shaky moment' when Corin came in as Hymen 'capped in a sort of war bonnet' while 'the forest lords with torches process to a chant not far removed from some ritual hymn of the Blackfeet tribe'. For most reviewers, however, Michael Elliott's response to the challenge of this final scene was a triumph, and something of its theatrical appeal is still discernible in the version made for television. It was presented as an evening scene. The promptbook has an elaborate plan (irreverently labelled 'Entry of the Gladiators') for a procession of eleven chanting forest lords. They carried flaming torches wreathed with roses and wound slowly in from the shadows, preceding two pages in white, then Corin, robed and crowned as Hymen. On the television film he speaks Hymen's lines carefully, with huge earnestness.

Then came Rosalind and Celia. Bernard Levin's report of Vanessa Redgrave's reappearance is perhaps the most rapturous account of any moment in any production of *As You Like It* in the many hundreds of reviews that research for this book has obliged me to read:

> like the arm which held Excalibur, clothed in white samite, mystic, wonderful and her sunny locks hang on her temples like the golden fleece ... If the word enchantment has any meaning it is here.
>
> (*D. Express*)

Many reviewers comment on the powerful effect of this moment (though none quite so ecstatically as this). Two others must speak for all: 'she is the embodiment of feminine radiance, fascination, and tenderness' (*Morn. Adv.*) and the spotlight in which she stands 'is superfluous: she could illuminate a universe' (*Bristol E. Post*, reviewing the Aldwych transfer). Whether Figure 42, which captures the moment, will convince the reader that these eulogies were justified is, as always, a question of taste.

After the princesses' entrance the four couples, 'seeming to awake slowly, as if in a dream' (*Birm. Post*), walked between two rows of torchbearers and were received by Hymen standing at the top of the aisle they formed like a priest at the altar. Jaques de Boys brought, along with his news of Frederick's conversion, the ducal coronet hidden beneath his cloak and presented it to Duke Senior on the line 'His crown bequeathing to his banish'd brother' (5.4.162). The Duke crowned himself and all knelt to him. The withdrawal of Max Adrian's remarkable Jaques – or so it is on the television film, anyway – was firm, sad, immovable: 'To see no pastime, I' (194) is said without the accusatory sneer that some performers of the role find in it, but is clear, absolute, utterly incontrovertible. His departure reminded Robert Speaight of 'Marcel Proust retiring to a monastery' (*SQ*, 434). The final dance, to music in the Elizabethan style that had been used throughout the production, was 'one of the loveliest dances ever planned for a Shakespeare play' (*Morn. Adv.*), sedate, a little wistful (the solitariness of the Duke is conspicuous in the film) and very much at the 'courtly' end of the spectrum of directorial choices in this series of productions, though during it the 'elephantine flirtatiousness' of Patsy Byrne's Audrey still delighted one reviewer (*Middles. E. Gaz.*).

At the end of David Jones's 1967 production John Higgins felt 'as the counterfeit faces are removed and forgiveness dominates, a rare feeling of humanity running through the theatre, as it does through a memorable last act of *Figaro*' (*FT*, reviewing the Aldwych transfer). The part of Hymen was listed in the programme, with the name of John Kaye against it; he is (presumably deliberately) not mentioned among the actors playing court or forest lords, though he had, in fact, been used to 'swell a scene or two' earlier. He came in slowly, escorting Rosalind and Celia, without special effects or machinery. He wore buskins for additional height, a full-length panelled gown, a tall crown of twigs with a half mask attached, and in his right hand he carried a flaming torch. Interestingly, although the costume and torch returned in the revival of the production the following year, it was now the Corin of Richard Moore who filled the role, theophany thus giving place

to amateur theatricals. The promptbook reveals that the 'wedlock hymn' (and the line referring to it – 5.4.136, 140–5) was cut, that each couple in turn knelt to Hymen, and that he remained on stage, presiding over events, until after the final dance.

In the world of denim jeans and rock music of Buzz Goodbody's 1973 *As You Like It* the final scene was obviously much more of a candidate for party treatment than for classical theophany. Michael Ensign, an actor whose name does not appear elsewhere in the programme, was nevertheless listed there against the role of Hymen and made a solemn entrance in a long, whitish, caped gown, looking vaguely monk-like and accompanied by a little procession of attendant forest lords carrying lanterns. There was no attempt to 'explain' this manifestation, which audiences presumably took as some sort of spiritual rite in the little hippy commune that Arden seemed to have become in this production. Jean Fuzier and Jean-Marie Maguin, lamenting the fact that the rest of the production seemed 'biased against poetry', remarked on the striking effect of Hymen's speaking of his verse, finding it 'all too brief and ... surprisingly out of place' (*Cahiers Elis.*). The promptbook makes it clear that at the end of his second speech, the first three lines of which were cut (5.4.124–64), Hymen moved to his 'marriage position' and that 'masquers' danced down stage and rose petals fell during the wedding hymn. This dance, complete with 'just married' signs and garlands for the participants, quickly became 'a rave-up to rock music' (*S. Telegraph*), a 'jazz festival finale ... with confetti fluttering from the roof' (*Listener*) while 'grinning supers threw confetti into the house' (*Observer*). After all this, remarked Peter Thomson, 'the unfortunate actor of

FIGURE 42 (*opposite*) The entry of Rosalind (Vanessa Redgrave, left) and Celia (Rosalind Knight) to a stage framed by torch-bearing forest lords: Oliver (David Buck) and Orlando (Ian Bannen) are in the left foreground, with Russell Hunter's Corin, playing Hymen, in front of them; in the right foreground are Jill Dixon's Phebe, Redmond Phillips's Duke Senior, Peter McEnery's Silvius and Patsy Byrne's Audrey. The moment received an extraordinarily enthusiastic critical response. (5.4, 1961)

Jaques de Boys must have felt even more like an unrequested encore' (*SS*, 149). Amid all the boisterousness two moments stood out: 'Rosalind's "I am yours" [116] to David Suchet's tender Orlando brought an uneven evening to a noble end' (*D. Telegraph*); and the exit of Richard Pasco's Jaques created a moment of chill in the proceedings, 'as if a cloud were passing over the sunlit world of Arden' (*Guardian*). Peter Thomson was struck by the same moment: 'having watched the modern frenzy of the wedding', he writes, Jaques 'spat out "so to your pleasures" [191] disconcertingly. It was only with some difficulty that Duke Senior recovered sufficient poise to restart the dance' (*SS*, 150). These are the first reviews to mention Jaques's exit in any post-war Stratford production of *As You Like It*. They come just a year after the publication of Anne Barton's seminal essay on the ending of the play, with its description of the exit of Jaques casting a 'tremor' over the proceedings, 'a tremor which guarantees the vitality of the moment itself but which also prefigures its imminent destruction' (Barton, 167).

The constant inclination of Trevor Nunn's 1977 *As You Like It* to turn into a baroque opera allowed him to treat the arrival of Hymen as an event in a seventeenth-century court masque – that form of entertainment so elusive for twentieth-century audiences to which the goddesses in *The Tempest* partly belong and to which this scene of *As You Like It* perhaps alludes. Hymen had, in fact, already appeared, in an added preludial trio with Art and Nature; his reappearance at the end was treated with all the arch theatrical self-consciousness with which the production abounded, and the episode was clearly more of a piece with the rest of the evening than is often the case. Just after Graham Crowden's very identifiable Le Beau (the last of this production's defectors from Frederick's court) had been welcomed to the forest community, the little cart, on which Corin and company had arrived, was removed. It had provided an affectionately mocking allusion to the play's recent Stratford performance history and a splendidly misleading prelude to the arrival of Hymen – for on this occasion he was anything but cart-borne. There was a clap of thunder and down he came from the flies on a puffy white cloud. It opened to present him seated under a rainbow, singing a pastiche Purcellian aria adapted (with repeats but no real additions) from the text, while the princesses made their entrances below on terra firma (see Figure 43). 'Rosalind has, presumably, contrived this with real, not pretended, magic', wrote B.A. Young (*FT*), but Roger Warren didn't enjoy its tongue-in-cheek tone and thought that Hymen's 'undifferentiated outpouring ... with an enormous sheepdoggy wobble' was 'rightly derided by the audience' (*SS*, 146). The exit of Jaques again drew comment: 'his final decision to leave the woodland merrymaking shocks ... after his having taken a full part in the preceding song-and-dance sequences' (*Morn. Star*).

From a singing, cloud-borne Hymen, fully credited in the programme, the pendulum swung back again in 1980. The god of marriage lost his billing to a Corin back in a cart. John Bowe, Orlando in the production, describes the moment:

> And so with the stage adorned with colourful blossom and foliage a cart appears, pulled by the forest lords, chariot-style. On board are Corin, commandeered to play Hymen in this pageant (with terrible verse supplied), Celia, and Rosalind, dressed as a girl again. All is resolved and all presumably live happily ever after ... To celebrate the cast dance and sing. It's a sort of fertility dance, rather like a Morris dance on the local village green; the audience clap to the beat.   (Bowe, 74–5)

Bowe's judgement of the quality of Hymen's verse was no doubt affected by its treatment: Michael Billington describes Corin's 'lighting up a particularly pungent briar pipe' for the occasion (*Guardian*), though Rosalind still kissed him for his delivery of what one felt sure were her lines. Hands's version of this scene must rank as one of its more boisterously energetic Stratford treatments, 'a pagan love-in and fertility feast involving the cast as a whole' (*New States.*), 'a pagan romp of corn dollies and ancient country gods' (*S. Mercury*). Inevitably its noise and energy and attempted inclusiveness left some unincluded: 'a bewilderingly

kitsch version of standard Stratford endings' sniffed Jeremy Treglown (*TLS*); Charles Spencer, on the other hand, found it 'near impossible to keep a smile off the face or a sentimental tear out of the eye' (*New Stand.*, reviewing the Aldwych transfer).

Into this turmoil of exuberance Michael Siberry's fresh-faced and eager Jaques de Boys came rushing with his good news; a dozen years later the same actor would walk out from the same scene in the role of the Jaques. The exit of Derek Godfrey's Jaques in 1980 made only a minor dent in the proceedings; Touchstone and Audrey defied his gloomy prognostications about their future with an energetic cuddle.

If the 'tremor' (to repeat Anne Barton's term) of Jaques's exit in 1980 registered little on the Richter scale of critical attention, that of Alan Rickman's Jaques in 1985 dominated reviewers' comments on the final scene. This was partly due to the physical prominence he was given in the preceding moments, silhouetted against the evening sky between the upstage mirror and grandfather clock for the entrance of Jaques de Boys, who fainted from exhaustion after delivering his extraordinary news. Revived and reunited with his brothers, Jaques de Boys was joined by Rickman's Jaques, with his questions about the newcomer's strange story. Both wore black, the only persons on stage so clothed: two Jaqueses, two Jacks, one to join the dance, one to walk out of it. Jaques (senior) then stood downstage to deliver his blessings on each of the couples, rejected contemptuously the Duke's plea to him to stay, and on 'To see no pastime, I' (5.4.194) ran upstage, forcing a passage through the assembly, and stepped through the mirror frame. Its glass came up after him, clonking gently into the upper frame as he sneered the words 'abandon'd cave' (195); just as the Duke gathered himself together and was about to reinstate the dancing, the grandfather

FIGURE 43 (*opposite*) In imitation of seventeenth-century masque form, Hymen (Michael Follis) descends in a rainbow on a cloud singing his lines in Purcellian operatic style. His attendants, and the lovers, assemble in deference below. (5.4, 1977)

clock resumed its ticking. Jaques 'the fastidious depressive departs through the pier glass, out of one exile into the next' wrote Michael Ratcliffe in the *Observer*; Nicholas Shrimpton saw it slightly more positively: 'Jaques steps through the mirror, abandoning cynicism for curiosity about the religious life' (*TES*). It was a striking theatrical moment, precisely balancing the moment when the same mirror had opened to let Duke Frederick through to become Duke Senior.

The 1985 production was also notable for providing the only invisible Hymen in a sequence of thirteen productions. Apart from Glen Byam Shaw's cutting it altogether in 1952, every other post-war Stratford director has offered an actor in the role; Adrian Noble tried a lighting effect. From a large, flickering, reddish disc over a temporarily darkened stage Hymen's words seemed to emanate, though an echo effect made their origin difficult to locate. The voice was unmistakably that of Griffith Jones, who had earlier appeared as Sir Oliver Martext. In a production in which the doubling of the Dukes was crucially significant, it was impossible not to connect the successful marriage celebrant of the final scene with his failed priestly counterpart earlier. Rosalind and Celia came in beneath the moon and the hymn to Hymen was sung by all four couples standing in a line holding candles, the great parachute silk that had once been the snows of Arden now suspended above the stage like an enormous bridal veil (see Figure 44). Eric Sams thought it worked 'quite well' and added 'only in such a dream world could Hymen ever appear to be a dénouement' (*TLS*). Nicholas Shrimpton, more grudgingly, felt that it was striving 'for a sense of magical reconciliation that it doesn't quite achieve' (*TES*). The Rosalind and Celia of the production describe the moment for themselves (and the changes to it when the production moved to London):

> In Stratford Hymen had been represented as a flickering silhouette on a lighted screen, placed upstage, obliging the actors to turn away from the audience to perceive him – this both threw the focus onto

FIGURE 44 Beneath the billowing silk sheet that earlier covered Arden in snow and has now become a gigantic bridal veil over the stage, the lovers, holding candles, line up (from left to right Silvius, Phebe, Orlando, Rosalind, Celia, Oliver, Audrey, Touchstone) to sing 'Wedding is great Juno's crown'. Hymen had spoken as a disembodied voice from a flickering point in the great disc visible upstage in the right of the photograph, the only non-human presentation of the god in this series of productions. (5.4.140, 1985)

an unlikely manifestation which threatened the audience's capacity to believe in what was going on, and deprived them of the characters' responses to the deity and his dictates. In London Hymen became a mere beam of light whose source was *behind* the audience, so that the actors beheld him facing out front. In this way the audience was able to focus not on the god, but on the faces of those whose futures he is deciding. (Shaw and Stevenson, 70)

The only *As You Like It* director at post-war Stratford to take the same basically theophanic approach to Hymen as his immediate predecessor was John Caird in 1989. His was a jovial giant of a Hymen, played by Andrew Tansey, the last of a trio of roles that had been preceded by Charles the wrestler and William. To the sound of Ilona Sekacz's 'measured, jangling anthem' (*FT*), he strode down the stage in a bright green suit, a child on his shoulders and two others in attendance. Rosalind and Celia followed as his speech forbidding confusion boomed out. Recalling that her Rosalind had no real idea what was going to happen as she made her appointment (at the end of 5.2) with Orlando, Silvius and Phebe, Sophie Thompson describes Rosalind's surprise at

> the arrival from the back of the stage of a figure out of William Blake, a strong man in a green costume with an angel perched on his back, leading two children by the hand. It happens because of faith, belief, magic. Rosalind didn't think when she went rushing off saying she will 'make these doubts all even' (V.iv.25) that she was going to get Hymen ready for his entrance ... It was the end of human control, as though something else had taken over ... I didn't really want to know where Hymen had come from, but I was very glad he had come.   (Thompson, 84–5)

Was this figure, one wondered, some version of the 'Green Man' of the Forest and, if so, what was the significance of his making his exit down the central aisle of the stalls? The production had begun with the stalls providing the only way onto or off the stage, but a route had been smashed through to the woodland playing space. The presiding forest god's final exit back into the audience's world was clearly making another of the director's metatheatrical points. After many doubts and grumbles about the production, John Gross confessed himself finally won over: 'By the end of the evening, as the masque of Hymen slips perfectly into place, it has achieved a magic that you would have thought quite beyond it at the beginning' (*S. Telegraph*).

Still to come, though, was the highly symbolic exit of Hugh Ross's exquisitely elegant Jaques. His blessings on the lovers crisply delivered and the Duke's plea that he should remain suavely dismissed, he strode upstage to a door we had not noticed in the rear wall, opened it, paused a moment, silhouetted in a strong back light, and then strode through. The moment vividly recalled Rosalind's opening of the great door to break the clock and escape into Arden – and to give us our play. But Jaques's door closed sharply behind him: the next play this observer of the world's stage was going to see, a most curious study of a converted duke, was to be a private show. Through the door he went and there was a pause as the stage seemed momentarily in darkness. Then up came the lights and an all-inclusive communal dance began, the state of undress – half the forest lords were in shorts and underpants – contrasting sharply with the buttoned-up formality of the evening's opening sequence on the dance-floor forestage.

Corin was back in the role of Hymen in 1992 with as simple an entrance as the god has had in this sequence of productions. Robed, and with a crown of leaves, he simply walked on over the little rustic bridge with Rosalind and Celia on either hand in white wedding dresses. The big effect was left to the music, an elaborate choral number for the wedding hymn that Garry O'Connor thought 'out-pastiches Andrew Lloyd Webber' (*Plays & P.*) and Charles Spencer felt created 'a wonderful sense of reconciliation' (*D. Telegraph*) – how remarkably instructive it is to observe the gulf in responses that the same theatrical moment can produce. Jaques's exit was less dramatic than in some recent productions, that distinctive rasping note in Michael Siberry's voice taking on a flatter, sadder tone as he declared himself 'for other than for dancing measures' (5.4.192). His downstage exit (in the sharpest contrast to his predecessor's flamboyant upstage departure) took him out, however, through the stalls, as though his withdrawal from the festivity was into our world. After it we watched the wreaths and high spirits of the final dance just a little more from the outside than would otherwise have been the case.

Steven Pimlott's version of Hymen in 1996 was one of the more notable in the history of the play on the Stratford stage. For the first time the god of marriage was played by a woman, a middle-aged woman who came onto the stage from the stalls wearing a black Marks and Spencer's trouser suit of the sort to be seen at suburban cocktail parties (see Figure 45). In a production dressed in Elizabethan costume this led many playgoers and several reviewers to suppose that a member of the audience must have taken a wrong turning, or suffered some sort of blackout – until, in a homely northern accent, she began to speak Hymen's blessings on the lovers. The ideas behind the moment were expounded by Pimlott in a lecture he gave as part of that year's Shakespeare Birthday celebrations and I paraphrase them here: if gods come from beyond the play's world, then can that not be well suggested by bringing into a play set in the Elizabethan period a figure from a later century; if a theatre performance derives its imaginative power from the audience's willingness to commit to its fiction, then what is more appropriate than to bring in the play's figure of ultimate power from the audience; and if this is primarily a play about a young woman in love, then does it not make sense to end it with the blessing of an older woman who may be supposed to have experienced love, marriage, motherhood and grandmotherhood? The persuasiveness of these ideas in the lecture room translated unfortunately (for most watchers of the production, anyway) into a moment of bathos in the theatre. The problem derived from one's fear that something had gone wrong, causing a momentary loss of belief in the theatrical event itself. When the production moved to the Barbican the episode was changed and Hymen's lines were spoken by a woman in Elizabethan costume who made an entrance from the stage, not from the auditorium.

Many reviewers grumbled about the presentation of Hymen – and several thought too that the attempted Elizabethan choreography of the final dance was simply clumsy ('the worst choreography of the lovers' dance I have yet witnessed in this house' snapped the *Birmingham Post*). Michael Billington was a notable exception, however, and his response is an interesting example of a reviewer perceiving something of the spirit of a production where others saw only its surface. One of Pimlott's 'best

FIGURE 45 A female Hymen (Doreen Andrew), having arrived on stage from the stalls in a modern trouser suit, contrasts surprisingly (and for some it proved to be bewilderingly) with the Elizabethan costumes of Liam Cunningham's Orlando (left), Niamh Cusack's Rosalind and Robert Demeger's Duke Senior. (5.4, 1996)

touches' he thought, was to make Hymen 'a sensible middle-aged lady in a black trouser suit. It is typical of the intelligence of this production: if these multiple, often patched-up couplings are to survive, you feel it will only be through the beneficence of enlightened womanhood' (*Guardian*).

Also unique in the final scene of the 1996 production was a little gift from Touchstone to the departing Jaques. The blessings on the lovers were spoken with the self-confident authority this Jaques had evinced all evening, and in response to the meanness of his prognostications for his and Audrey's future Touchstone intoned a hollow, deathly 'ha ... ha' and dropped a skull into Jaques's hands. In his interview for the programme Pimlott refers more than once to Jaques as a 'death's-head' and remarks disapprovingly of his having become 'a Hamlet figure in some recent versions of the play'. Jaques, he says, must be old – and the text offers evidence for that (5.1.3), though few directors have felt bound to observe it – and Touchstone young; if Jaques has any affinities with Hamlet, therefore 'it is a Hamlet who lived on into old age' (1996 programme). And so, before the dancing began and everyone took their partners, Touchstone, the play's Yorick, gave its ageing Hamlet a skull to keep him company as he stalked off in search of the converted Duke.

In the embroidered, colourful world of Stratford's 2000 *As You Like It* such a moment would have been inconceivable. Cut-out festoons of flowers had come down from the flies at the end of 'It was a lover and his lass' (5.3.37) and the stage for the final scene was awash with colour, not at all to the taste of Charles Spencer, who thought it 'a Disneyland technicolour nightmare' (*D. Telegraph*). Audreys over the years at Stratford have been caught in various thoughtlessly undignified moments when admonished by Touchstone to bear their bodies 'more seeming' (5.4.68) – adjusting sleeves or bra straps, showing slightly too much cleavage, sitting, or lolling, a little too nonchalantly, staring too interestedly at the young men. It seemed a measure of this production's over-anxiety and exaggeration that its Audrey was so astonished by the brave new world of dukes and lords that she stood gawping in blank amazement, gradually hoisting the hem of her skirt and revealing her undergarments – it seemed unconsciously rather than in any overt sexual invitation, though the promptbook refers to her 'flirting'; either way, it is a curious 'Stratford first' to have to record.

There were other Stratford firsts about the scene, though the flower-decorated, fluffy-cloud-painted cart that brought in Hymen was scarcely one of them. That Peter Copley's ancient Adam was speaking Hymen's lines was an innovation, however, in a half-century of productions, and his hesitant care in getting them right seemed to suggest the difficulty Rosalind must have had in teaching them to him. The wedding hymn, in the production's usual smoochy jazz style, seemed ill at ease, as so much of the music had, with the faux-naïf of the setting. After it we saw Phebe weeping at the loss of her love for Ganymede; and then Jaques de Boys arrived in the dark court costume that we hadn't seen since the beginning of the evening. He was the first Jaques de Boys since 1961 to bring on the ducal coronet, which he carried in a large box. Duke Senior held it aloft on 'our returned fortune' (5.4.173), but the production then scored another first for this history when he decided not to put it on but handed it, rather nonchalantly, to one of his followers and determined to 'forget this new-fall'n dignity' (175). Thirteen productions on, and seconds from the end of the play, and Shakespeare's text is still yielding interesting innovatory choices to directors. It is the pleasure of such moments of discovery that illuminates the 'harmless drudgery' of gathering information for a performance history such as this.

There was nothing actually innovatory about the departure of Declan Conlon's rather subdued Jaques, but it was unusual in its mildness. He was quietly interested in his namesake's story, kindly in his farewells to the lovers and genuinely affectionate in his leave-taking with the Duke. The Duke's plea that he should 'stay, Jaques, stay' (5.4.193) was positively forlorn in its urgency, but Jaques's response, though profoundly gentle, was not to be gainsaid. And, as so often, the 'tremor' was felt, and it took a few seconds for the Duke to find the will to set the dances going. William was there, and with a new partner (yet another rarity), and the lovers' dance, brief and simple, ended with a kiss between each couple before Alexandra Gilbreath stepped down to the forestage to address the audience in her epilogue.

Epilogues are comparatively rare in Shakespeare's plays and where they occur are usually spoken by some sort of framing chorus-figure (as in *Henry V* and *Pericles*). Rosalind is the only female character in a Shakespeare play to be given the responsibility of an epilogue – as is immediately clear from the way she begins: 'It is not the fashion to see the lady the epilogue; but it is no more unhandsome than to see the lord the prologue' (5.4.198–200). A joke was made of that in 1989 when the dancing stopped and

Orlando stepped forward as if about to address the audience – just as he had done at the beginning, when Orlando's speech to Adam had been treated very much as 'the lord the prologue'. But he could only manage a little inarticulate sound of embarrassment that brought Sophie Thompson's Rosalind to his rescue; she kissed him in reassurance before taking over the task.

For all that the epilogue to *As You Like It* makes clear that it was very precisely created for the boy actor who had just played Rosalind, it has always been played in post-war Stratford productions, and nearly always left uncut. Just twice, the promptbooks reveal, there were changes to the words 'If I were a woman' (5.4.214–15): in 1973 they were deleted and in 1992 they were altered to 'As I am a woman'. Apart from that, and the removal of the reference to the lord as the prologue in 1946, the epilogue has always been given in full and unchanged.

Comment on its treatment by reviewers is sadly rare, the imminence of that first-night rush from the theatre to phone in copy for the morning edition perhaps taking minds off these closing moments. J.C. Trewin, though, clearly took a special interest in it and nearly always managed to pay its speaker a compliment. In 1957, for example, he wrote that he would 'long remember Peggy Ashcroft's delivery of the Epilogue before the house assured her of its affection and loyalty' (*Birm. Post*); and elsewhere he referred to her 'glowing charm' in the speech (*Illus. Lon. News*). The falling cadences of the epilogue's prose, ending in the gracious request to be bidden farewell, do have an extraordinary way of 'conjuring' (5.4.208) affection from the house. Ruth Lodge, whom several reviewers in 1946 had felt was not, on the first night, as at home in the role as they hoped she would later become, was described as giving, in her epilogue, 'a glimpse of what she can do when she comes out into the open' (*Evesham J.*), and Margaret Leighton, in 1952, made sure that we 'miss not a syllable of the Epilogue, so often a scamper' (Trewin again, in the *Lady*). Vanessa Redgrave, in 1961, 'sent shivers down the spine' (*Guardian*) and Eileen Atkins, after all the rock-band high jinks of the final dance in 1973, stilled the audience wonderfully for the epilogue when, 'with the house lights up, as they should be' (*Observer*), she was 'Rosalind's very self' (Trewin once more, *Birm. Post*). Kate Nelligan, in 1977, had seemed to Trewin a little too 'calculated' in her spontaneity at times during the evening but in her epilogue she was 'in complete repose … much her happiest passage' (*Birm. Post*), and Frank Marcus felt that Nelligan's epilogue 'touches our hearts' (*S. Telegraph*). Susan Fleetwood, stepping out from the high-voltage energies of the dance in 1980, seemed to her Orlando to be speaking to 'a sea of smiling, happy faces. I think they've had a good time' (Bowe, 75).

Reviewers' silence on the epilogue in 1985 and 1989 is replaced by actors' comment. Both Juliet Stevenson and Sophie Thompson clearly worried about how to deal with this moment and in Stevenson's case it was changed between Stratford and London:

> In Stratford the dance had lulled the play to its close and the dancers remained on stage for Rosalind's closing address to the audience. We came to realize that this created problems for the audience, who did not know whether the characters were staying in Arden or not, or *who*, exactly, was talking to them in the epilogue. In London the dance culminated in a moment of still suspension, as the characters took in the Arden they were about to leave … They then exited, through the moon-shaped hole in the backdrop, which both told the story more clearly and laid emphasis on the fantastical nature of the whole event. With Rosalind alone on stage, the epilogue then clearly became a separate event. (Shaw and Stevenson, 71)

More simply, Sophie Thompson describes her Orlando's failure to speak the epilogue and her needing to take over:

> I liked that because it made you remember him at the beginning of the play, unable to put his feelings about Rosalind into words. I liked the fact that here you saw a bit of their being 'together' – Mrs helping Mr in a rather 'social' situation. (Thompson, 85)

She then goes on to describe how she always began the speech as if she were making it up as she went along, but that when she got to

'My way is to conjure you' (5.4.208) that idea disappeared and 'it somehow changed and reminded us of the magic we'd seen'. She goes on to use the Epilogue as a way of looking into the future, offering a hopeful vision of the marriage of Rosalind and Orlando: 'They understand now that love isn't all romance, and that you have to work at it every single day' (Thompson, 85).

Whether one discerns such prognostications in the Epilogue or not, Thompson's response to the energy and buoyancy of its prose, to what she calls its 'magic', is something that many Rosalinds have evinced. Samantha Bond conveyed it vividly in 1992 as she was caught, almost unawares, in a downstage spotlight while the rest of the cast sat watching her from the forest slope of the stage. Niamh Cusack, too, in 1996, responded joyously to the Epilogue's challenge as she engaged the audience, all 'energy and shrewdness' (*Independent*), with an openness and sparkle that even survive on the archival video. And in the last of this sequence of productions, Alexandra Gilbreath's Rosalind, stepping forward from her embroidered Arden, found in the Epilogue the emotional directness, the wit and vivacity, and the grace, that are the play's gift to the player of Rosalind (see Figure 46). As the 2000 season was drawing towards its close, there was much discussion in Stratford of the possibility of a new theatre to replace the 1932 building, and one found oneself wondering, as one watched this thirteenth in the extraordinarily various, and distinguished, sequence with which this book has been concerned, how many more Rosalinds there might be, before a new building came along, who would stand at the front of that stage and secure, with that Epilogue, 'the affection and loyalty of the house'.

FIGURE 46 (*opposite*) Alexandra Gilbreath's Rosalind breaks from the final dance and comes down stage to address the audience in the Epilogue. (5.4, 2000)

PRODUCTION CREDITS
AND CAST LISTS

Programmes supply production credits and cast lists; in every case the listing is that announced for the first performance. The catalogue of the Shakespeare Centre Library and its index to the production archives provide the incidental details, such as press night and transfer dates. The opening date given is that of the Stratford press night; since the 1970s a small number of 'preview' performances have been given prior to press night. All productions were at the Royal Shakespeare Theatre (known before 1961 as the Shakespeare Memorial Theatre). Characters are listed in the order of Agnes Latham's Arden edition, that is in a roughly hierarchical sequence, with the women's roles separate and a single group for anonymous lords (some of whom have a few lines to speak), ladies and foresters. Theatre programmes, on the other hand, usually divide the play's characters into 'Court' and 'Forest' groups, and not infrequently create a separate section also for 'The de Boys Household'. Court lords almost always reappear as forest lords; only in productions where the same actor plays Duke Senior and Duke Frederick is this interpretational. Another frequent (and fairly neutral) double is that of Charles and William. A number of recent programmes have included the role of Hisperia, Celia's 'gentlewoman' (2.2.10), whose presence on stage is not quite demanded by the text. The Arden cast list does not include Hymen; the role has been added in the lists below when it appears in a programme. The recent disappearance of the two pages who used to be such a prominent feature in earlier productions is clear from these lists; they are gradually subsumed into a pool of pages or 'children', not all of whom would have appeared at every performance, and in the three most recent productions 'It was a lover and his lass' has been sung by adult actors. Numbers in recent RSC *As You Like It* companies are generally much lower than those in the earlier productions in these lists, sometimes as little as half.

1946

Director	Herbert M. Prentice
Set designer	Joyce Hammond
Costume designer	Osborne Robinson
Music	Julius Harrison
Choreography	June Rousselle

DUKE SENIOR	William Avenell
DUKE FREDERICK	Duncan Ross
LE BEAU	Donald Sinden
CHARLES	Anthony Hooper
TOUCHSTONE	Hugh Griffith
OLIVER	Paul Scofield
ORLANDO	Myles Eason
JAQUES DE BOYS	Anthony Groser
DENNIS	David Hobman
ADAM	Douglas Seale
AMIENS	Dudley Jones
JAQUES	Julian Somers
CORIN	Patrick Ross
SILVIUS	Trevor Barker
WILLIAM	Donald Sinden
SIR OLIVER MARTEXT	Anthony Groser

ROSALIND	Ruth Lodge
CELIA	Joy Parker
PHEBE	Muriel Davidson
AUDREY	Nancy Nevinson

PAGES	Sulwen Morgan, David O'Brien

LORDS, LADIES AND FORESTERS ATTENDING ON THE DUKES
Pat Brewer, Eileen Clark, Jennifer Coverdale, Duncan Goddard, Robin Griffin, Anthony Hooper, Lyndon Mason, June Monkhouse, Christian Morrow, Barbara Ormerod, Richard Renny, Michael Rose, John Shaw, Leonard White

Number in company	33
Press night	31 May 1946

1952

Director	Glen Byam Shaw
Designer	Motley
Music	Clifton Parker
Lighting	Julia Wootten
Wrestling	Charles Alexis

DUKE SENIOR	Jack Gwillim
DUKE FREDERICK	Powys Thomas
LE BEAU	Aubrey Woods
CHARLES	Alan Townsend
TOUCHSTONE	Michael Bates
OLIVER	David Dodimead
ORLANDO	Laurence Harvey
JAQUES DE BOYS	Jerome Willis
DENNIS	Brendon Barry
ADAM	James Wellman
AMIENS	Michael Turner
JAQUES	Michael Hordern
CORIN	Mervyn Blake
SILVIUS	Alexander Davion
WILLIAM	Michael Hayes
SIR OLIVER MARTEXT	Edward Atienza

ROSALIND	Margaret Leighton
CELIA	Siobhan McKenna
PHEBE	Maureen Quinney
AUDREY	Jill Showell

PAGES	Derek Hodgson, Thomas Moore

LORDS, LADIES AND FORESTERS ATTENDING ON THE DUKES
Ian Bannen, Margaret Chisholm, Leo Ciceri, Eric Evans, Peter Halliday, Charles Howard, Peter Johnson, John Calvert Lee, Richard Martin, Philip Morant, John Nettleton, William Peacock, Judy Storm, John Turner, Zena Walker, Veronica Wells, Jerome Willis, Kenneth Wynne

Number in company	39
Press night	29 April 1952

1952 (revival)

Director	Glen Byam Shaw
Designer	Motley
Music	Clifton Parker
Lighting	Julia Wootten
Wrestling	Charles Alexis
Choreography	Pauline Grant

DUKE SENIOR	Jack Gwillim
DUKE FREDERICK	Raymond Westwell
LE BEAU	Derek Godfrey
CHARLES	John Turner
TOUCHSTONE	Leo McKern
OLIVER	Terence Longdon
ORLANDO	Keith Michell
JAQUES DE BOYS	Peter Jackson
DENNIS	John Nettleton
ADAM	Kenneth Wynne
AMIENS	Eric Lander
JAQUES	Anthony Quayle
CORIN	Edward Atienza
SILVIUS	Ian Bannen
WILLIAM	James Grout
SIR OLIVER MARTEXT	Derek Godfrey

ROSALIND	Barbara Jefford
CELIA	Charmian Eyre
PHEBE	Zena Walker
AUDREY	Joan MacArthur

PAGES	Derek Hodgson, Thomas Moore

LORDS AND FORESTERS ATTENDING ON THE DUKES
Geoffrey Curtis, Peter Halliday, Ian Mullins, John Nettleton

Number in company	24
Press night	2 December 1952
Tour	Australia and New Zealand, February–March 1953

1957

Director	Glen Byam Shaw
Designer	Motley
Music	Clifton Parker
Lighting	Peter Streuli
Wrestling	Charles Alexis
Choreography	Pauline Grant

DUKE SENIOR	Cyril Luckham
DUKE FREDERICK	Mark Dignam
LE BEAU	Peter Cellier
CHARLES	Ron Haddrick
TOUCHSTONE	Patrick Wymark
OLIVER	Robin Lloyd
ORLANDO	Richard Johnson
JAQUES DE BOYS	John Murray Scott
DENNIS	Derek Mayhew
ADAM	James Wellman
AMIENS	Rex Robinson
JAQUES	Robert Harris
CORIN	Donald Eccles
SILVIUS	Robert Arnold
WILLIAM	Toby Robertson
SIR OLIVER MARTEXT	Donald Layne-Smith
HYMEN	Gordon Wright

ROSALIND	Peggy Ashcroft
CELIA	Jane Wenham
PHEBE	Doreen Aris
AUDREY	Stephanie Bidmead

PAGES	Michael Saunders, Peter Whitmarsh

LORDS, LADIES AND FORESTERS ATTENDING ON THE DUKES
Thane Bettany, Christopher Bond, Antony Brown, Edward Caddick, Simon Carter, John Davidson, Henry Davies, Mavis Edwards, William Elmhirst, Elizabeth Evans, Kenneth Gilbert, Julian Glover, John Grayson, Norman Miller, Peter Palmer, John Salway, Gordon Souter, Roy Spencer, Molly Tapper, Pamela Taylor, Barry Warren

Number in company	44
Press night	2 April 1957

1961

Director	Michael Elliott
Designer	Richard Negri
Music	George Hall
Lighting	Richard Pilbrow
Wrestling	Charles Alexis
Movement	Litz Fisk

DUKE SENIOR	Redmond Phillips
DUKE FREDERICK	Tony Church
LE BEAU	Ian Richardson
CHARLES	Sebastian Breaks
CHARLES'S SECOND	Paul Bailey
TOUCHSTONE	Colin Blakely
OLIVER	David Buck
ORLANDO	Ian Bannen
JAQUES DE BOYS	Ian Richardson
DENNIS	Paul Bailey
ADAM	Clifford Rose
AMIENS	Eric Flynn
JAQUES	Max Adrian
CORIN	Russell Hunter
SILVIUS	Peter McEnery
WILLIAM	Gordon Gostelow
SIR OLIVER MARTEXT	William Wallis

ROSALIND	Vanessa Redgrave
CELIA	Rosalind Knight
PHEBE	Jill Dixon
AUDREY	Patsy Byrne

PAGES	Michael Stephens, Barry Stockwell

LORDS, LADIES AND FORESTERS ATTENDING ON THE DUKES
Richard Barr, Michael Blackham, Sebastian Breaks, Maroussia Frank, Peter Holmes, Roger Jerome, James Kerry, Narissa Knights, Bruce McKenzie, Gareth Morgan, Michael Murray, Rosemary Mussell, William Wallis, Georgina Ward, Brian Wright

Number in company	34
Press night	4 July 1961
Transfer	London, Aldwych Theatre, 10 January 1962
Video recording	Filmed for BBC television (redirected by Ronald Eyre and broadcast March 1963; a copy is in the Shakespeare Centre Library)

1967

Director	David Jones
Designer	Timothy O'Brien
Music	William Mathias
Lighting	John Bradley
Wrestling	Roy Scammell
Choreography	Sheila Falconer

DUKE SENIOR	Patrick Stewart
DUKE FREDERICK	Morgan Sheppard
LE BEAU	Tim Wylton
CHARLES	Michael Goldie
TOUCHSTONE	Roy Kinnear
OLIVER	Charles Thomas
ORLANDO	Michael Williams
JAQUES DE BOYS	Robert East
DENNIS	Seymour Matthews
ADAM	George Cormack
AMIENS	Martin Best
JAQUES	Alan Howard
CORIN	Terrence Hardiman
SILVIUS	John Kane
WILLIAM	Tim Wylton
SIR OLIVER MARTEXT	Richard Simpson
HYMEN	John Kaye

ROSALIND	Dorothy Tutin
CELIA	Janet Suzman
PHEBE	June Watts
AUDREY	Frances de la Tour

PAGES	Rufus Frampton, Richard Kahn

LORDS, LADIES AND FORESTERS ATTENDING ON THE DUKES
Tom Georgeson, Sarah Hyde, Trevor Kent, Ben Kingsley, Robert Lloyd, Ursula Mohan, Gregg Palmer, Roger Rees, Gregory Reid, Derek Steen, Mark York

Number in company	33
Press night	15 June 1967
Transfer	London, Aldwych Theatre, 19 July 1967
Tour	Britain, September–November 1967
	Los Angeles, January–February 1968

1968 (revival of 1967 production)

Director	David Jones
Designer	Timothy O'Brien
Music	William Mathias
Lighting	John Bradley
Wrestling	Roy Scammell
Choreography	Christie Dickason

DUKE SENIOR	Terrence Hardiman
DUKE FREDERICK	Clifford Rose
LE BEAU	Richard Simpson
CHARLES	John Shrapnel
TOUCHSTONE	Patrick Stewart
OLIVER	Bernard Lloyd
ORLANDO	Michael Williams
JAQUES DE BOYS	Eric Allan
DENNIS	John York
ADAM	George Cormack
AMIENS	Ben Kingsley
JAQUES	Alan Howard
CORIN	Richard Moore
SILVIUS	Bruce Myers
WILLIAM	Bryan Robson
SIR OLIVER MARTEXT	Richard Simpson
HYMEN	Richard Moore

ROSALIND	Janet Suzman
CELIA	Rowena Cooper
PHEBE	June Watts
AUDREY	Susan Fleetwood

PAGES	Rufus Frampton, Paul Stratford

LORDS, LADIES AND FORESTERS ATTENDING ON THE DUKES
Trevor Adams, Hugh Keays Byrne, Madelaine Cannon, Ralph Cotterill, Julian Curry, David Firth, Stephen Greif, John Kay, Stuart McGugan, Philip Manikum, Lyn Moore, Robert Oates, Gareth Thomas, Ted Valentine

Number in company	35
Press night	15 May 1968

1973

Director	Buzz Goodbody
Designer	Christopher Morley
Music	Guy Woolfenden
Lighting	Brian Harris
Wrestling	Brian Glover
Choreography	John Broome

DUKE SENIOR	Tony Church
DUKE FREDERICK	Clement McCallin
LE BEAU	Anthony Pedley
CHARLES	Brian Glover
TOUCHSTONE	Derek Smith
OLIVER	Charles Keating
ORLANDO	David Suchet
JAQUES DE BOYS	John Abbott
DENNIS	Nickolas Grace
ADAM	Sydney Bromley
AMIENS	Ray Armstrong
JAQUES	Richard Pasco
CORIN	Jeffery Dench
SILVIUS	Peter Machin
WILLIAM	Lloyd Maguire
SIR OLIVER MARTEXT	Richard Mayes
HYMEN	Michael Ensign

ROSALIND	Eileen Atkins
CELIA	Maureen Lipman
HISPERIA	Janet Whiteside
PHEBE	Janet Chappell
AUDREY	Annette Badland

PAGES	Ian Collins and Simon Walker *or*
	Merlin Milner and Neil Weerdmeester

LORDS, LADIES AND FORESTERS ATTENDING ON THE DUKES
John Abbott, Janet Chappell, Michael Ensign, Nickolas Grace, Wilfred Grove, Catherine Kessler, Lloyd McGuire, Peter Machin, Colin Mayes, Leon Tanner

Number in company	29
Press night	12 June 1973

1977

Director	Trevor Nunn
Designer	John Napier
Music	Stephen Oliver
Lighting	John Watts
Wrestling	Peter Woodward
Choreography	Gillian Lynne

DUKE SENIOR	Oliver Ford-Davies
DUKE FREDERICK	John Rhys-Davies
LE BEAU	Graham Crowden
CHARLES	Jack Klaff
TOUCHSTONE	Alan David
OLIVER	Charles Dance
ORLANDO	Peter McEnery
JAQUES DE BOYS	Bille Brown
DENNIS	Michael Bertenshaw
ADAM	Jeffery Dench
AMIENS	Michael Bulman
JAQUES	Emrys James
CORIN	Edwin Richfield
SILVIUS	Ian Gelder
WILLIAM	David Shaw-Parker
SIR OLIVER MARTEXT	Paul Imbusch
HYMEN	Michael Follis
NATURE	Michael Bulman
FORTUNE	Ann Holloway

ROSALIND	Kate Nelligan
CELIA	Judith Paris
HISPERIA	Roberta Taylor
PHEBE	Lynsey Baxter
AUDREY	Ann Holloway

PAGES	Andrew Coonan, Alberto Fernandez, Owen James, William James

ATTENDANTS ON HYMEN
Jill Baker, Andrew Coonan, Alberto Fernandez, Owen James, William James, Roberta Taylor

LORDS, LADIES AND FORESTERS ATTENDING ON THE DUKES
Jill Baker, Michael Bertenshaw, Bille Brown, Pat Connell, Michael
Follis, Ann Holloway, Dominic Jephcott, Morris Perry, Roy Purcell,
David Shaw-Parker, Roberta Taylor

Number in company	31
Press night	6 September 1977
Transfer	Newcastle, Theatre Royal, 13 February 1978
	London, Aldwych Theatre, 15 September 1978

1980

Director	Terry Hands
Designer	Farrah
Music	Guy Woolfenden
Lighting	Terry Hands, with Clive Morris
Wrestling	Ian McKay
Choreography	David Toguri

DUKE SENIOR	Trevor Baxter
DUKE FREDERICK	Bruce Purchase
LE BEAU	Bille Brown
CHARLES	Terry Wood
TOUCHSTONE	Joe Melia
OLIVER	Jonathan Hyde
ORLANDO	John Bowe
JAQUES DE BOYS	Michael Siberry
DENNIS	Michael Fitzgerald (Rolf Saxon in 1981 revival)
ADAM	Jimmy Gardner
AMIENS	Philip Dennis
JAQUES	Derek Godfrey
CORIN	Tom Wilkinson (Raymond Westwell in 1981 revival)
SILVIUS	Allan Hendrick
WILLIAM	Terry Wood
SIR OLIVER MARTEXT	Bille Brown

ROSALIND	Susan Fleetwood
CELIA	Sinead Cusack
PHEBE	Julia Tobin
AUDREY	Corrina Seddon

PAGES	Matthew Beacham, Kevin Brannen, Christopher Cattle (not in 1981 revival), Melanie Leach, Nicholas Storr

LORDS, LADIES AND FORESTERS ATTENDING ON THE DUKES
Gordon Dulieu, Michael Fitzgerald (Rolf Saxon in 1981 revival),
Arthur Kohn, Pip Miller, Brett Usher

Number in company	27 (26 in 1981 revival)
Press night	3 April 1980
Transfer	Newcastle, Theatre Royal, 31 March 1981
Revival	Stratford, 4 May 1981
Transfer	London, Aldwych Theatre, 22 July 1981

1985

Director	Adrian Noble
Designer	Bob Crowley
Music	Howard Blake
Lighting	David Hersey
Wrestling	Ian McKay
Choreography	Stuart Hopps
Sound	John A. Leonard
DUKE SENIOR	Joseph O'Conor
DUKE FREDERICK	Joseph O'Conor
LE BEAU	Griffith Jones
CHARLES	Campbell Morrison
TOUCHSTONE	Nicky Henson
OLIVER	Bruce Alexander
ORLANDO	Hilton McRae
JAQUES DE BOYS	Paul Spence
DENNIS	Russell Boulter
ADAM	Mark Dignam
AMIENS	Andrew Yeats
JAQUES	Alan Rickman
CORIN	Colin Douglas
SILVIUS	Roger Hyams
WILLIAM	Campbell Morrison
SIR OLIVER MARTEXT	Griffith Jones
ROSALIND	Juliet Stevenson
CELIA	Fiona Shaw
PHEBE	Lesley Manville
AUDREY	Mary Jo Randle
PAGES	Alan Brookes, Mark Brooks, Simon Page, Christopher Storr

LORDS, LADIES AND FORESTERS ATTENDING ON THE DUKES
Russell Boulter, Richard Conway, Brian Horstead, Hugh Simon, Paul Spence, Alexander Wilson

Number in company	25
Press night	23 April 1985
Transfer	London, Barbican Theatre, 17 December 1985
Video recording	12 November 1985

1989

Director	John Caird
Designer	Ultz
Music	Ilona Sekacz
Lighting	Alan Burrett
Wrestling	Jannica Svärd
Choreography	Matthew Bourne
Sound	Charles Horne

DUKE SENIOR	Clifford Rose
DUKE FREDERICK	Clifford Rose
LE BEAU	Hugh Ross
CHARLES	Andrew Tansey
TOUCHSTONE	Mark Williams
OLIVER	Howard Ward
ORLANDO	Jerome Flynn
JAQUES DE BOYS	Jason Flemyng
DENNIS	Adrian Hilton
ADAM	Eric Francis
AMIENS	Craig Pinder
JAQUES	Hugh Ross
CORIN	George Malpas
SILVIUS	Alan Cumming
WILLIAM	Andrew Tansey
SIR OLIVER MARTEXT	Andrew Hesker
HYMEN	Andrew Tansey

ROSALIND	Sophie Thompson
CELIA	Gillian Bevan
PHEBE	Cassie Stuart
AUDREY	Joanna Mays

CHILDREN
Paul Brookes, Andrew Kwan, Robert Langley, Ray Lawley, Charlene O'Dowd, Louise Potter, Charlotte Potts, Minna Zouhou

LORDS, LADIES AND FORESTERS ATTENDING ON THE DUKES, AND 'GOATGIRLS'
Judith Brydon, Alan Cumming, Simon D'Arcy, Jason Flemyng, Eric Francis, Andrew Hesker, Adrian Hilton, Maxwell Hutcheon, David

Joyce, George Malpas, Joanna Mays, Clara Onyemere, Craig Pinder,
Alison Ruffelle, Cassie Stuart

Number in company	31
Press night	13 September 1989
Transfer	Newcastle, Theatre Royal, 20 February 1990
	London, Barbican Theatre, 11 April 1990
Video recording	14 September 1989

1992

Director	David Thacker
Designer	Johan Engels
Music	Gary Yershon
Lighting	Jimmy Simmons
Wrestling	Terry King
Movement	Lesley Hutchison
Sound	Paul Slocombe

DUKE SENIOR	Jeffery Dench
DUKE FREDERICK	Andrew Jarvis
LE BEAU	Nick Kemp
CHARLES	Nick Holder
TOUCHSTONE	Anthony O'Donnell
OLIVER	Adrian Lukis
ORLANDO	Peter de Jersey
JAQUES DE BOYS	Alan Cox
DENNIS	Jack Waters
ADAM	Alfred Burke
AMIENS	David Burt
JAQUES	Michael Siberry
CORIN	John Bott
SILVIUS	Andrew Cryer
WILLIAM	Nick Holder
SIR OLIVER MARTEXT	James Walker

ROSALIND	Samantha Bond (Kate Buffery from 23 September)
CELIA	Phyllida Hancock (Samantha Bond in Barbican transfer)
HISPERIA	Susie Lee Hayward
PHEBE	Emma Gregory
AUDREY	Susan-Jane Tanner

LORDS, LADIES, FORESTERS, 'SOLDIERS' (AT DUKE FREDERICK'S COURT), AND 'SHEPHERDESSES'
David Burt, Jonathan Cake, Alan Cox, Andrew Cryer, Bella Enahoro, Emma Gregory, Susie Lee Hayward, Nick Holder, Andrew Jarvis, Nick Kemp, Jenna Russell, Susan-Jane Tanner, James Walker, Jack Waters

Number in company	23
Press night	22 April 1992
Transfer	Newcastle, Theatre Royal, 22 February 1993
	London, Barbican Theatre, 21 April 1993
Video recording	15 January 1993

1996

Director	Steven Pimlott
Designer	Ashley Martin-Davies
Music	Jason Carr
Lighting	Mimi Jordan Sherin
Wrestling	Terry King
Movement	Liz Ranken
Sound	Paul Arditti

DUKE SENIOR	Robert Demeger
DUKE FREDERICK	Colum Convey
LE BEAU	Raymond Bowers
CHARLES	Ross O'Hennessy
TOUCHSTONE	David Tennant
OLIVER	Sebastian Harcombe
ORLANDO	Liam Cunningham
JAQUES DE BOYS	Mark Gillis
DENNIS	Brian Abbott
ADAM	John Quayle
AMIENS	Blair Wilson
JAQUES	John Woodvine
CORIN	Arthur Cox
SILVIUS	Joseph Fiennes
WILLIAM	Simeon Defoe
SIR OLIVER MARTEXT	Raymond Bowers

ROSALIND	Niamh Cusack
CELIA	Rachel Joyce
HISPERIA	Emma Poole
PHEBE	Victoria Hamilton
AUDREY	Susannah Elliott-Knight

HYMEN	Doreen Andrew

LORDS AND FORESTERS ATTENDING ON THE DUKES
Nathaniel Duncan, Colin Farrell, Simon Westwood

Number in company	24
Press night	25 April 1996
Transfer	London, Barbican Theatre, 23 October 1996
Video recording	17 May 1996

2000

Director	Gregory Doran
Designers	Kaffe Fassett and Niki Turner
Music	Django Bates
Lighting	Howard Harrison
Wrestling	Terry King
Movement	Siân Williams
Sound	Martin Slavin

DUKE SENIOR	Ian Hogg
DUKE FREDERICK	Ian Hogg
LE BEAU	David Mara
CHARLES	Joshua Richards
TOUCHSTONE	Adrian Schiller
OLIVER	Tom Smith
ORLANDO	Anthony Howell
JAQUES DE BOYS	Christian Mahrle
DENNIS	Gavin Abbott
ADAM	Peter Copley
AMIENS	Paul Ewing
JAQUES	Declan Conlon
CORIN	Barry McCarthy
SILVIUS	Andrew Pointon
WILLIAM	Gavin Abbott
SIR OLIVER MARTEXT	David Acton

ROSALIND	Alexandra Gilbreath
CELIA	Nancy Carroll
HISPERIA	Emma Pallant
PHEBE	Danielle Tilley
AUDREY	Nina Conti

LORDS, LADIES AND FORESTERS ATTENDING ON THE DUKES
Vincent Brimble (First Forest Lord); other parts played by members of the company

Number in company	20
Press night	23 March 2000
Transfer	Newcastle, Theatre Royal, 30 October 2000
	London, Barbican (The Pit), 2 January 2001
Video recording	5 October 2000

REVIEWS CITED

Unless otherwise stated in the text, all references are to reviews of the original production, not the transfer or revival.

1946

Berrow's Worcester Journal, 8 June 1946
Birmingham Evening Despatch, 1 June 1946
Birmingham Post, 1 June 1946, T.C. K[emp]
Birmingham Weekly Post, 7 June 1946
Daily Telegraph, 1 June 1946, W.A. Darlington
Evesham Journal, 8 June 1946
Leamington Spa Courier, 7 June 1946
Malvern Gazette, 8 June 1946
News Chronicle, 7 June 1946, Alan Dent
Stage, 6 June 1946
Stratford-upon-Avon Herald, 7 June 1946
Times, 3 June 1946
Warwick Advertiser, 14 June 1946

1952

Birmingham Evening Despatch, 30 April 1952
Birmingham Gazette, 30 April 1952
Birmingham Mail, 30 April 1952
Birmingham Post, 1 May 1952
Birmingham Weekly Post, 2 May 1952
Bolton Evening News, 3 May 1952
Coventry Evening Telegraph, 30 April 1952
Coventry Standard, 2 May 1952
Daily Express, 30 April 1952
Daily Herald, 30 April 1952

Daily Mail, 30 April 1952
Daily Telegraph, 30 April 1952, W.A. Darlington
Evening News, 30 April 1952
Evening Standard, 30 April 1952
Jack O'London's Weekly, 16 May 1952, J.C. Trewin
Lady, 15 May 1952, J.C. Trewin
Leamington Spa Courier, 2 May 1952
Manchester Daily Despatch, 30 April 1952
Manchester Guardian, 30 April 1952
Manchester Guardian Weekly, 3 May 1952, Philip Hope-Wallace
News Chronicle, 30 April 1952, Alan Dent
New Statesman, 10 May 1952, T.C. Worsley
Nottingham Guardian, 1 May 1952
Observer, 4 May 1952, Ivor Brown
Sketch, undated cutting in RSC theatre records collection
Solihull News, 3 May 1952
Spectator, 9 May 1952, Peter Fleming
Stage, 1 May 1952
Stratford-upon-Avon Herald, 2 May 1952
Sunday Times, 4 May 1952
Time and Tide, 10 May 1952
Times, 30 April 1952
Truth, 9 May 1952
Warwick Advertiser, 2 May 1952
Western Daily Press, 4 May 1952

STRATFORD REVIVAL

Leamington Spa Courier, 4 December 1952
Stage, 4 December 1952
Stratford-upon-Avon Herald, 5 December 1952

1957

Birmingham Evening Despatch, 3 April 1957
Birmingham Mail, 3 April 1957
Birmingham Post, 3 April 1957, J.C. T[rewin]
Birmingham Weekly Post, 5 April 1957

Coventry Evening Telegraph, 3 April 1957
Daily Mail, 3 April 1957, Cecil Wilson
Daily Telegraph, 3 April 1957, W.A. Darlington
Evening Standard, 3 April 1957, Milton Shulman
Financial Times, 3 April 1957, Derek Granger
Illustrated London News, 13 April 1957, J.C. Trewin
Liverpool Post, 3 April 1957
Manchester Guardian, 4 April 1957
New Statesman, 13 April 1957
Oxford Mail, 3 April 1957
Oxford Times, 5 April 1957
Punch, 10 April 1957
Shakespeare Quarterly, 8 (1957), 480–2, Muriel St Clare Byrne
Stage, 4 April 1957
Star, 3 April 1957
Stratford-upon-Avon Herald, 5 April 1957, Rosemary Anne Sisson
Sunday Times, 7 April 1957
Time and Tide, 13 April 1957, Philip Hope-Wallace
Times, 3 April 1957
Warwick Advertiser, 5 April 1957
Western Daily Press, 5 April 1957
Western Independent, 7 April 1957
Yorkshire Post, 3 April 1957

1961

Birmingham Mail, 5 July 1961
Birmingham Post, 5 July 1961, J.C. Trewin
Coventry Evening Telegraph, 5 July 1961
Daily Express, 5 July 1961, Bernard Levin
Daily Herald, 5 July 1961, David Nathan
Daily Mail, 5 July 1961, Robert Muller
Evening News, 5 July 1961
Financial Times, 5 July 1961, T.C. Worsley
Glasgow Herald, 7 July 1961
Guardian, 6 July 1961, Gerard Fay
Jack O'London's Weekly, 13 July 1961, Caryl Brahms
Leamington Spa Courier, 6 July 1961

Liverpool Post, 5 July 1961
Middlesbrough Evening Gazette, 5 July 1961
Morning Advertiser, 10 July 1961, Geoffrey Tarran
New Statesman, 14 July 1961
Oxford Mail, 5 July 1961
Oxford Times, 7 July 1961
Shakespeare Quarterly, 12 (1961), 432–4, Robert Speaight
South Wales Evening Argus, 5 July 1961
Spectator, 14 July 1961, Bamber Gascoigne
Stage, 6 July 1961
Stratford-upon-Avon Herald, 7 July 1961, Edmund Gardner
Sunday Mercury, 9 July 1961
Sunday Times, 9 July 1961, J.W. Lambert
Tatler, 9 July 1961
Times, 5 July 1961
Warwick Advertiser, 8 July 1961
Yorkshire Post, 5 July 1961

ALDWYCH TRANSFER (1962)

Bristol Evening Post, 11 January 1962
Daily Telegraph, 11 January 1962, W.A. Darlington
Evening News, 11 January 1962, Felix Barker
Evening Standard, 11 January 1962, Milton Shulman
Guardian, 11 January 1962, Philip Hope-Wallace
Liverpool Post, 13 January 1962
New Statesman, 19 January 1962, Roger Gellert
Observer, 15 January 1962, Irving Wardle
Sunday Times, 15 January 1962, J.W. Lambert
Times, 11 January 1962

1967

Birmingham Post, 16 June 1967, J.C. Trewin
Bristol Evening Post, 17 June 1967
Daily Express, 16 June 1967, Herbert Kretzmer
Daily Mail, 16 June 1967, Peter Lewis
Daily Telegraph, 16 June 1967, W.A. Darlington

Evening News, 16 June 1967, Felix Barker
Evening Standard, 16 June 1967, Milton Shulman
Financial Times, 16 June 1967, B.A. Young
Guardian, 16 June 1967, Gareth Lloyd Evans
Illustrated London News, 24 June 1967, J.C. Trewin
Leamington Spa Courier, 23 June 1967
Liverpool Post, 16 June 1967
Morning Star, 17 June 1967
New Statesman, 23 June 1967, D.A.N. Jones
Observer, 18 June 1967, Ronald Bryden
Queen, 15 July 1967, Gerard Fay
Spectator, 23 June 1967, Hilary Spurling
Stratford-upon-Avon Herald, 23 June 1967
Sun, 16 June 1967, Ann Pacey
Sunday Telegraph, 18 June 1967, Alan Brien
Times, 16 June 1967, Irving Wardle
Yorkshire Post, 16 June 1967

ALDWYCH TRANSFER

Birmingham Post, 20 July 1967, J.C. Trewin
Daily Telegraph, 20 July 1967, W.A. Darlington
Financial Times, 20 July 1967, John Higgins
Liverpool Echo, 28 July 1967
Nottingham Observer, 1 August 1967
Time and Tide, 27 July 1967

STRATFORD REVIVAL (1968)

Birmingham Post, 22 May 1968, J.C. Trewin
Daily Mail, 22 May 1968, Barry Norman
Daily Telegraph, 22 May 1968, Eric Shorter
Financial Times, 22 May 1968, B.A. Young
Guardian, 22 May 1968, Gareth Lloyd Evans
Liverpool Post, 22 May 1968
Oxford Mail, 22 May 1968
Shakespeare Quarterly, 19 (1968), 370–1, Robert Speaight
South Wales Evening Argus, 24 May 1968

Stage, 23 May 1968
Stratford-upon-Avon Herald, 24 May 1968
Times, 22 May 1968, Michael Billington

1973

Berrow's Worcester Journal, 14 June 1973
Birmingham Post, 14 June 1973, J.C. Trewin
Cahiers Elisabéthains, 4 (1973), 51–2, Jean Fuzier and Jean-Marie
    Maguin
Coventry Evening Telegraph, 13 June 1973
Daily Express, 13 June 1973, Herbert Kretzmer
Daily Mail, 13 June 1973, Jack Tinker
Daily Telegraph, 13 June 1973, John Barber
Evening Standard, 13 June 1973, Milton Shulman
Financial Times, 13 June 1973, B.A. Young
Guardian, 13 June 1973, Michael Billington
Jewish Chronicle, 15 June 1973, David Nathan
Listener, 21 June 1973, John Elsom
Malvern Gazette, 14 June 1973
New Statesman, 22 June 1973, Benedict Nightingale
Nottingham Guardian, 14 June 1973
Observer, 17 June 1973, Robert Cushman
Oxford Mail, 15 June 1973
Punch, 20 June 1973, Jeremy Kingston
Shakespeare Survey 27 (1974), 149–50, Peter Thomson
Spectator, 23 June 1973, Kenneth Hurren
Stage, 21 June 1973, Wendy Monk
Sunday Telegraph, 17 June 1973, Frank Marcus
Sunday Times, 17 June 1973, J.W. Lambert
Times, 13 June 1973, Irving Wardle

1977

Birmingham Post, 12 September 1977, J.C. Trewin
Coventry Evening Telegraph, 9 September 1977
Daily Mail, 13 September 1977, Jack Tinker
Daily Telegraph, 9 September 1977, John Barber

Evening News, 9 September 1977
Financial Times, 8 September 1977, B.A. Young
Guardian, 10 September 1977, Michael Billington
Jewish Chronicle, 16 September 1977, David Nathan
Listener, 15 September 1977, John Elsom
Morning Star, 15 September 1977, Gordon Parsons
Observer, 11 September 1977, Robert Cushman
Oxford Mail, 9 September 1977
Oxford Times, 16 September 1977
Shakespeare Quarterly, 29 (1978), 215–16, J.C. Trewin
Shakespeare Survey 31 (1978), 146–7, Roger Warren
Stratford-upon-Avon Herald, 16 September 1977, Gareth Lloyd Evans
Sunday Telegraph, 11 September 1977, Frank Marcus
Sunday Times, 11 September 1977, John Peter
Times, 9 September 1977, Irving Wardle

NEWCASTLE TRANSFER (1978)

Newcastle Journal, 20 February 1978

ALDWYCH TRANSFER (1978)

Financial Times, 18 September 1978, B.A. Young
Observer, 24 September 1978, Robert Cushman
Spectator, 23 September 1978, Peter Jenkins

1980

Birmingham Mail, 11 April 1980
Birmingham Post, 7 April 1980, J.C. Trewin
Country Life, 24 April 1980, Ian Stewart
Coventry Evening Telegraph, 4 April 1980
Daily Telegraph, 7 April 1980, Eric Shorter
Financial Times, 5 April 1980, B.A. Young
Guardian, 5 April 1980, Michael Billington
Listener, 17 April 1980, Alan Drury
New Statesman, 11 April 1980, Benedict Nightingale
Observer, 13 April 1980, Robert Cushman
Oxford Mail, 8 April 1980

Plays and Players, May 1980, Sally Aire
Punch, 30 April 1980, Sheridan Morley
Shakespeare Quarterly, 32 (1981), 163–4, J.C. Trewin
Shakespeare Survey 34 (1981), 149–51, Roger Warren
Stratford-upon-Avon Herald, 11 April 1980, Gareth Lloyd Evans
Sunday Mercury, 6 April 1980
Sunday Times, 6 April 1980, John Peter
Times, 5 April 1980, Irving Wardle
Times Literary Supplement, 18 April 1980, Jeremy Treglown
Yorkshire Post, 5 April 1980, Desmond Pratt

ALDWYCH TRANSFER (1981)

Birmingham Post, 24 July 1981, J.C. Trewin
Daily Telegraph, 23 July 1981, John Barber
Financial Times, 23 July 1981, Michael Coveney
Guardian, 23 July 1981, Michael Billington
New Standard, 23 July 1981, Charles Spencer
Observer, 26 July 1981, Robert Cushman

1985

Daily Telegraph, 25 April 1985, John Barber
Financial Times, 25 April 1985, Martin Hoyle
Guardian, 26 April 1985, Michael Billington
Observer, 28 April 1985, Michael Ratcliffe
Oxford Mail, 24 April 1985
Plays and Players, June 1985, David Nathan
Shakespeare Quarterly, 37 (1986), 116–18, Roger Warren
Shakespeare Survey 39 (1987), 199–202, Nicholas Shrimpton
Spectator, 18 May 1985, Christopher Edwards
Stage, 2 May 1985, R.B. Marriott
Times, 24 April 1985, Irving Wardle
Times Educational Supplement, 10 May 1985, Nicholas Shrimpton
Times Literary Supplement, 3 May 1985, Eric Sams

BARBICAN TRANSFER

Daily Mail, 18 December 1985, Jack Tinker

Financial Times, 18 December 1985, Michael Coveney
Guardian, 19 December 1985, Nicholas de Jongh
Times, 18 December 1985, Irving Wardle

1989

Birmingham Post, 15 September 1989, Richard Edmonds
Country Life, 21 September 1989, Michael Billington
Financial Times, 15 September 1989, Michael Coveney
Guardian, 15 September 1989, Michael Billington
Independent, 15 September 1989, Peter Kemp
New York Herald Tribune, 20 September 1989, Michael Billington
Shakespeare Quarterly, 41 (1990), 491–3, Robert Smallwood
Shakespeare Survey 44 (1991), 162–3, Peter Holland
Spectator, 16 September 1989, Christopher Edwards
Stratford-upon-Avon Herald, 22 September 1989, Paul Lapworth
Sunday Correspondent, 17 September 1989, Hugo Williams
Sunday Telegraph, 17 September 1989, John Gross
Sunday Times, 17 September 1989, John Peter
Times Educational Supplement, 22 September 1989, Rex Gibson
Times Literary Supplement, 22 September 1989, Katherine Duncan-Jones
Yorkshire Post, 15 September 1989

BARBICAN TRANSFER (1990)

Birmingham Post, 16 April 1990, Stanley Slaughter
Guardian, 13 April 1990, Nicholas de Jongh

1992

Birmingham Mail, 23 April 1992, Michael Davies
Birmingham Post, 24 April 1992, Terry Grimley
Daily Mail, 23 April 1992, Jack Tinker
Daily Telegraph, 24 April 1992, Charles Spencer
Evening Standard, 23 April 1992, Nicholas de Jongh
Financial Times, 24 April 1992, David Murray
Guardian, 24 April 1992, Michael Billington
Independent, 24 April 1992, Paul Taylor
Observer, 26 April 1992, Michael Coveney

Plays and Players, June 1992, Garry O'Connor
Shakespeare Quarterly, 44 (1993), 347–9, Robert Smallwood
Shakespeare Survey 46 (1993), 177–80, Peter Holland
Stratford-upon-Avon Herald, 1 May 1992, Paul Lapworth
Sunday Telegraph, 26 April 1992, John Gross
Sunday Times, 26 April 1992, John Peter
Times, 24 April 1992, Benedict Nightingale
Times Literary Supplement, 8 May 1992, Lindsay Duguid

BARBICAN TRANSFER (1993)

Daily Express, 22 April 1993, Maureen Paton
Daily Mail, 22 April 1993, Jack Tinker
Evening Standard, 22 April 1993, Michael Arditti
Stage, 13 May 1993, Peter Roberts
Times, 24 April 1993, Martin Hoyle

1996

Birmingham Post, 27 April 1996, Richard Edmonds
Daily Telegraph, 27 April 1996, Charles Spencer
Evening News, 27 April 1996, Karen Harbridge
Evening Standard, 26 April 1996, Nicholas de Jongh
Financial Times, 29 April 1996, David Murray
Guardian, 30 April 1996, Michael Billington
Independent, 27 April 1996, Robert Hanks
Observer, 28 April 1996, Michael Coveney
Shakespeare Quarterly, 48 (1997), 208–10, Russell Jackson
Shakespeare Survey 50 (1997), 203–7, Robert Smallwood
Sunday Mercury, 28 April 1996
Sunday Times, 4 May 1996, John Peter
Time Out, 1 May 1996
Times, 27 April 1996, Benedict Nightingale
Times Literary Supplement, 17 May 1996, John Mullan

BARBICAN TRANSFER

What's On, 30 October 1996

2000

Cahiers Elisabéthains, 58 (2000), 78–80, Peter J. Smith
Daily Telegraph, 27 March 2000, Charles Spencer
Guardian, 25 March 2000, Michael Billington
Independent, 28 March 2000, Paul Taylor
Independent on Sunday, 26 March 2000, Robert Butler
Observer, 26 March 2000, Susannah Clapp
Shakespeare Quarterly, 52 (2001), 109–10, Russell Jackson
Shakespeare Survey 54 (2001), 271–3, Michael Dobson
Stratford-upon-Avon Herald, 30 March 2000, Anne Tugwell
Sunday Telegraph, 26 March 2000, John Gross
Sunday Times, 2 April 2000, John Peter
Times, 27 March 2000, Benedict Nightingale

BARBICAN (PIT) TRANSFER (2001)

Financial Times, 5 January 2001, Ian Shuttleworth
Guardian, 4 January 2001, Phil Daoust
What's On, 10 January 2001, John Thaxter

ABBREVIATIONS

Berrow's Worcs. J.	*Berrow's Worcester Journal*
Birm. E. Desp.	*Birmingham Evening Despatch*
Birm. Mail	*Birmingham Mail*
Birm. Post	*Birmingham Post*
Birm. W. Post	*Birmingham Weekly Post*
Bolton E. News	*Bolton Evening News*
Bristol E. Post	*Bristol Evening Post*
Cahiers Elis.	*Cahiers Elisabéthains*
Country L.	*Country Life*
Coventry E. Tel.	*Coventry Evening Telegraph*
Coventry Sta.	*Coventry Standard*
D. Express	*Daily Express*
D. Herald	*Daily Herald*
D. Mail	*Daily Mail*
D. Telegraph	*Daily Telegraph*
E. News	*Evening News*
E. Standard	*Evening Standard*
Evesham J.	*Evesham Journal*
FT	*Financial Times*
Glasgow Her.	*Glasgow Herald*
Illus. Lon. News	*Illustrated London News*
Indep. Sun.	*Independent on Sunday*
Jack O'L.	*Jack O'London's Weekly*
Jewish Chron.	*Jewish Chronicle*
Leam. Spa Cour.	*Leamington Spa Courier*
Liv. Echo	*Liverpool Echo*
Liv. Post	*Liverpool Post*
Malvern Gaz.	*Malvern Gazette*
Man. D. Desp.	*Manchester Daily Despatch*
Man. Guardian	*Manchester Guardian*

Man. Guardian W.	*Manchester Guardian Weekly*
Middles. E. Gaz.	*Middlesbrough Evening Gazette*
Morn. Adv.	*Morning Advertiser*
Morn. Star	*Morning Star*
Newcastle J.	*Newcastle Journal*
New Stand.	*New Standard*
New States.	*New Statesman*
News Chron.	*News Chronicle*
Nott. Guardian	*Nottingham Guardian*
Nott. Observer	*Nottingham Observer*
Oxf. Mail	*Oxford Mail*
Oxf. Times	*Oxford Times*
Plays & P.	*Plays and Players*
S. Corresp.	*Sunday Correspondent*
S. Mercury	*Sunday Mercury*
S. Telegraph	*Sunday Telegraph*
S. Times	*Sunday Times*
S. Wales E. Arg.	*South Wales Evening Argus*
SA Herald	*Stratford-upon-Avon Herald*
Solihull N.	*Solihull News*
SQ	*Shakespeare Quarterly*
SS	*Shakespeare Survey*
TES	*Times Educational Supplement*
Time & T.	*Time and Tide*
TLS	*Times Literary Supplement*
Warwick Adv.	*Warwick Advertiser*
West. D. Press	*Western Daily Press*
West. Indep.	*Western Independent*
Yorks. Post	*Yorkshire Post*

BIBLIOGRAPHY

PRODUCTION ARCHIVES

The primary source for all productions at Stratford-upon-Avon is the collection of the Shakespeare Centre Library. Its holdings include promptbooks, programmes and other theatre documents for all post-war productions of *As You Like It*, as well as press cuttings ('Theatre Records'), photographs and (for productions from the 1957 one onwards) colour slides. There are also fixed-camera archival video recordings for the 1985, 1989, 1992, 1996 and 2000 productions. (That for the 1992 production was made late in the season, after Samantha Bond had been replaced as Rosalind by Kate Buffery.) The library also holds a copy of the BBC television film version of the 1961 production.

BOOKS AND ARTICLES

Addenbrooke, David, *The Royal Shakespeare Company: The Peter Hall Years* (London, 1974)

Barber, C.L., *Shakespeare's Festive Comedy* (Princeton, N.J., 1959)

Barton, Anne, '*As You Like It* and *Twelfth Night*: Shakespeare's sense of an ending', in Malcolm Bradbury and David Palmer (eds), *Shakespearian Comedy*, Stratford-upon-Avon Studies, 14 (London, 1972), 160–80

Bate, Jonathan and Russell Jackson (eds), *Shakespeare: An Illustrated Stage History* (Oxford, 1996)

Beauman, Sally, *The Royal Shakespeare Company: A History of Ten Decades* (Oxford, 1982)

Bowe, John, 'Orlando in *As You Like It*', in Philip Brockbank (ed.), *Players of Shakespeare 1* (Cambridge, 1989), 67–76

Brissenden, Alan (ed.), *As You Like It*, The Oxford Shakespeare (Oxford, 1993)

Crowl, Samuel, *Shakespeare Observed: Studies in Performance on Stage and Screen* (Athens, Ohio, 1992)

David, Richard, *Shakespeare in the Theatre* (Cambridge, 1978)

Dawson, Anthony B., *Watching Shakespeare: A Playgoer's Guide* (London, 1988)

Dobson, Michael, 'Shakespeare performances in England, 2000', *Shakespeare Survey 54* (2001), 246–82

Faucit, Helena, Lady Martin, *On Some of Shakespeare's Female Characters*, 5th edition (London, 1893)

Gardner, Helen, '*As You Like It*', in John Garrett (ed.), *More Talking of Shakespeare* (London, 1959), 17–32

Grimley, Terry, 'Playing with a Bond' (interview with Samantha Bond), *Birmingham Post*, 23 March 1992

Hattaway, Michael (ed.), *As You Like It*, The New Cambridge Shakespeare (Cambridge, 2000)

Hemming, Sarah, 'Taking Strides' (interview with past and current players of Rosalind), *Independent*, 15 April 1992

Holland, Peter, *English Shakespeares: Shakespeare on the English Stage in the 1990s* (Cambridge, 1997)

Holland, Peter, 'Shakespeare in the twentieth-century theatre', in Margreta de Grazia and Stanley Wells (eds), *The Cambridge Companion to Shakespeare* (Cambridge, 2001), 199–216

Jenkins, Harold, '*As You Like It*', *Shakespeare Survey 8* (1955), 40–51

Kemp, T.C. and J.C. Trewin, *The Stratford Festival: A History of the Shakespeare Memorial Theatre* (Birmingham, 1953)

Kennedy, Dennis, *Looking at Shakespeare: A Visual History of Twentieth-century Performance* (Cambridge, 1993)

Latham, Agnes (ed.), *As You Like It*, The Arden Shakespeare (London, 1975)

Leggatt, Alexander, *Shakespeare's Comedy of Love* (London, 1974)

Mullin, Michael, *Design by Motley* (Newark, Del., and London, 1996)

Oliver, H.J. (ed.), *As You Like It*, The New Penguin Shakespeare (Harmondsworth, 1968)

Pimlott, Steven, 'As Who Likes It?: Steven Pimlott in conversation with Robert Smallwood', *RSC Magazine*, 13 (1996), 17–19

Pringle, Marian J., *The Theatres of Stratford-upon-Avon, 1875–1992: An Architectural History* (Stratford-upon-Avon, 1994)

Rickman, Alan, 'Jaques in *As You Like It*', in Russell Jackson and Robert Smallwood (eds), *Players of Shakespeare 2* (Cambridge, 1988), 73–80

Shaw, Fiona and Juliet Stevenson, 'Celia and Rosalind in *As You Like It*', in Russell Jackson and Robert Smallwood (eds), *Players of Shakespeare 2* (Cambridge, 1988), 55–72

Shaw, George Bernard, *Shaw on Shakespeare*, ed. Edwin Wilson (London, 1961)

Smallwood, Robert, '"To seek my uncle in the Forest of Arden": plot manipulation and the happy ending of *As You Like It*', in Jean-Paul Debax and Yves Peyré (eds), '*As You Like It': Essais Critiques* (Toulouse, 1998), 27–43

Smallwood, Robert, 'Twentieth-century Performance: the Stratford and London companies', in Sarah Stanton and Stanley Wells (eds), *The Cambridge Companion to Shakespeare on the Stage* (Cambridge, 2002), 98–117

Sprague, Arthur Colby, *The Doubling of Parts in Shakespeare's Plays* (London, 1966)

Tennant, David, 'Touchstone in *As You Like It*', in Robert Smallwood (ed.), *Players of Shakespeare 4* (Cambridge, 1998), 30–44

Thompson, Sophie, 'Rosalind (and Celia) in *As You Like It*', in Russell Jackson and Robert Smallwood (eds), *Players of Shakespeare 3* (Cambridge, 1993), 77–86

Trewin, J.C., *Shakespeare on the English Stage, 1900–1964* (London, 1964)

Wells, Stanley and Gary Taylor, with John Jowett and William Montgomery (eds), *William Shakespeare: The Complete Works* (Oxford, 1986)

THEATRE YEARBOOKS AND SOUVENIRS

The Shakespeare Memorial Theatre, 1951–1953: A Photographic Record with an Introduction by Ivor Brown (London, 1953)

The Shakespeare Memorial Theatre, 1957–1958: A Photographic Record with an Introduction by Ivor Brown (London, 1959)

The Royal Shakespeare Company, 1960–63, ed. John Goodwin (London, 1964)

The Royal Shakespeare Company Yearbook, 1980–1981, ed. Simon Trussler (Stratford-upon-Avon, 1981)

The Royal Shakespeare Company Yearbook, 1985–1986, 1986–1987, ed. Peter Harlock (Stratford-upon-Avon, 1987)

FILM

As You Like It, directed for the RSC by Michael Elliott, redirected for BBC television by Ronald Eyre and broadcast March 1963. (A copy is in the Shakespeare Centre Library.)

GRAMOPHONE RECORD

Shakespeare: Twenty Sonnets and Scenes from 'As You Like It', with Dame Edith Evans and Michael Redgrave (Columbia Gramophone Company, 33CX: 1375, n.d.)

INDEX

This index includes actors, directors, critics and other individuals mentioned in the main text who are connected with a production of *As You Like It*. It also includes references to other Shakespeare plays. Individual productions, listed under Shakespeare, are identified by director and year. Page numbers in bold refer to illustrations.